A bit misty now
A smart wall might still hurt you
A woman. A man. No only
Always the impossible as stupid as reality
As predictable as tides, as trainable as pets
Babe I'm poetry, just read between the lines. . .
Be the lover you never received
Be yourself, but don't overdo it
Beloved are they who sit down
Bender
Brush past me
Chemical rushes
Closer scrub
Coral, not moral
Cover me
Crimson
Dear blue I'm just like you
Desperate for tenderness, to raw for the greeting of senses. . .
Different roots; same destination
Do you want to fall without knowing who took you?
Don't breathe out (but I know you will)
Due to not wanting to, I will not
Each burden, each great catch
Everything arrived as sealed
French-kiss in chaos
Glamour requires this space
Go home once in a while
How brave is your brain?
How to cope inside of it
I am now the one looking
I got a lot of space in my brain for you
I kill a part of me to keep you alive
I like the sky because I don't believe it's infinite
I like to see how red the flag can get. . .
I missed my reds (I didn't miss my reds)
I remember love, but I can't remember you
I slept where you slept so I slept with you
I touched the beginning. . .
I want it all, but slowly
I want it all, give me your money and your phone!
I want to lick you in places that leave my tongue bacterial
I will never be satisfied with just one part of you. . .
If I could bottle you up into a cologne, I would call you initiative!
If you got the truth, you can keep it
If you want the rainbow, you need to put up with a little bit of rain. . .
If you want to control someone love them
Initially I too appear between the legs
It isn't spiritual arrogance
It would only bring an exhausting demand for explanation
It's a nasty piece of work
It's curiously beautiful, like a loyalty we do not share
It's deeper than you think
I hate the game but I love to do it
I'm the war you can never win
I've been planning while you're playing
Just when I discovered the meaning of life they changed it
Keep the side rooms less exclusive
Line

Lost it to the left
Memory is a monster, you think you got memories, but it got you
More than ever and once again
My love life definitely skews towards crimson
My nipples are freer than yours
No rain no flowers
Not true but helpful
Nothing to prove, move to move
Of course I'm not sorry
On I go
Once bitten, twice shy
Past in the present
Pastel me not
Philosophy is probably homesickness
PMS is my definition of time
Point black
Raunchy humour, fairly specific sex
Repeated spots
Respect pop, but we're broken up. . .
Second-hand lingerie
Self-conscious sabotage
Self-regarding attitudes
Shovels of coals (I no longer feel the shovel. . .)
Smile now, cry later
Smoother tomorrow, easier than yesterday
So many unsaid things on the tip of my tongue
Someone amongst the breathing knows. . .
The best is yet to come
The circle is a spiral, it will be OK I promise
The day I met you never ended for me
The intimidation of sexual wealth
The jokes on you I'm biding my time
The platform isn't any colour
The universe doesn't allow perfection
They come, they go. . .
To get lost is to learn the way
Toothpaste for trespassers
Total existence needs meaning and myth
Victorian promenade of self-sabotage
Wake up alone!
We don't see things as they are, we see things as we are
We should take a deep breath
What we think we become
When I notice, I don't enjoy, I see!
When I wear a swimsuit I just don't swim
When love is gone where does it go?
White lines, blue eyes
Why do you mostly speak in quotations?
Will always be the opposite
Words I wish I had said
You are experienced, but still pissing towards the moon. . .
You didn't make it to heaven
You taught me a lesson I didn't want to learn
You truly are awash of good ideas
You were once blue
Your loneliness is the symptom, not the sickness!
You'll be the first to drown in a desert
You're not a complete idiot, some parts are still missing

Of Course I'm Not Sorry

Tyra Tingleff

Mousse Publishing

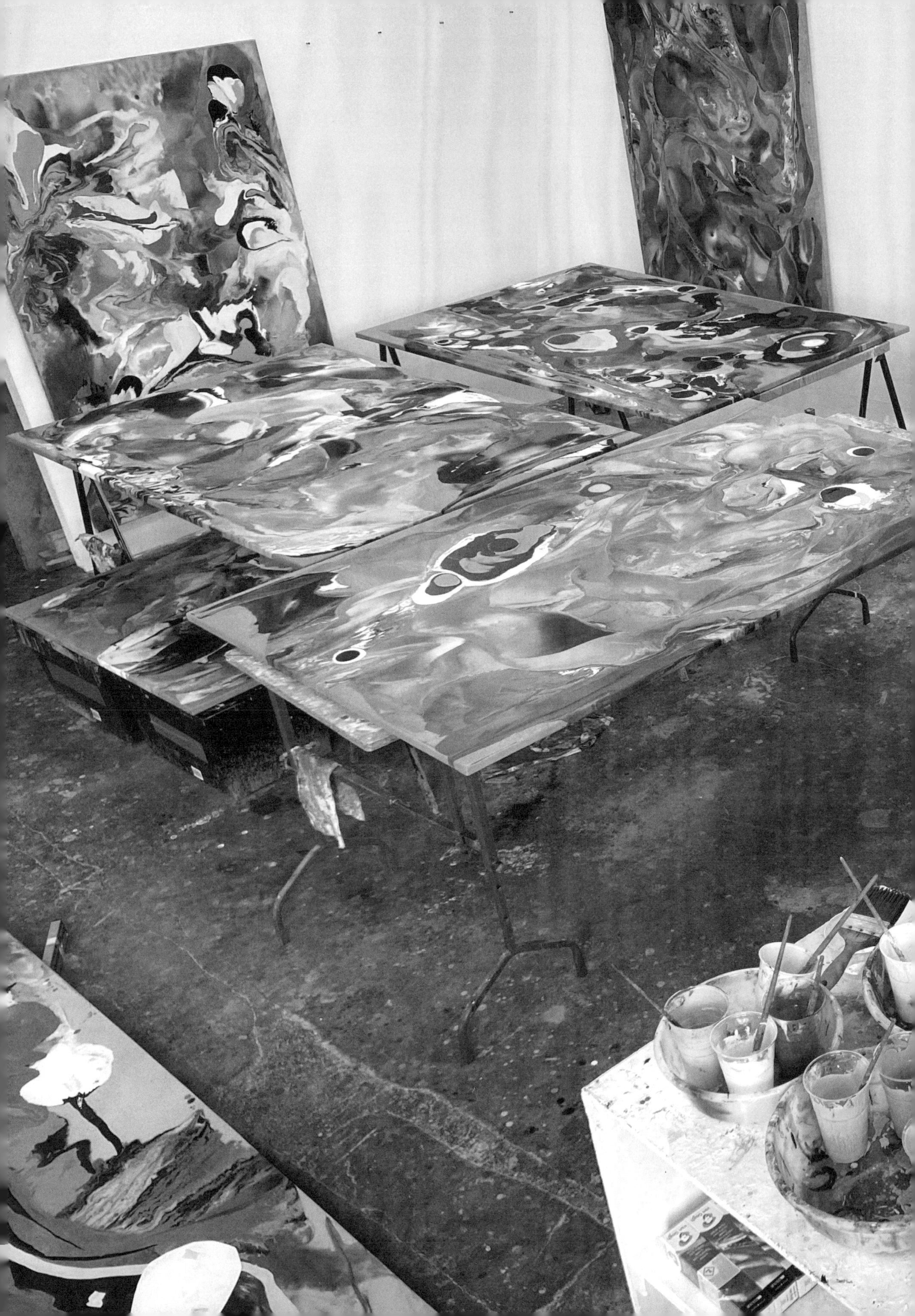

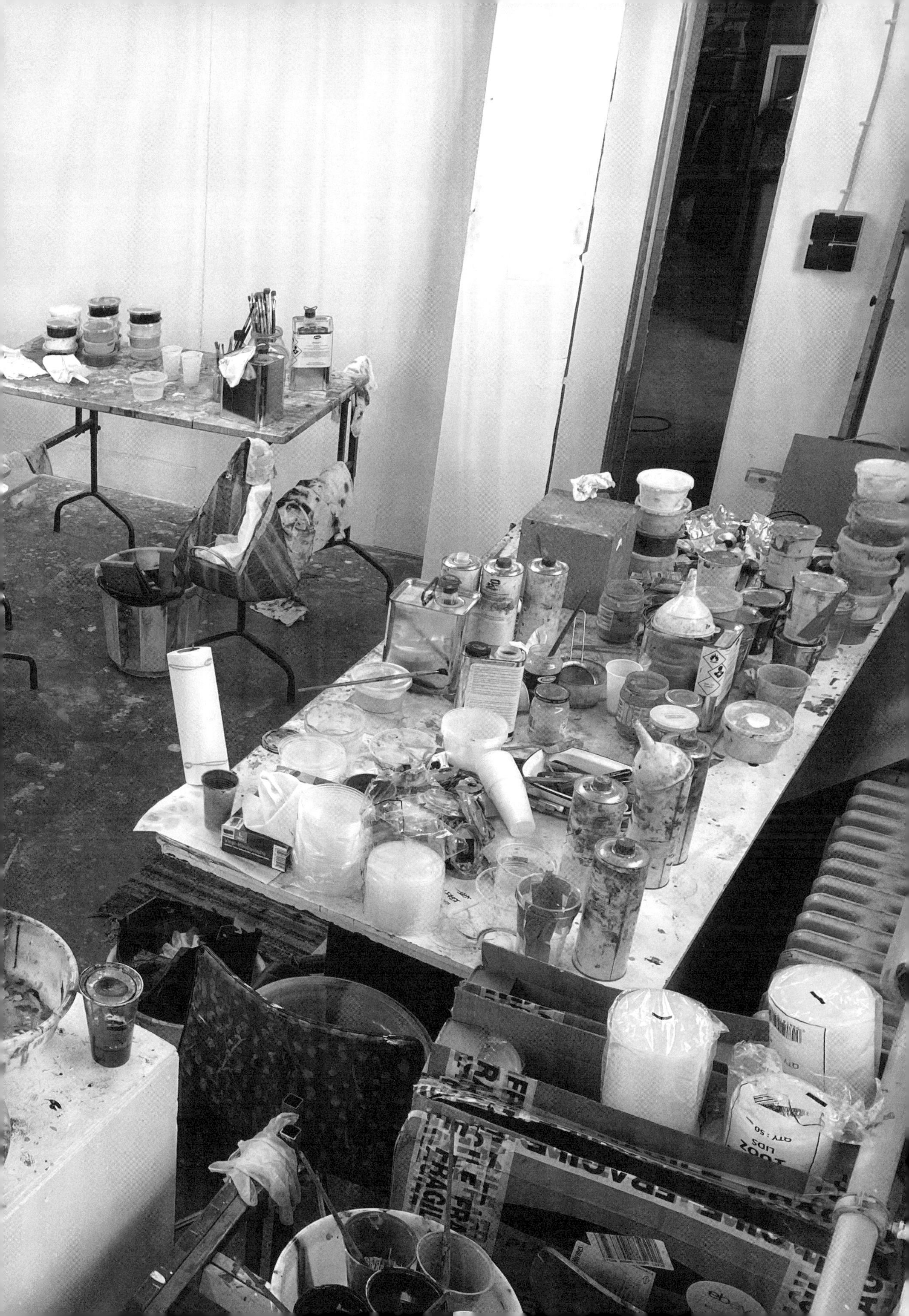

The Möbius Strip Theory of Painting

Amy Sherlock

During a studio visit with an artist friend—an abstract painter—a couple of years ago, the topic turned to the question of how to know when a painting is finished. It's an endlessly intriguing proposition when applied to the process of painting, which, unlike, say, a cast sculpture or a fired ceramic, always remains open to additions or subtractions, to things being painted in or out. After hesitating for a moment, she told me: "When I can see how it started." It's a good answer, I think. What I understood her to mean was: a canvas is like a puzzle, where the last piece reveals the pattern of the whole. The beginning and end might be thought of as two undifferentiated points on a continuous loop; the canvas can be read forward and backward. Though not a painting, Henri Matisse's exquisitely simple monumental late cutout *The Snail* (1953) is a useful way of thinking about this. The image resolves only when—voilà!—the final, central block of color is placed, from which the composition then seems to spiral outward. You know that a certain type of painting has finished because it has come *full circle*.

Two images spring to mind to describe this kind of painting: the first is the ouroboros, the ancient serpent continually devouring its own tail; the second is the Möbius strip, a mathematical object named for its mid-nineteenth-century German discoverer that, when visualized in three-dimensional space, usually looks like a figure eight with a twist in the middle. A Möbius strip has only one surface and boundary. The mathematically minded Dutch illustrator M.C. Escher famously depicted ants processing around one in *Möbius Strip II (Red Ants)* (1963). By indicating the motion of the ants, the drawing shows how one might set out from a given point and return to that same point upside down. The ant would have to do two complete circuits to get back to the same point the right way around.

I'm thinking of paintings like Tyra Tingleff's *My love life definitely skews towards crimson* (2021), in which pastel ribbons, diaphanous as chiffon, twist and contort against a seared red-purple background. The palette is a little sweet, a little sour—a kind of toxic sherbet. The effect is vaporous. The whole painting feels like it's in motion, as though you might look away and turn back to find the formation changed. It is difficult to pick out how and where the looping forms begin and end, in the same way that it's impossible to identify at exactly what point one cloud formation becomes another. (The patches of raw linen that are frequently visible in Tingleff's compositions compound this impression—like glimpses of sky.) The form of such a work does not resolve easily when you look at it. It leads your eye around in circles, returning you compulsively, but never to quite the same point.

There is another way of thinking about the question "Where does a painting begin?" that, rather than answer in terms of form, would give its history, its art-historical antecedents. Tingleff's painting is part of a tradition that began in earnest with the gestural gymnastics of Abstract Expressionism, although it also quivers with earlier cosmic energies:

the pastel-hued mandalas of the nineteenth-century mystic Hilma af Klint, for instance, whose hand was led by her spirit guide, or the self-taught US artist Eugene Von Bruenchenhein, whose seared landscapes are like apocalyptic updates of the Romantic sublime. But while these examples are conduits between interior psychology and the astral plane, Tingleff's works feel deeply embedded in the urban texture of the present. They're open to the possibility of ugliness. A little more punk. Her clashing colors nod ever so slightly to the world of graffiti, but more than that, she taps into its spirit of trespass, of making marks where one shouldn't—especially as a woman in the field of abstract painting, which has historically been, and continues to be, dominated by men. (Let's not forget that it was not until decades after af Klint's works were first shown that they were acknowledged as the earliest examples of Western abstraction, preceding Wassily Kandinsky's canonical efforts by some five years.)

In the studio, Tingleff's raw-linen canvases are laid flat. She thins her paints with a lot of turpentine before applying them, and then moves the canvases around to create a marbled effect. It's a physical process and an instinctive one. The larger paintings require the help of a studio assistant to hold the other end of the canvas and maneuver it up and down. In this way, they index a kind of dancing, and have a distinct rhythm. There is a stage after the marbling happens, Tingleff says, where the paintings are *too beautiful*. The marbled surface is so smooth, so delicious, that our eye just slips over it without properly looking. There has to be something that catches us, some texture. So then comes the laborious process of squeegee-ing, blurring, overpainting—the work of imperfecting, basically. As a painter, one must be on one's guard against beauty. This is painting caught in the push-pull between seduction and revulsion, an internal tension that accounts for the delicious tension of its many contortions. The works accrue in numerous layers, but because the oils are thinned, they acquire intensity without density. All the action pushes up against the surface. They are resolutely flat. (The sense they create of twisting in three-dimensional space accounts for some of the headfuckery that makes me think of Möbius strips.)

In the last century, Modernist painting achieved flatness, ironically, by means of a tool used since fourteenth-century Florence to create perspective, which is to say the illusion of depth: the grid. The grid is often thought of as *the* operating principle of twentieth-century abstraction, from the fractured images of Cubism through Piet Mondrian's checkerboards to Jackson Pollock's diffuse surfaces to Agnes Martin's trembling renditions. (It made waves among art historians when, in 2015, restoration work on Pollock's early poured painting *Alchemy* [1947] revealed a grid of delicate white lines beneath its densely textured surface.) For Rosalind Krauss, who had pretty much the conclusive word on the subject in her 1979 essay "Grids" in the journal *October*, the grid "is what art looks like when it turns its back on nature."[1] It was the tool that allowed Modernism to claim autonomy for the artwork: the lines of the grid as a portcullis to keeps the world out.

A Möbius-strip painting knows that art is a bit messier than that. *Life is the shit that happens when you are waiting for the moment that never comes* reads the title of one of Tingleff's paintings from 2019. It depicts a knot-like structure that weaves across the canvas, looping and folding back in on itself—beginnings that turn into ends that turn into beginnings. Tingleff's titles, with their fortune-cookie wisdom, are drawn from expressions overheard, platitudes, quotations from friends. Her most recent solo exhibition at The Sunday Painter in London was titled *Smile now, cry later*—a sentiment with a particularly universal bathos that also nods to *The best is yet to come* (2019), *Beloved are they who sit down* (2016), or *Just when I discovered the meaning of life they changed it* (2019). The titles don't describe the work, but rather are snippets of speech that attach themselves to the forms, miring painting in the language of the world, with all of its mishearings and misunderstandings. This is painting as small talk—ironic hyperbole, not grand pronouncement. That 2019 title could be lightly amended to double as a philosophy of painting: "Painting is the shit that happens when you are waiting for the moment that never comes." Painting happens in the process, not by grand designs. It's the labor of working every day, trying new techniques and relearning old ones, so that the end point might arrive unexpectedly—a surprise even to the artist—revealing its logic only at the moment of conclusion.

Tingleff's verbose titles are by turns witty, sassy, guru-ish, and funny. They send up the faux solemnity of calling a work *Untitled*, which I have always found slightly haughty—a way of closing down, rather than opening up to, differing interpretations ("I know what this is, but I'm not going to tell you"). Giving a painting a precisely articulated title that describes something not, in any real sense, depicted on the canvas amounts to something like Frank Stella's immortal line, given in an interview in 1964, when he was at the height of his minimalist powers: "What you see is what you see."[2] Tingleff's paintings, which are a kind of delinquent grandniece to Stella's patrician abstractions, are saying, "Don't ask me to describe what I am, not because it is self-evident, but because every person will see it differently." (Fortune cookies work that way, too; it's the art of optimal generalization.) To look too hard for a definitive connection between paintings and title is a red herring, another twist in the play of dissonance and disorientation. A Möbius strip painting eludes absolutes. Just as you think you know what you are looking at, it turns into something else.

I've started to think about Tingleff's paintings in terms of resistance: of the layers of paint to one another, to a beauty that's too obvious, to a form that's too identifiable, to titles that would pin them down. But also to the viewer. *Smile now, cry later* was dominated by a large-scale canvas—her largest yet—that occupied the double height of the lower gallery, leaning against a steel beam in the middle of the ceiling with a punkish loucheness. From the street, all you saw of *Don't breathe out (but I know you will)* (2021) was the upper section of the canvas, like the tip of a hallucinatory iceberg. Once you were downstairs with it, the painting screened off part of the space. It was intrusive and a little confrontational; it pushed you out. I like this idea of painting as physical obstacle, not just something pretty hanging on a wall. The fact that it's leaning adds a certain gravitational menace: be careful or it might just squash you flat.

There is something else new about this canvas, which you note from the street: it's looking back at you. It has eyes. In fact, these are the initial pours, where Tingleff's paints pool in layers before she begins the marbling process. This time, she's left them. They were the last additions to the composition. How do you know when a painting is finished? When you can see where it began.

1   Rosalind Krauss, "Grids," *October* 9 (Summer 1979): 50.
2   "Questions to Stella and Judd," interview by Bruce Glaser, edited by Lucy R. Lippard, *ARTnews* (September 1966).

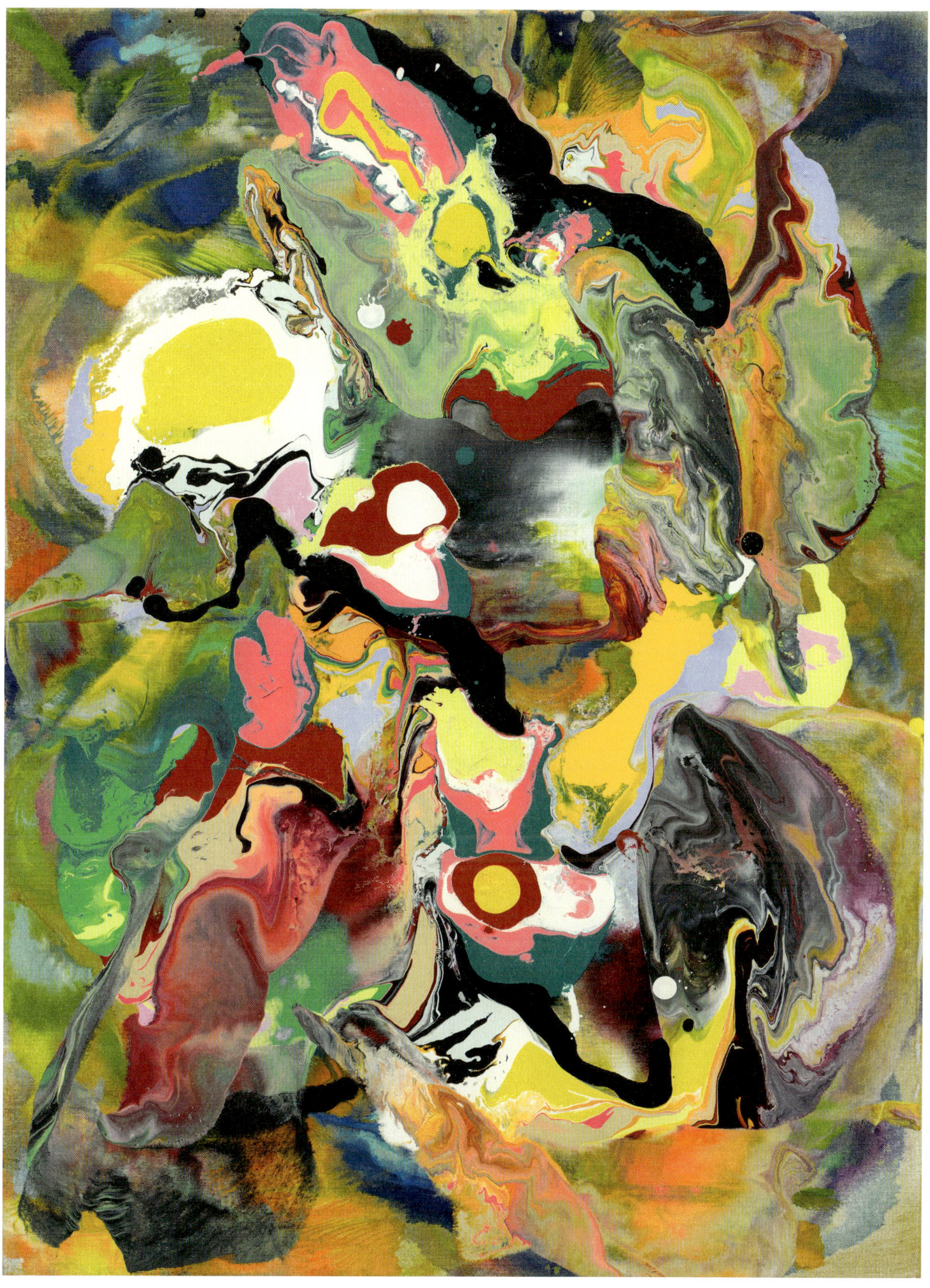

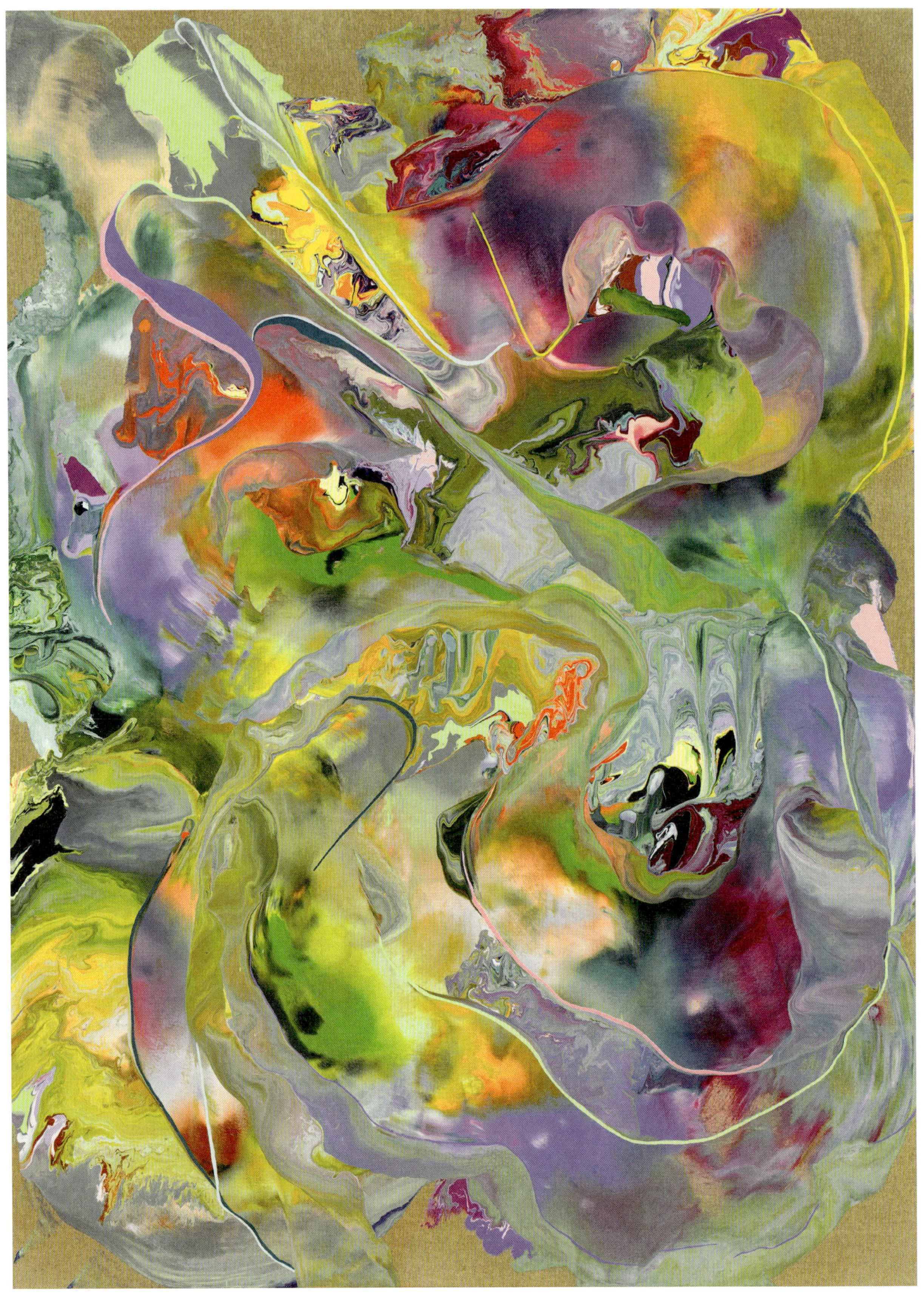

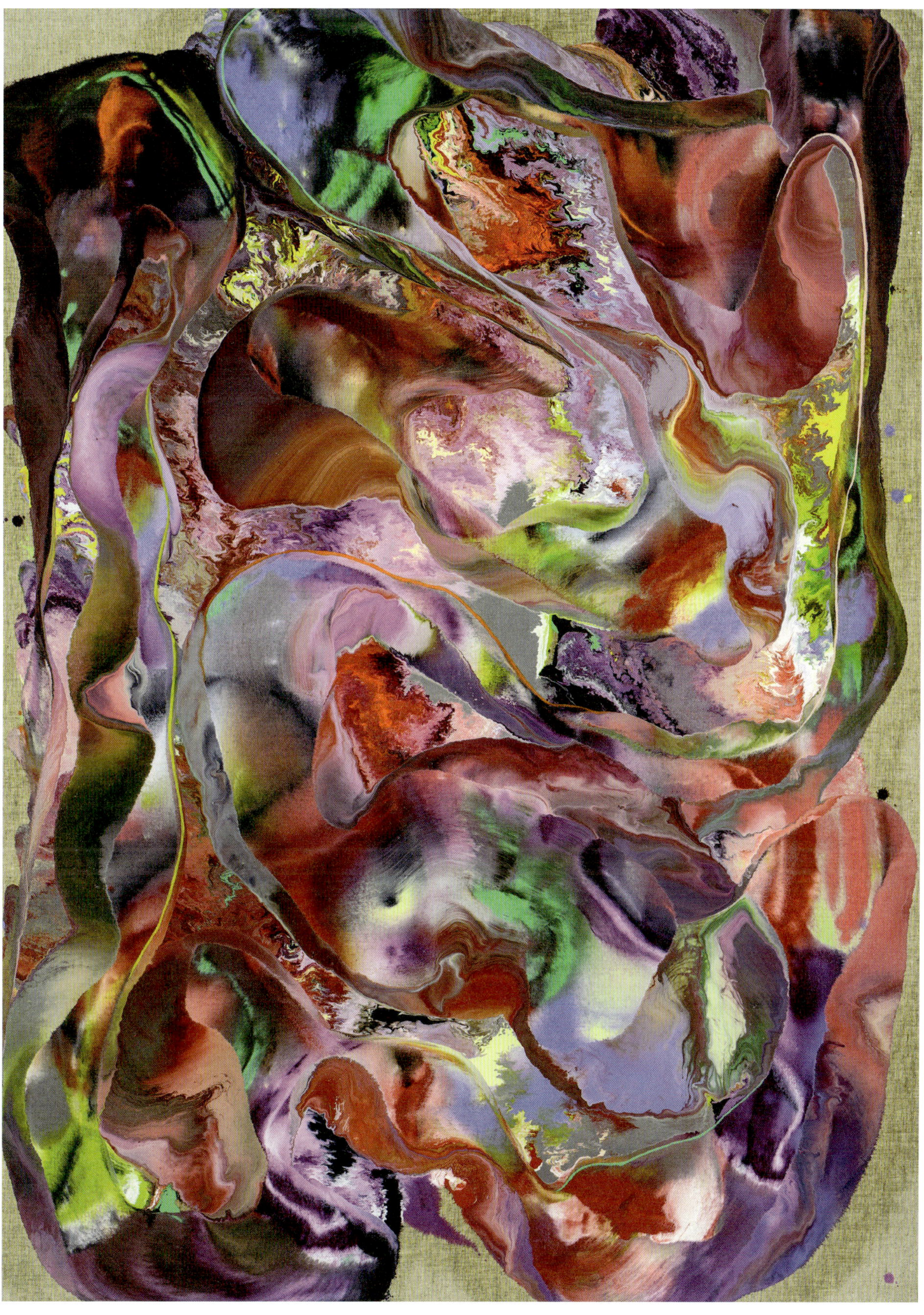

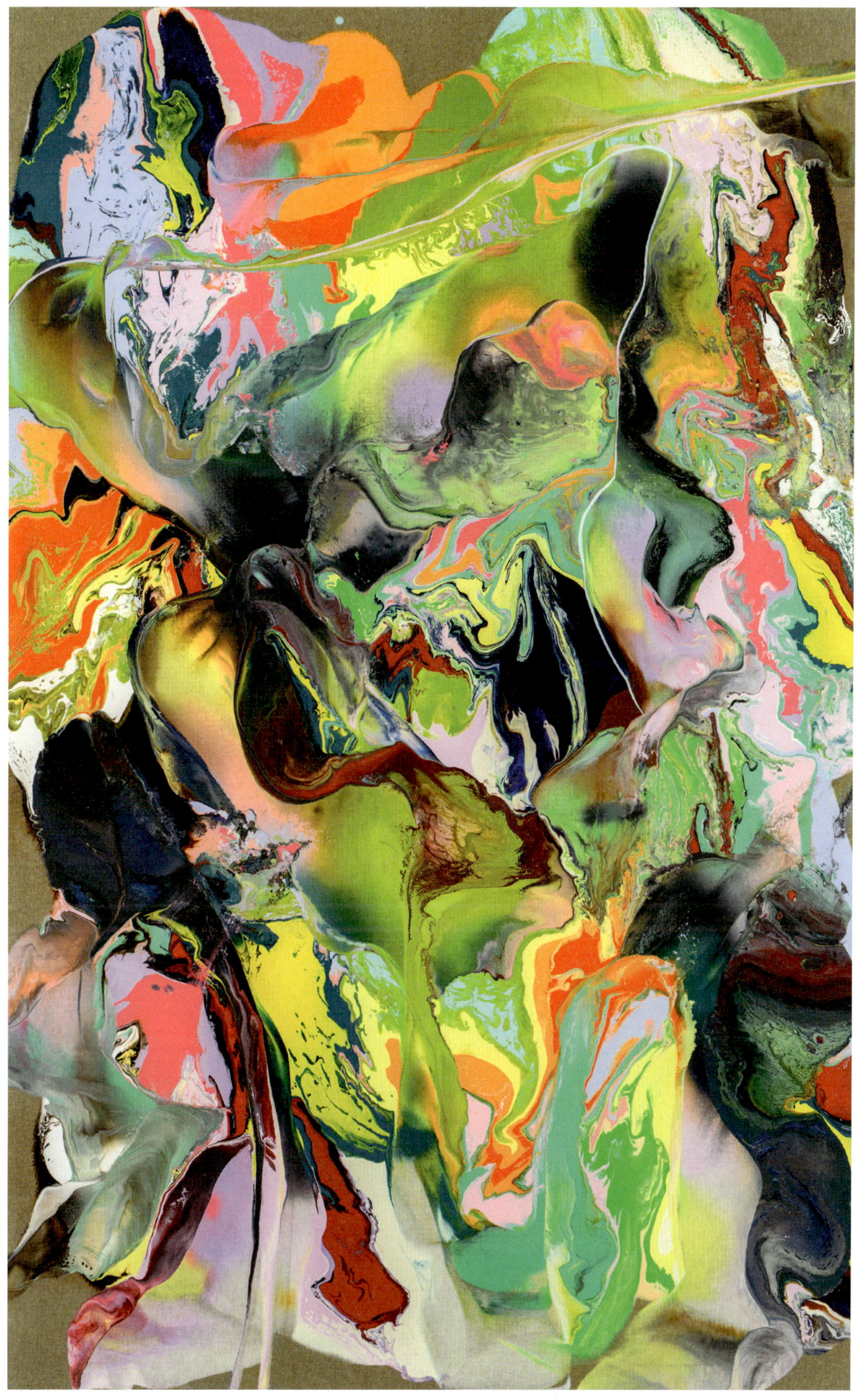

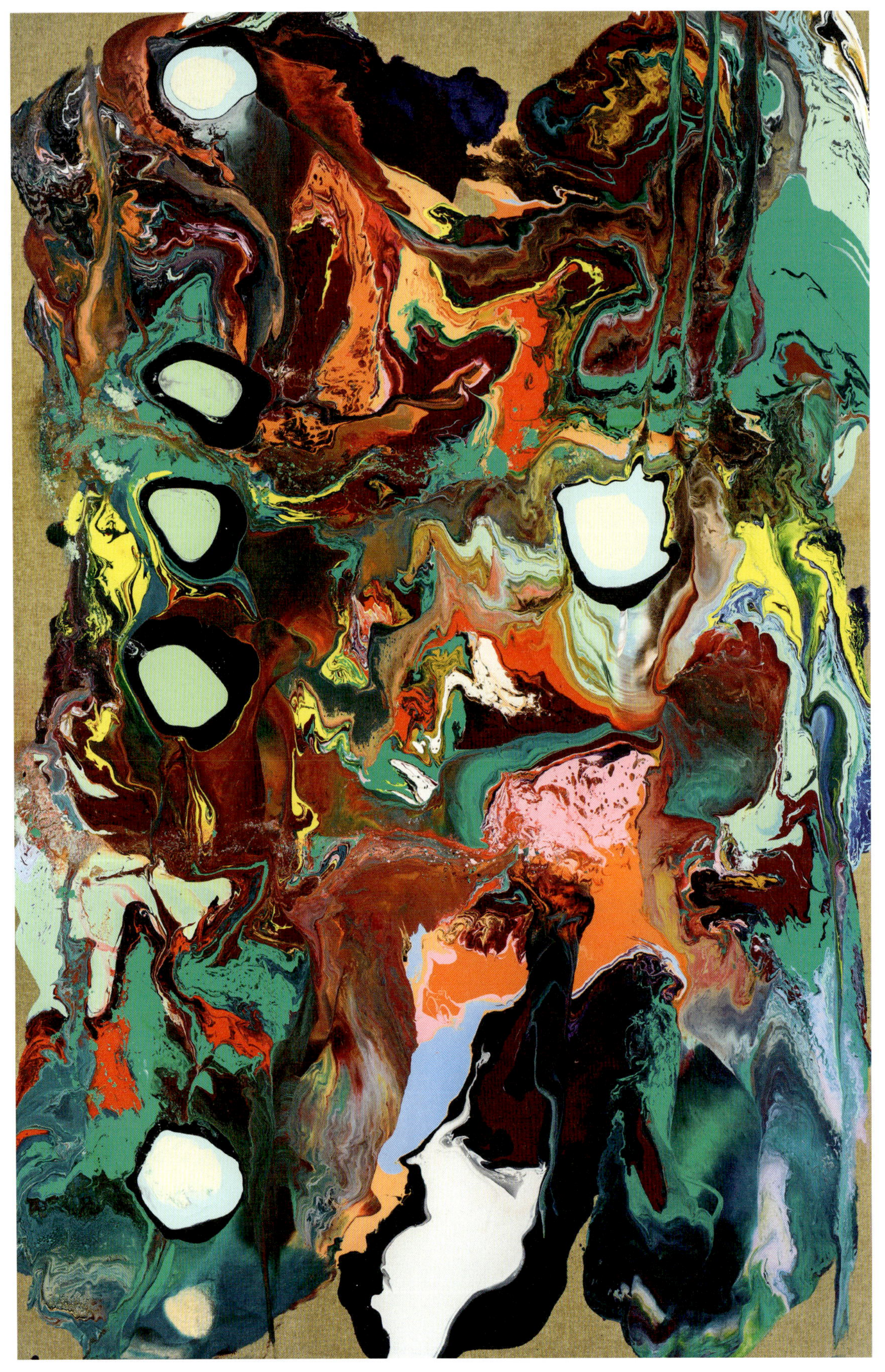

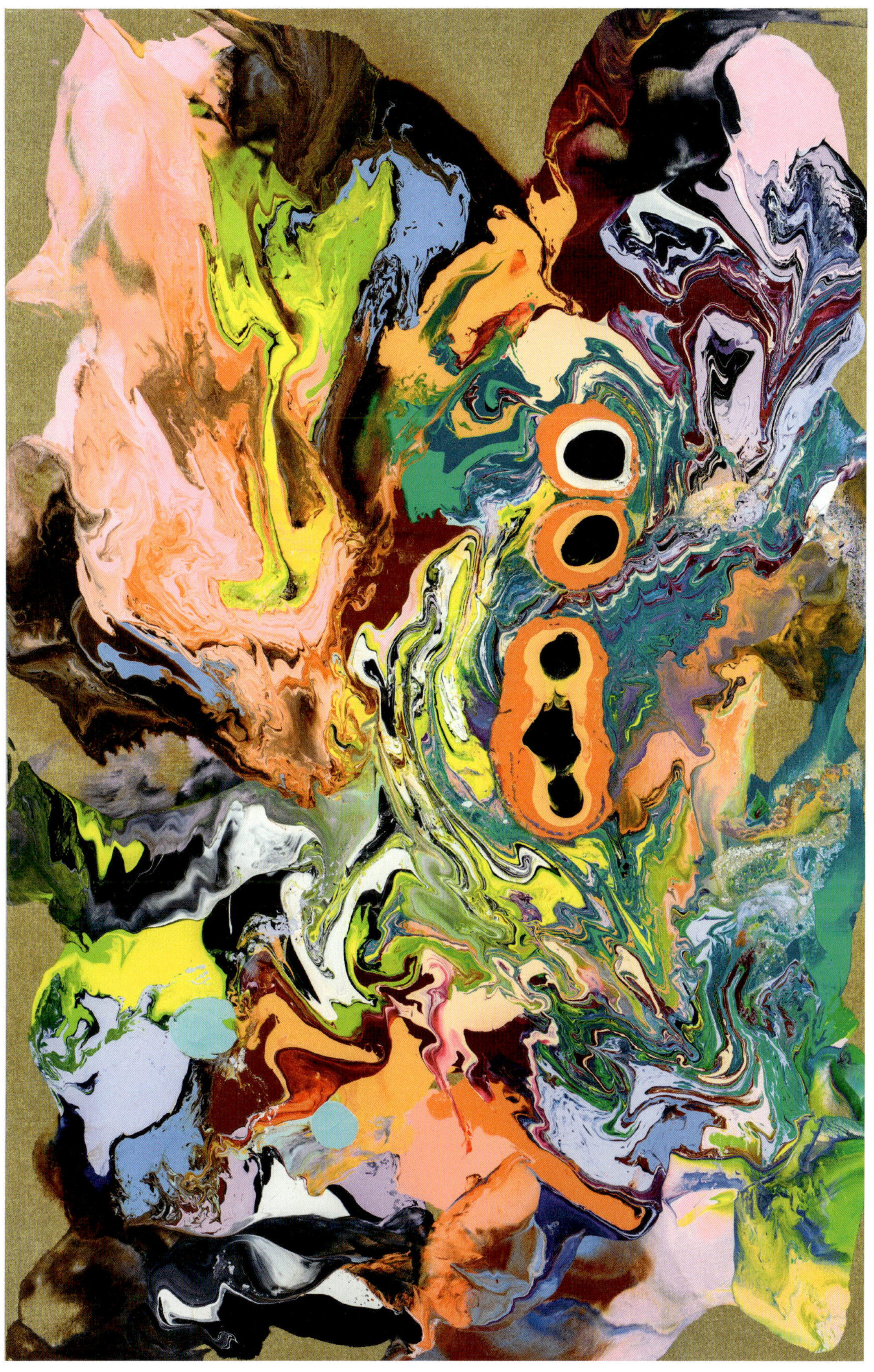

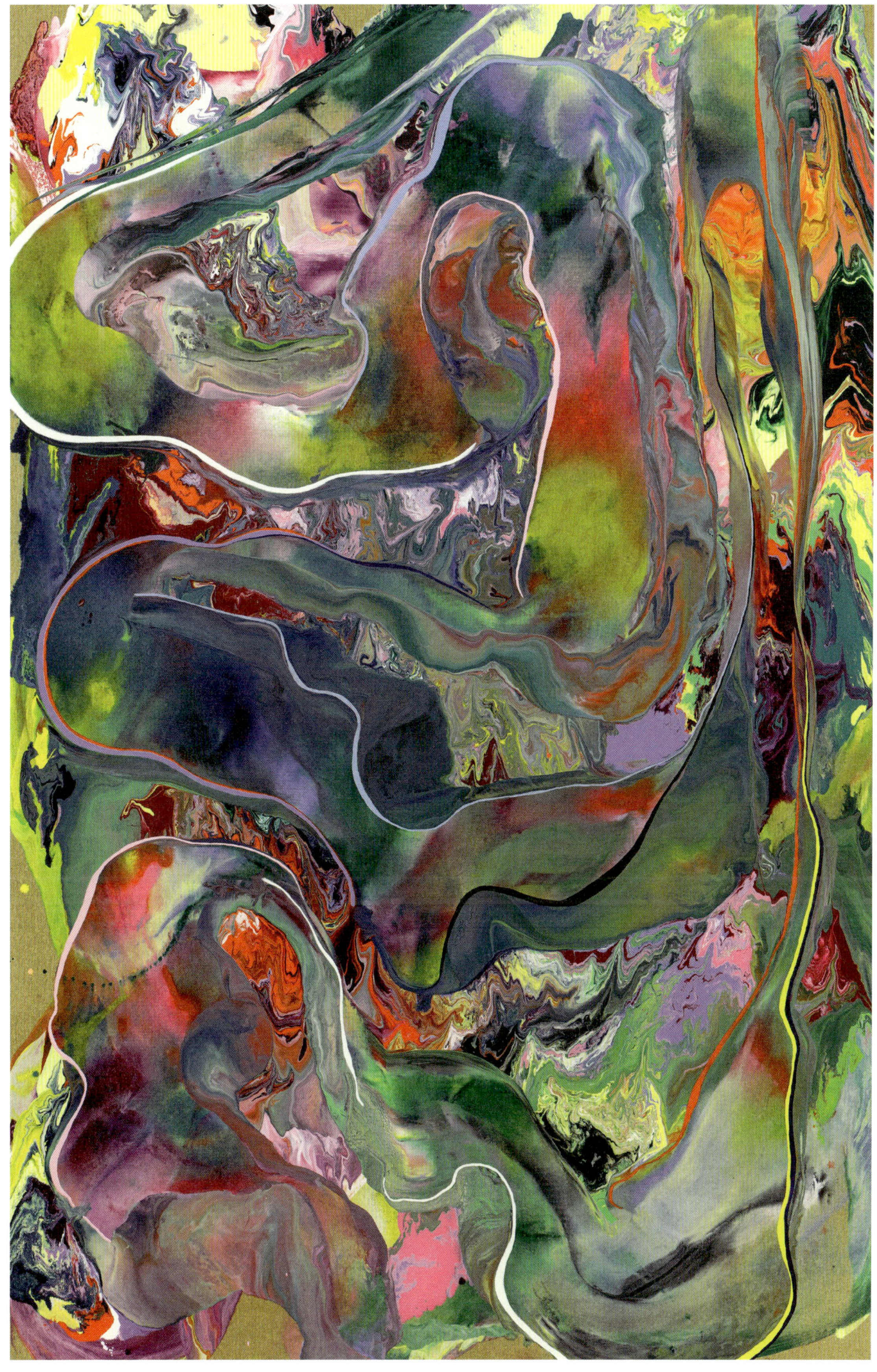

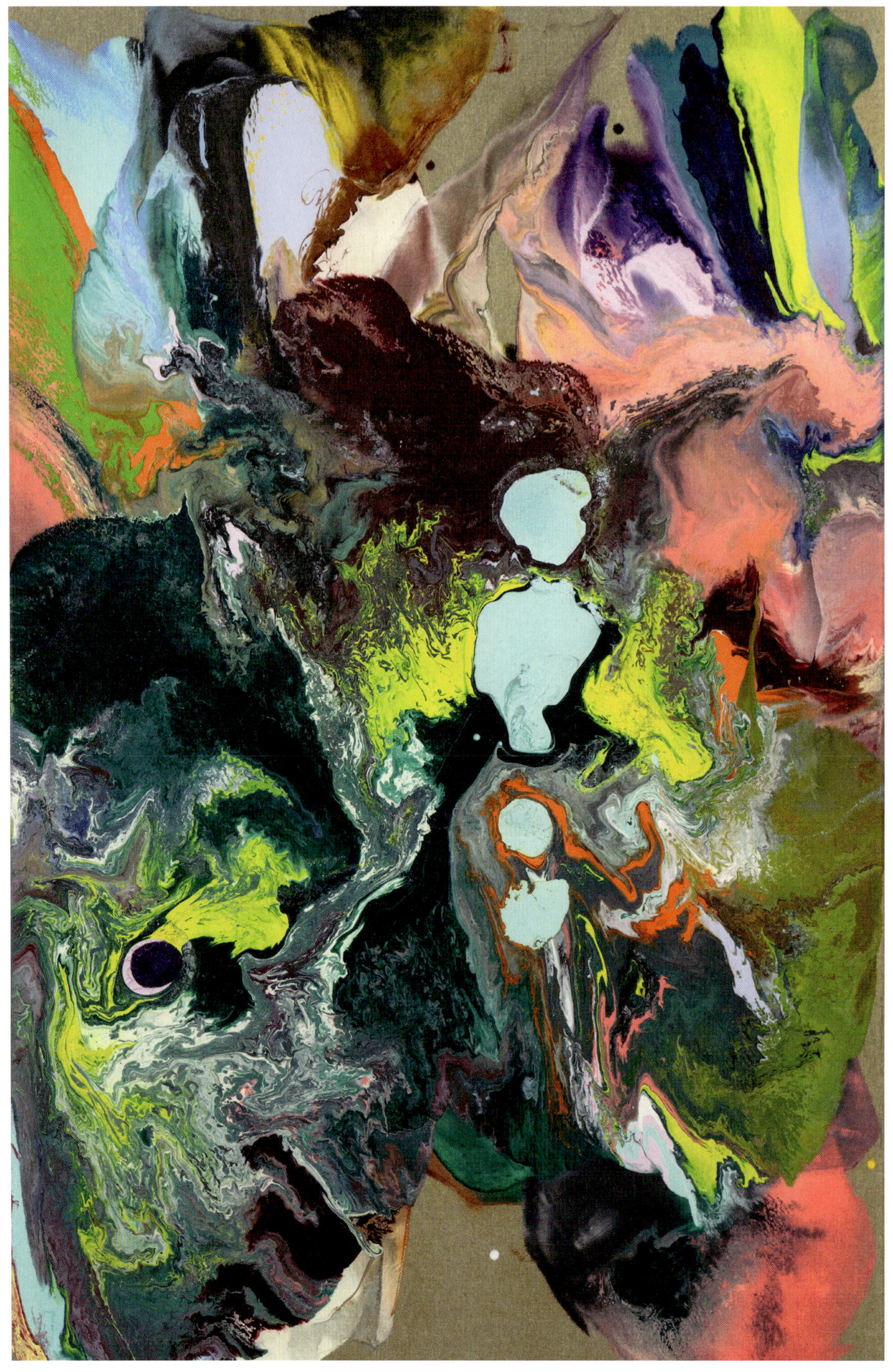

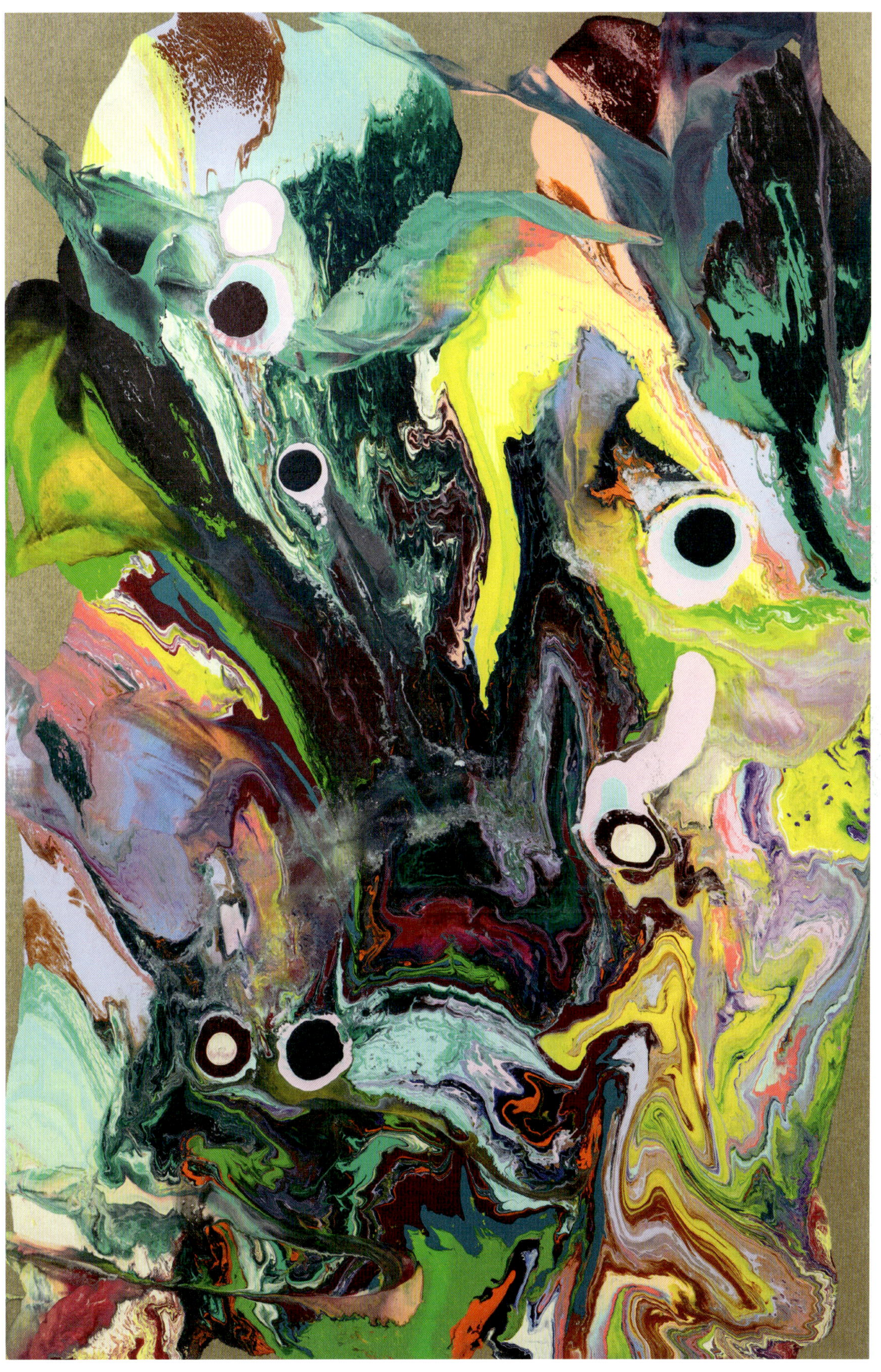

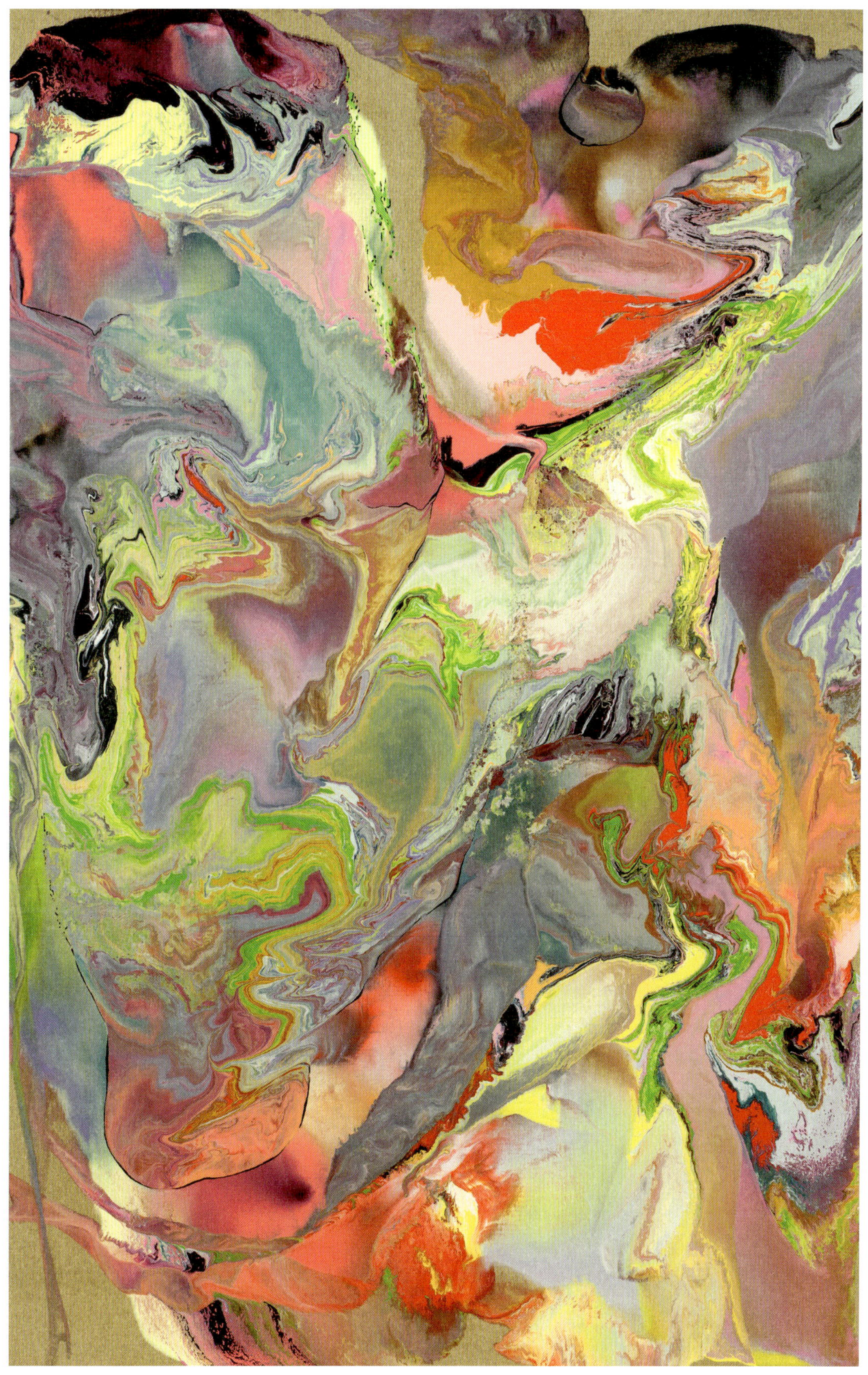

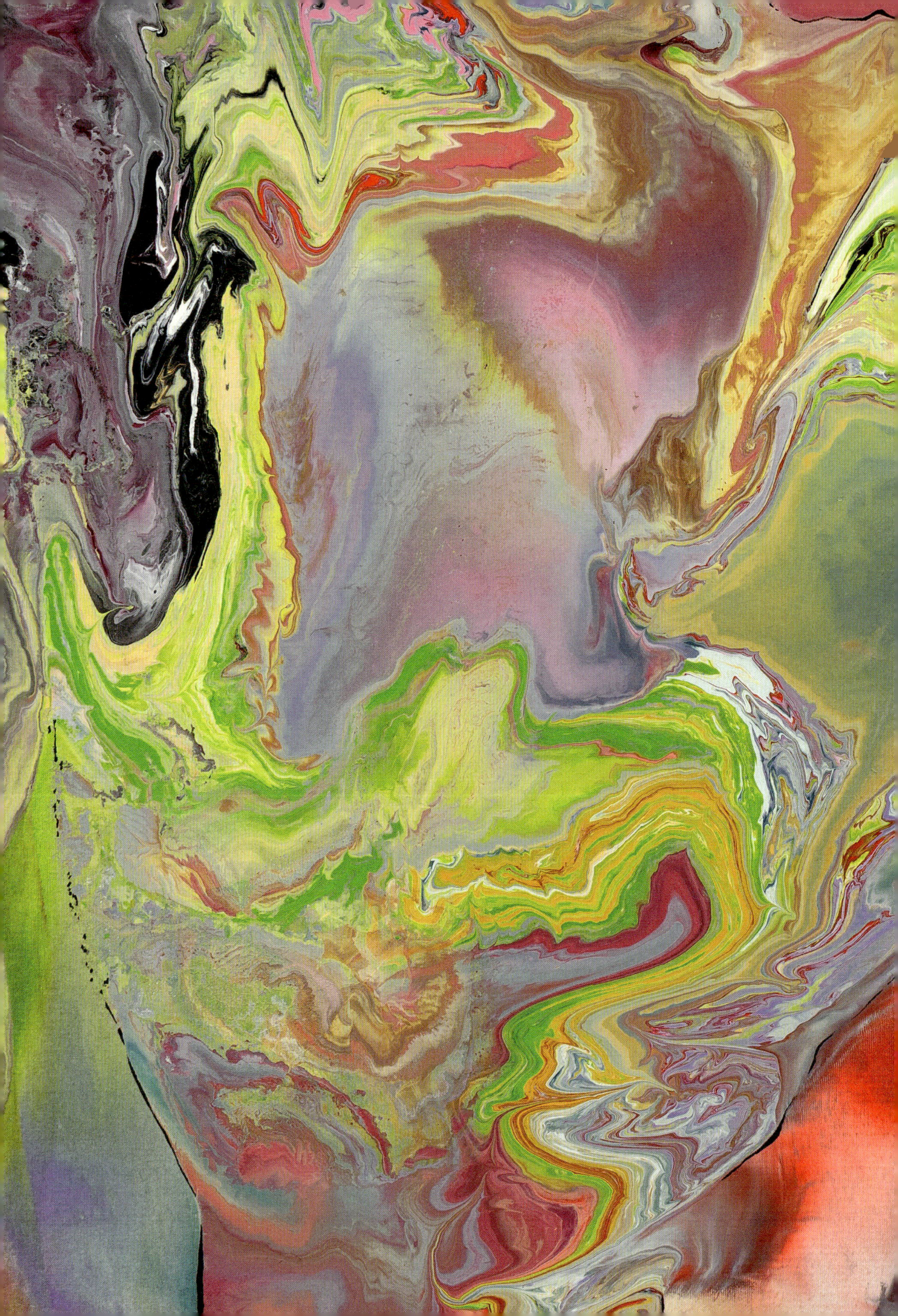

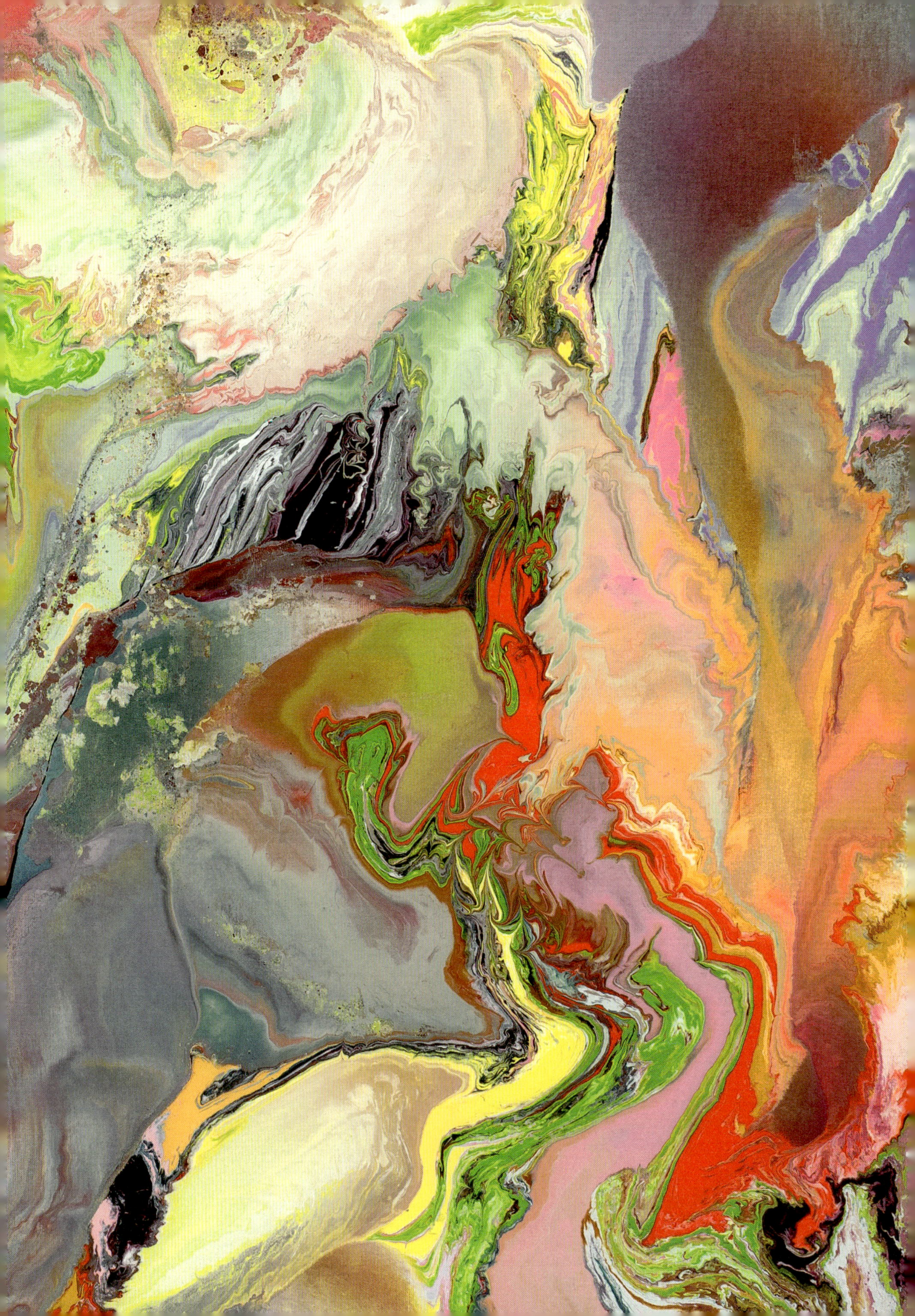

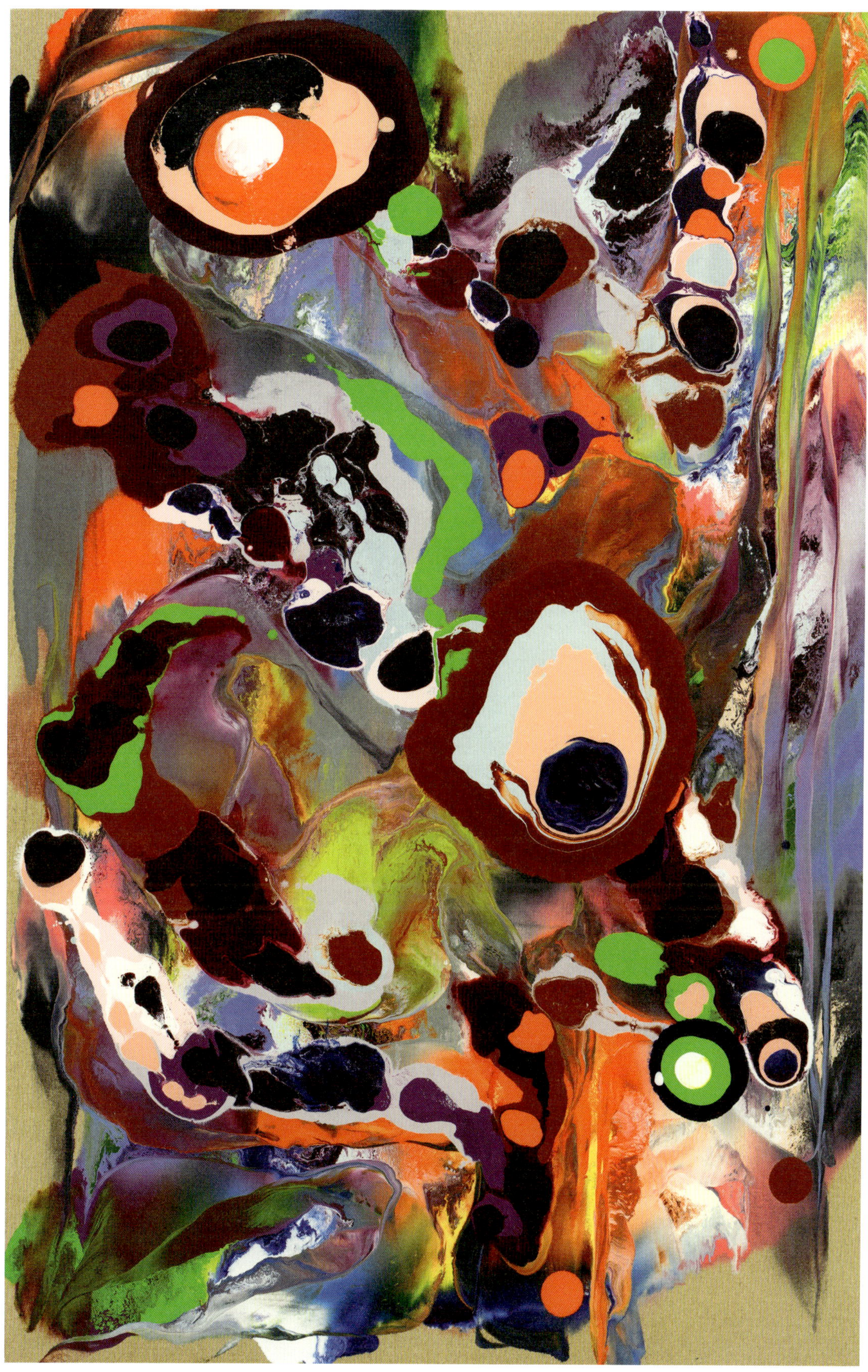

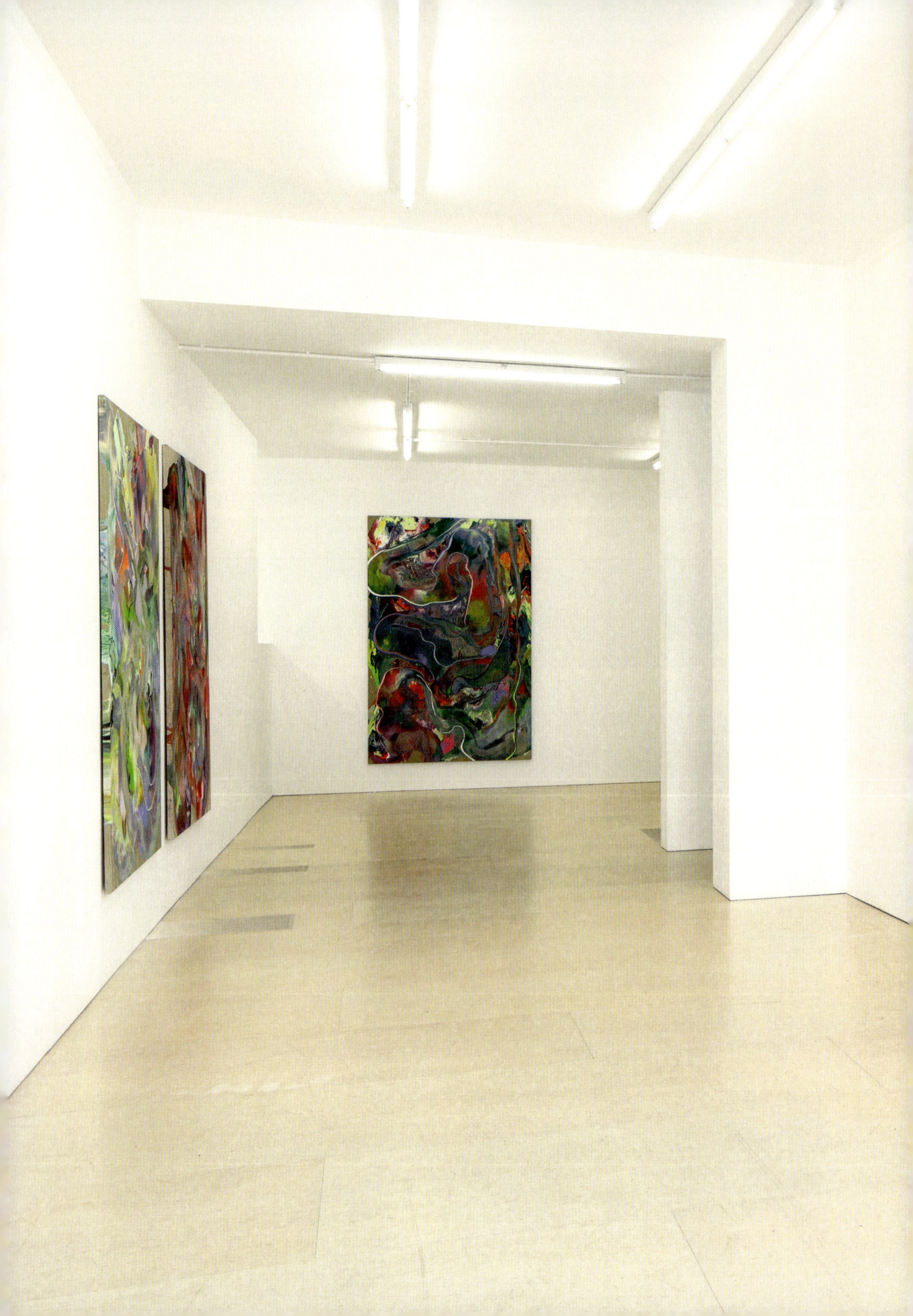

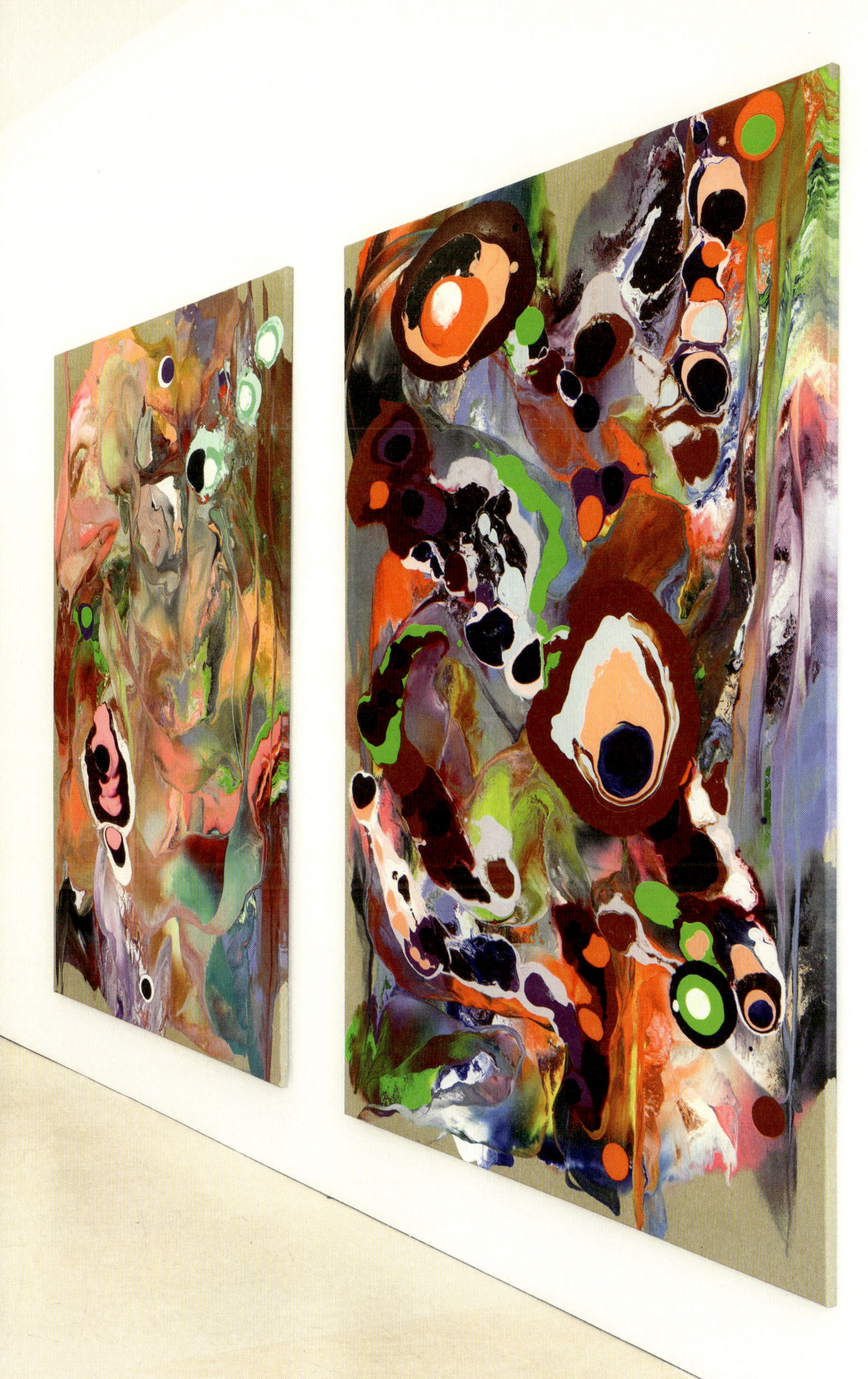

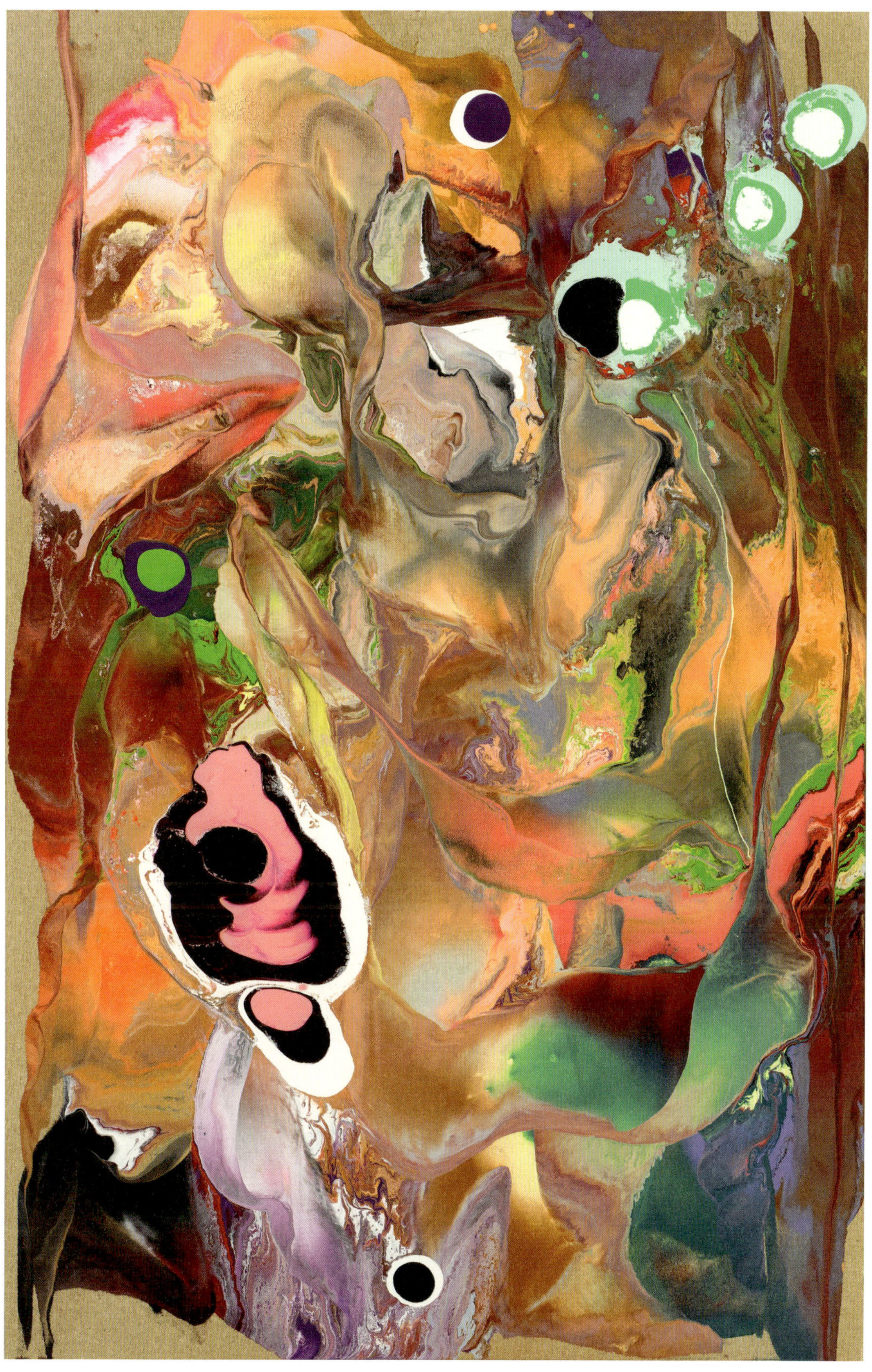

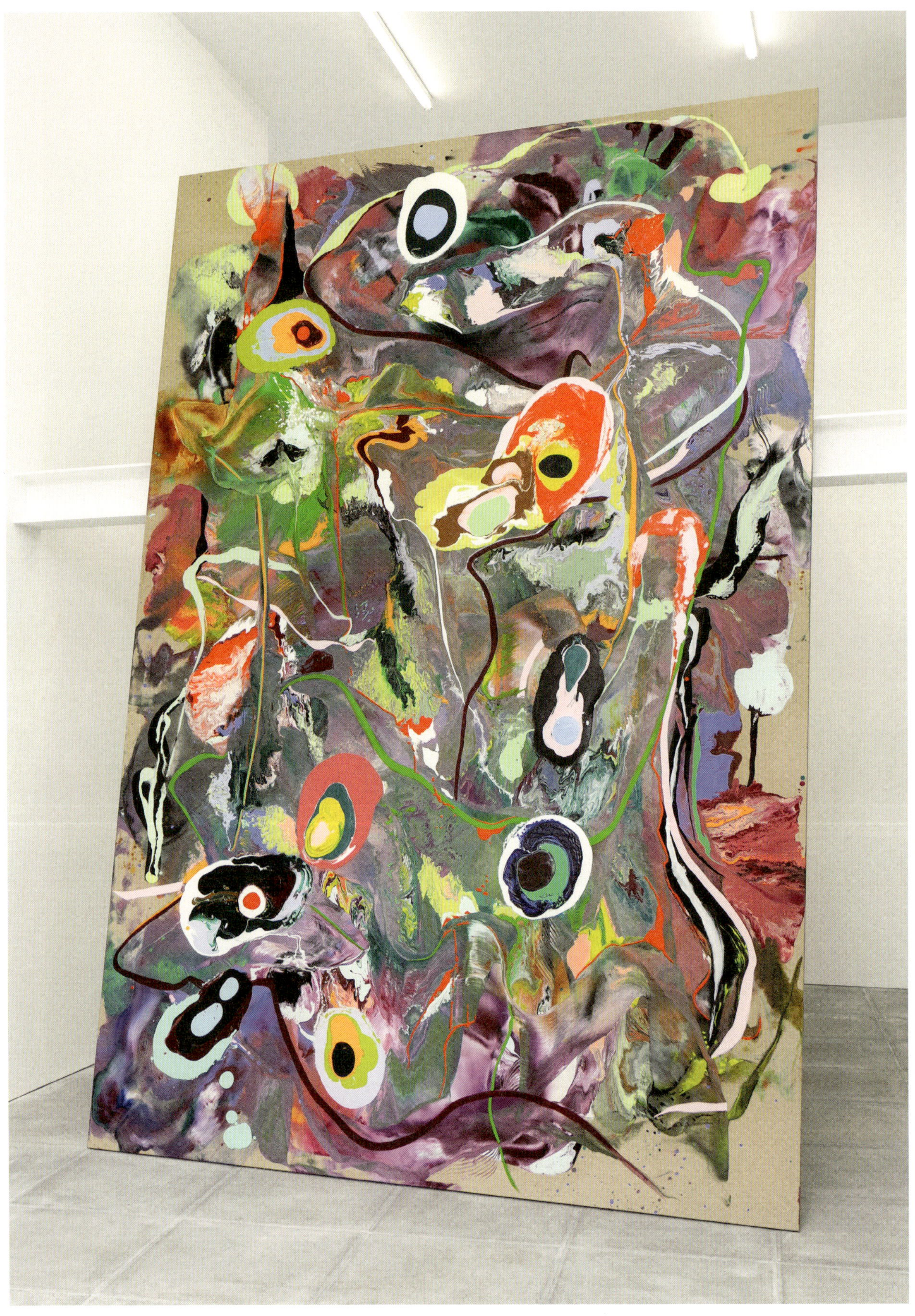

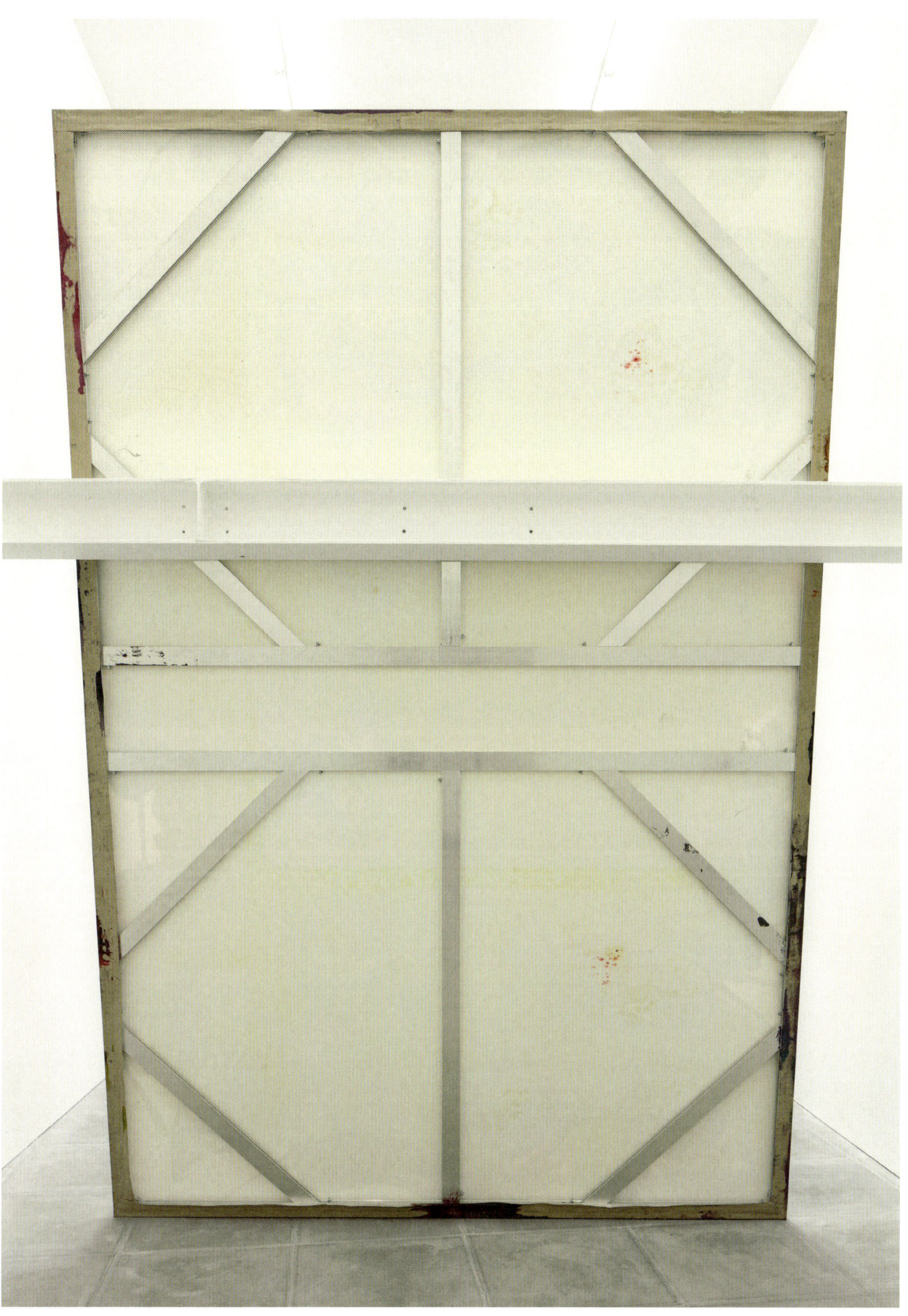

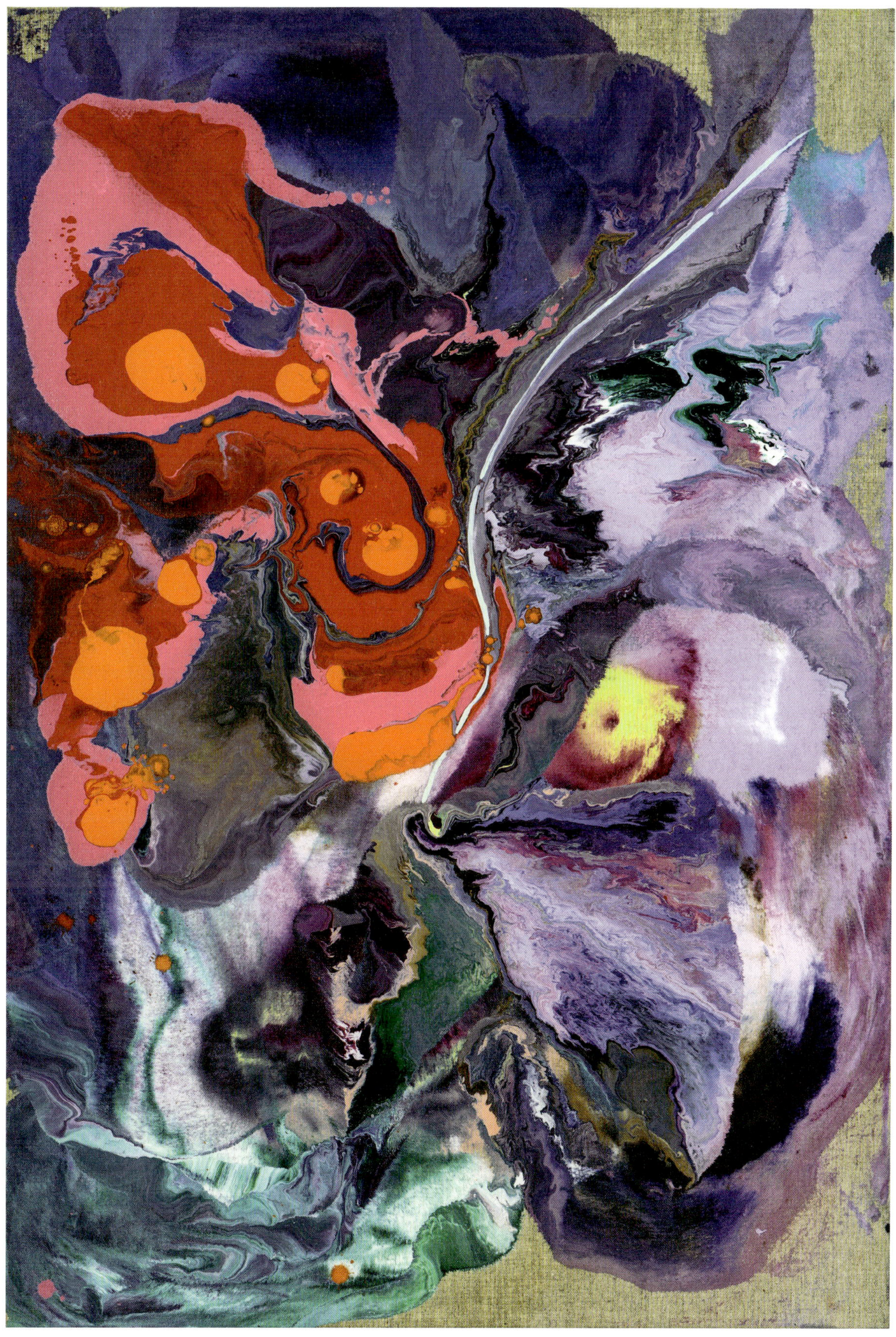

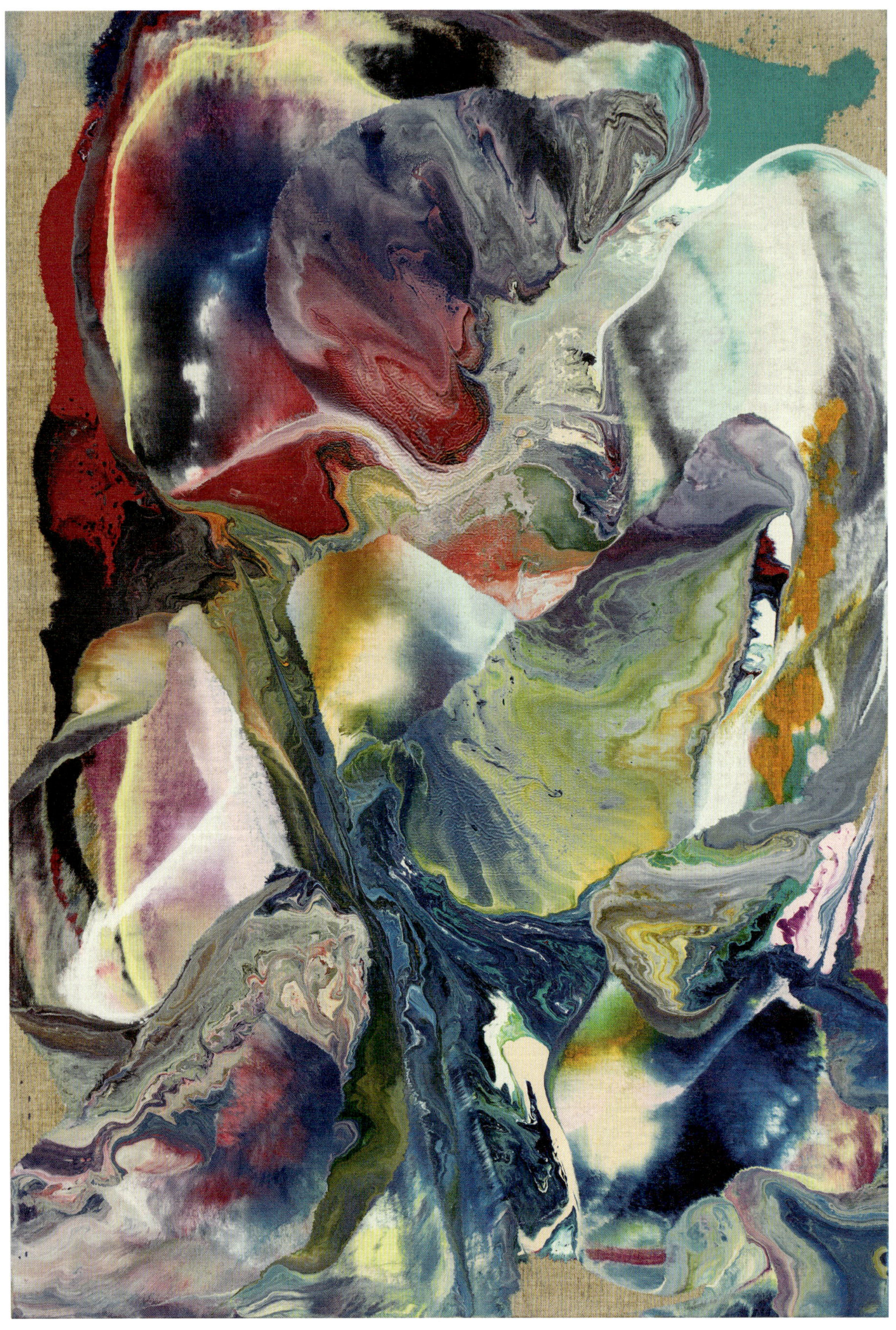

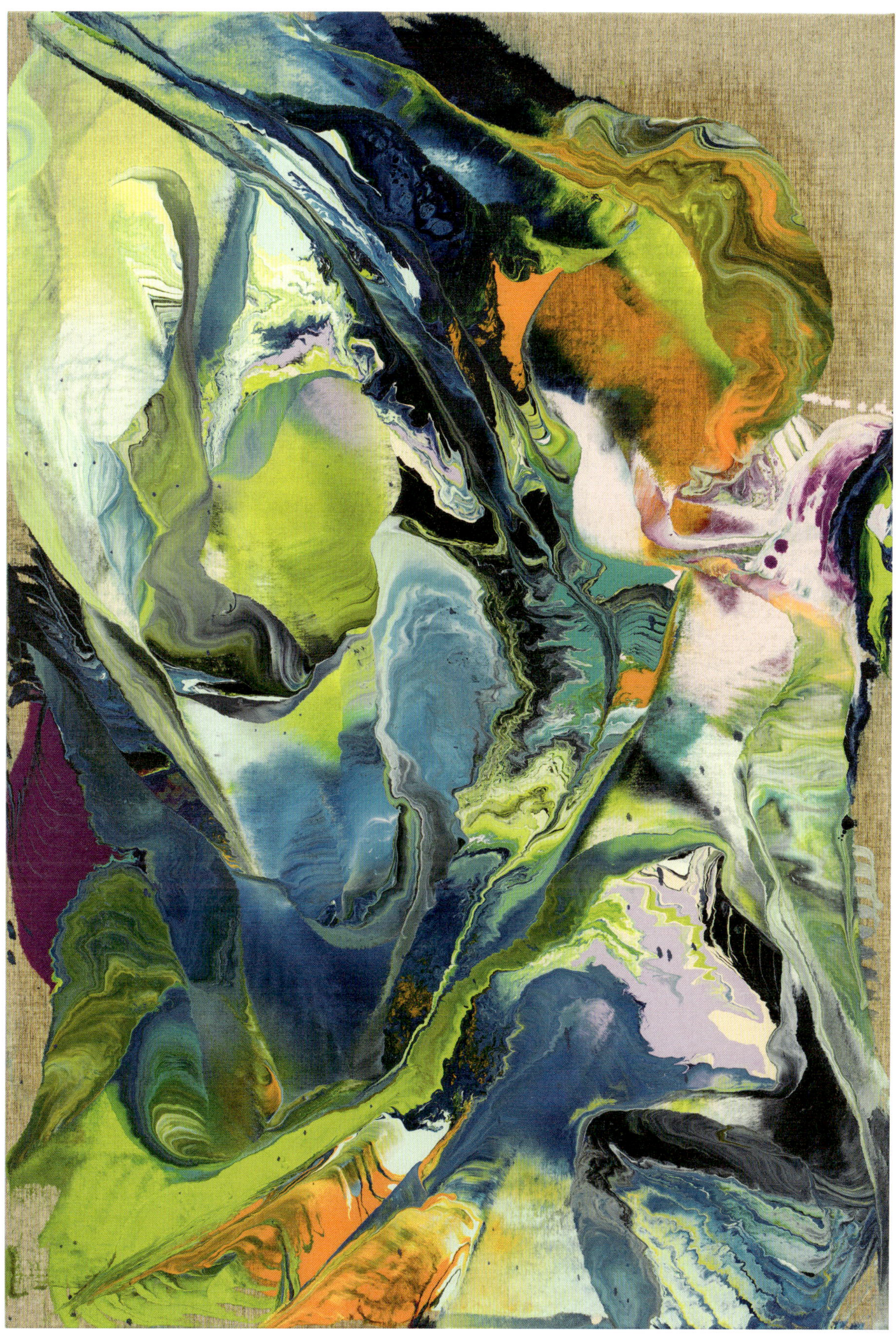

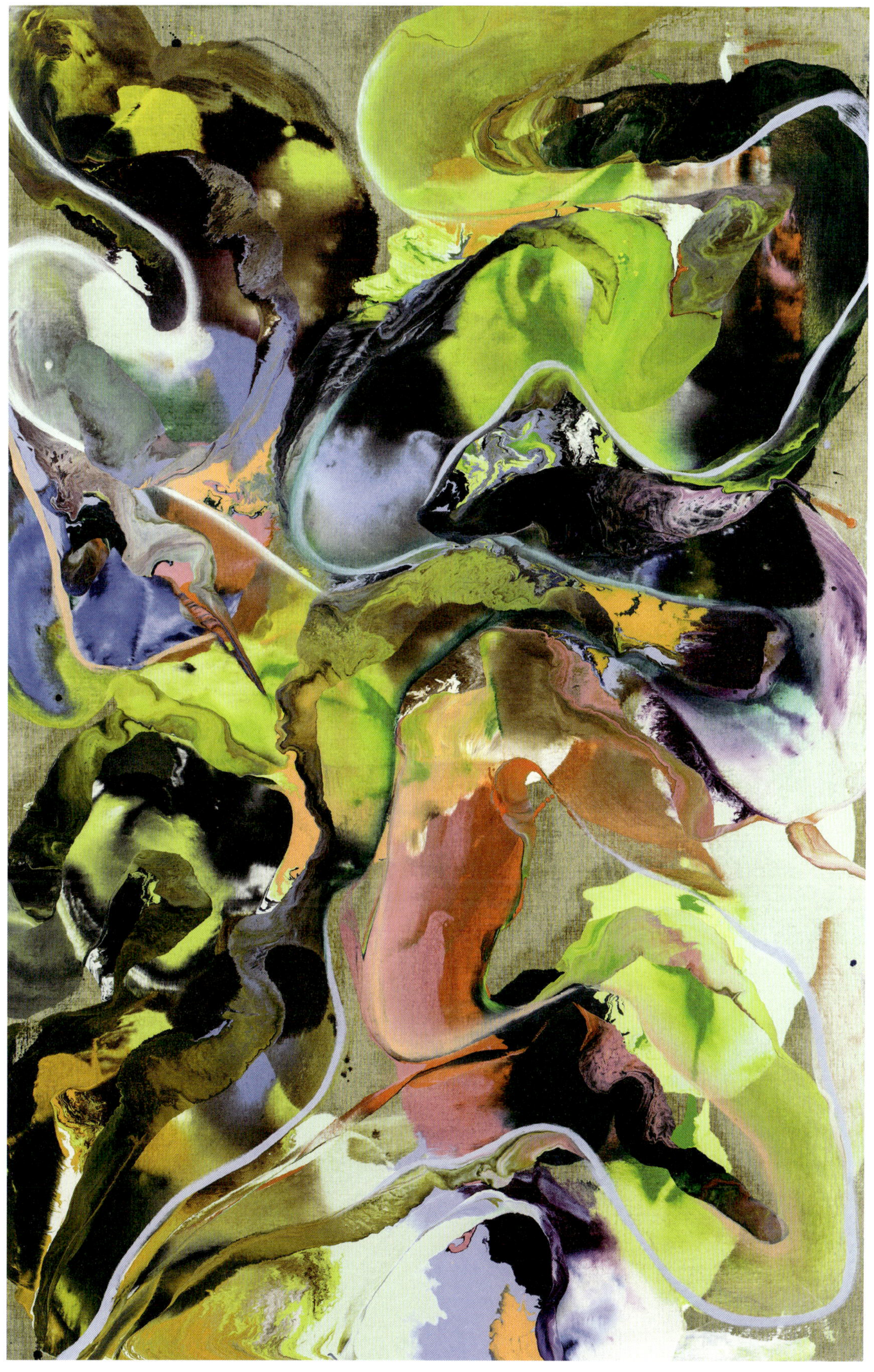

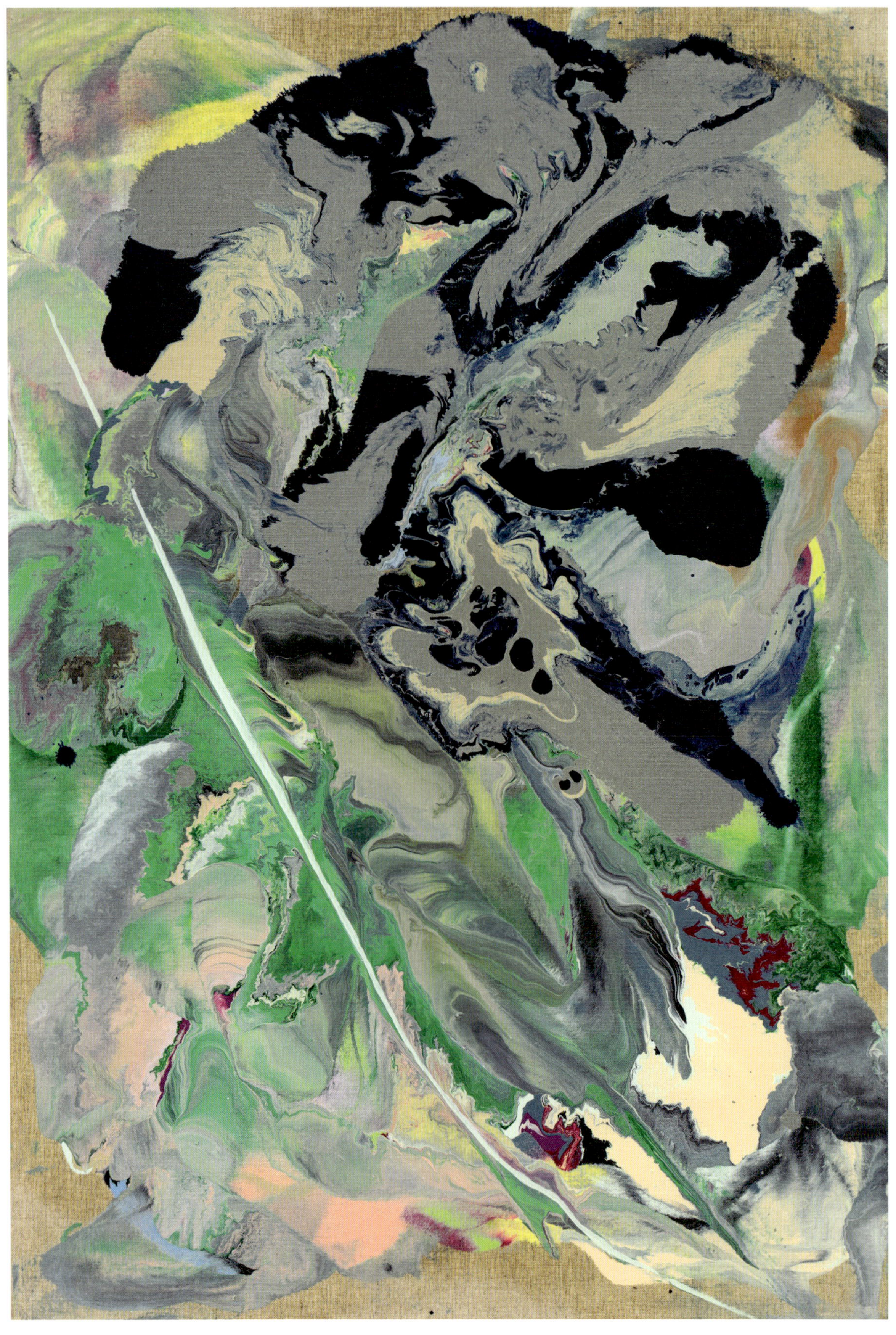

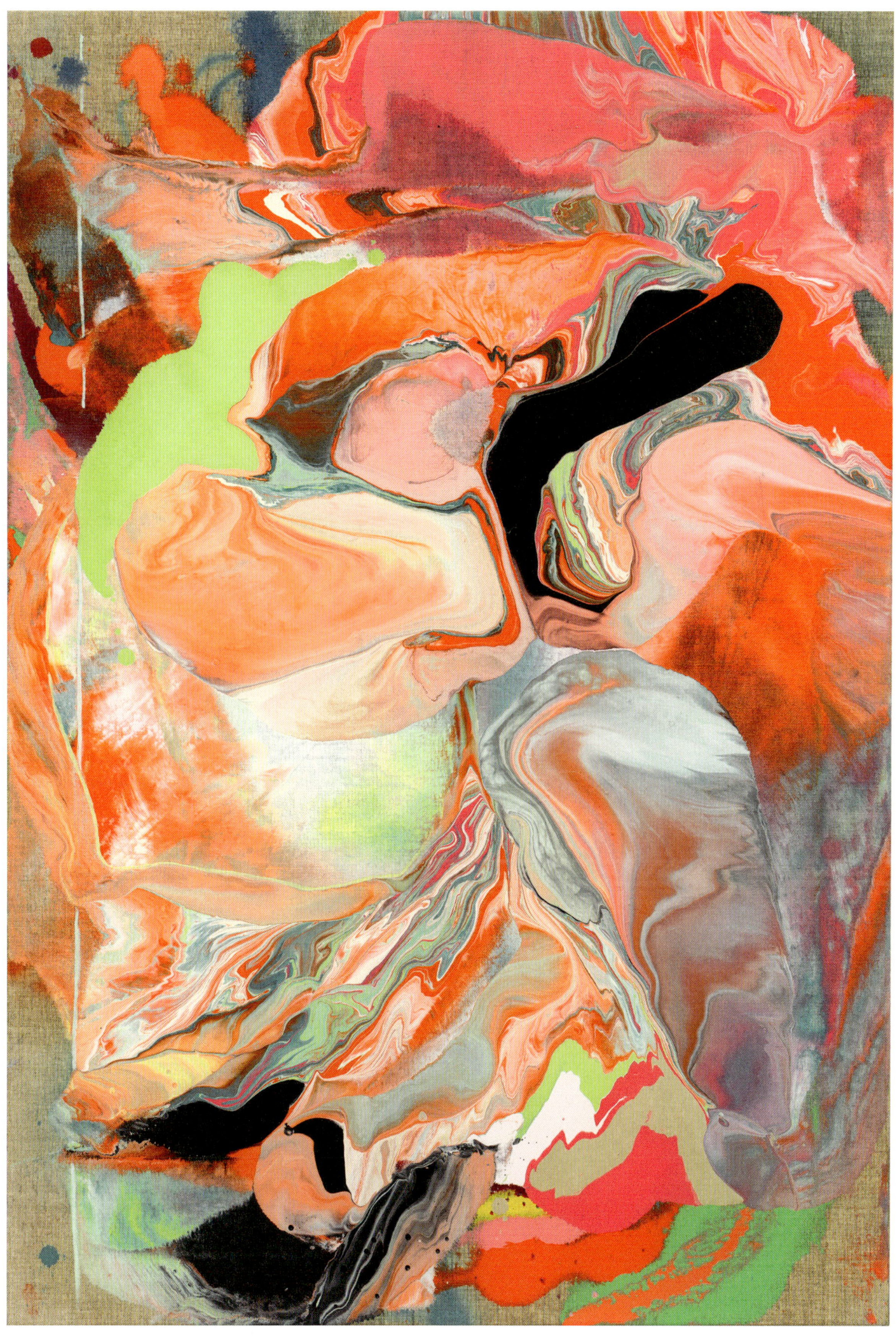

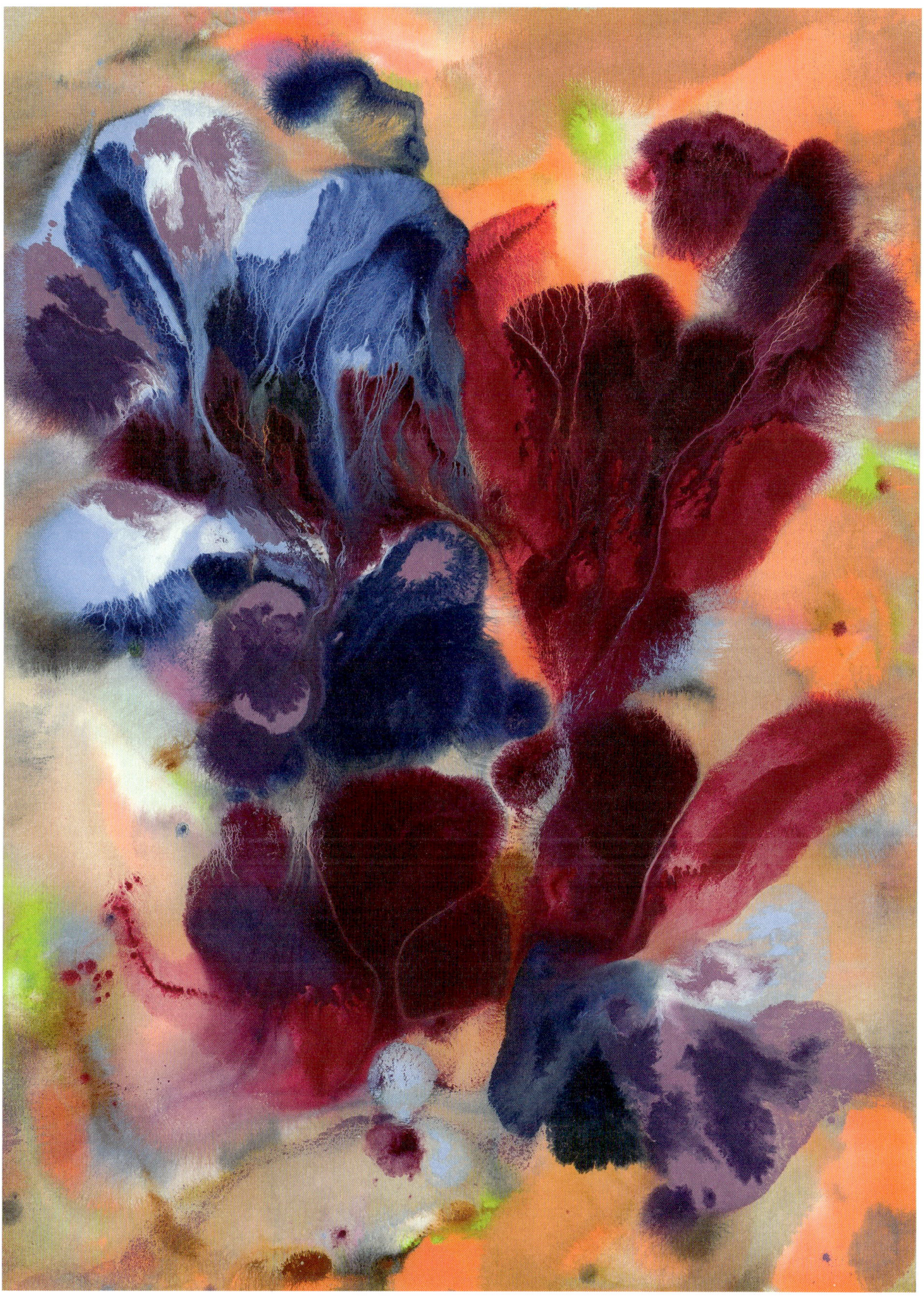

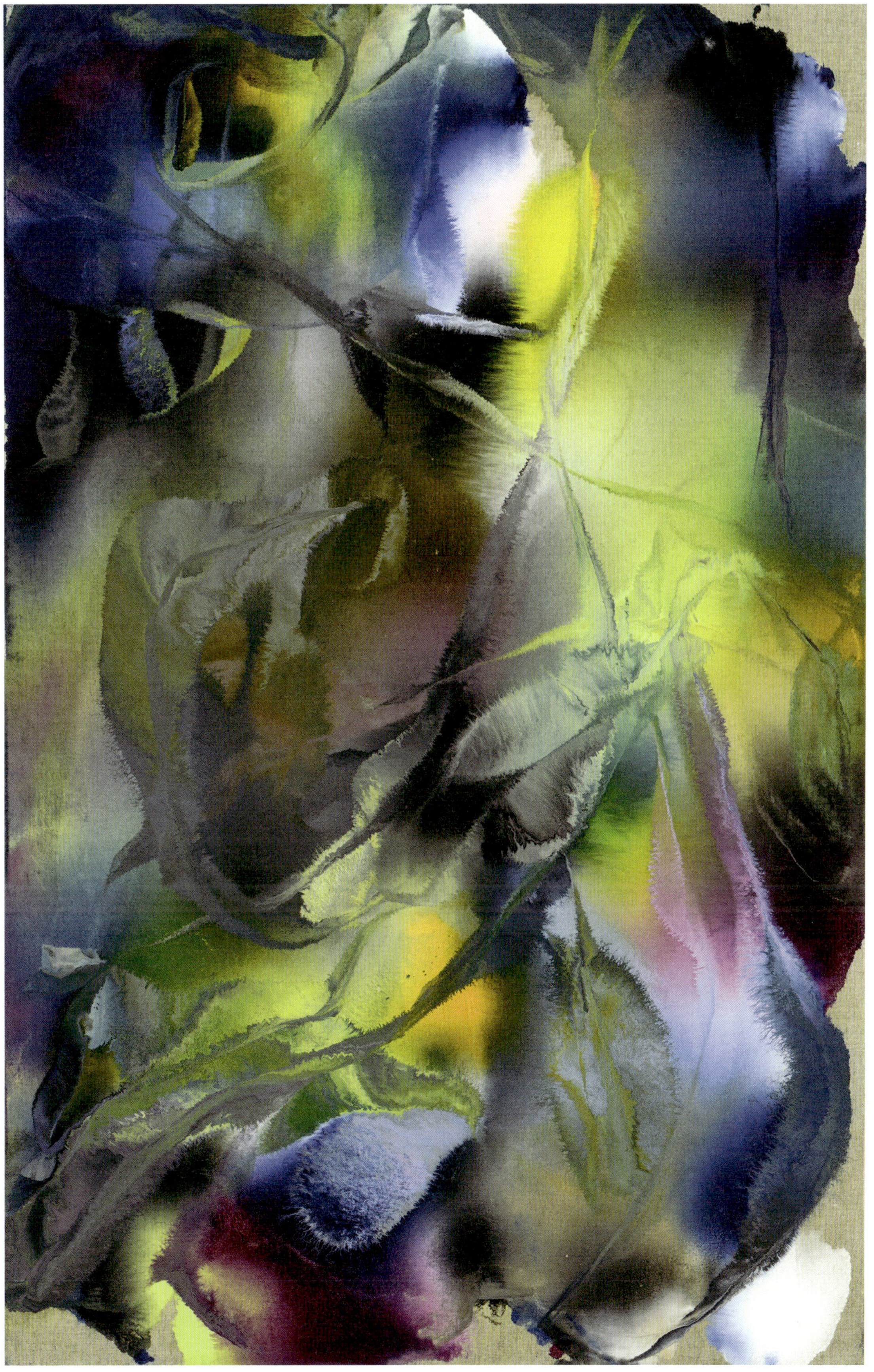

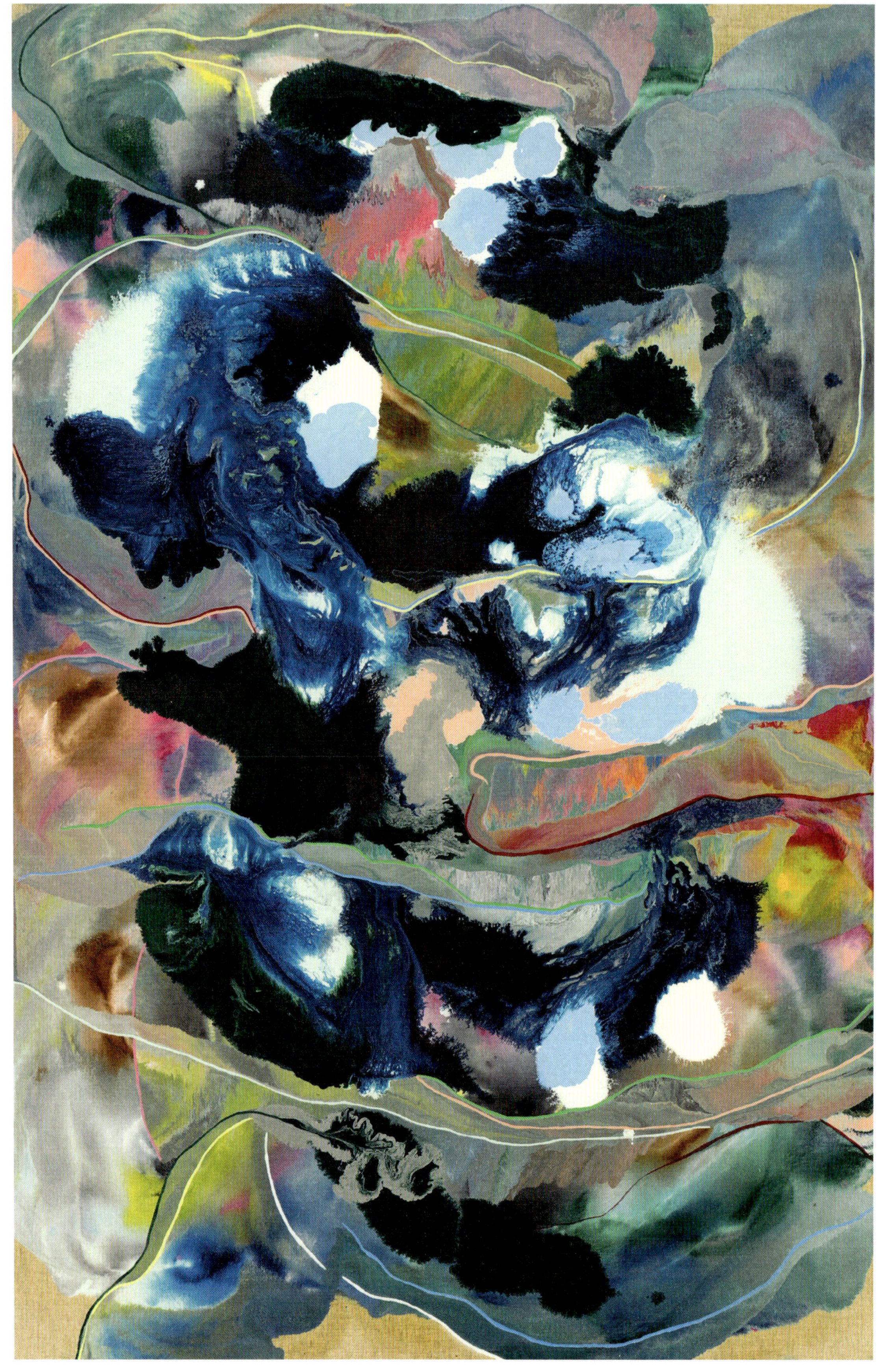

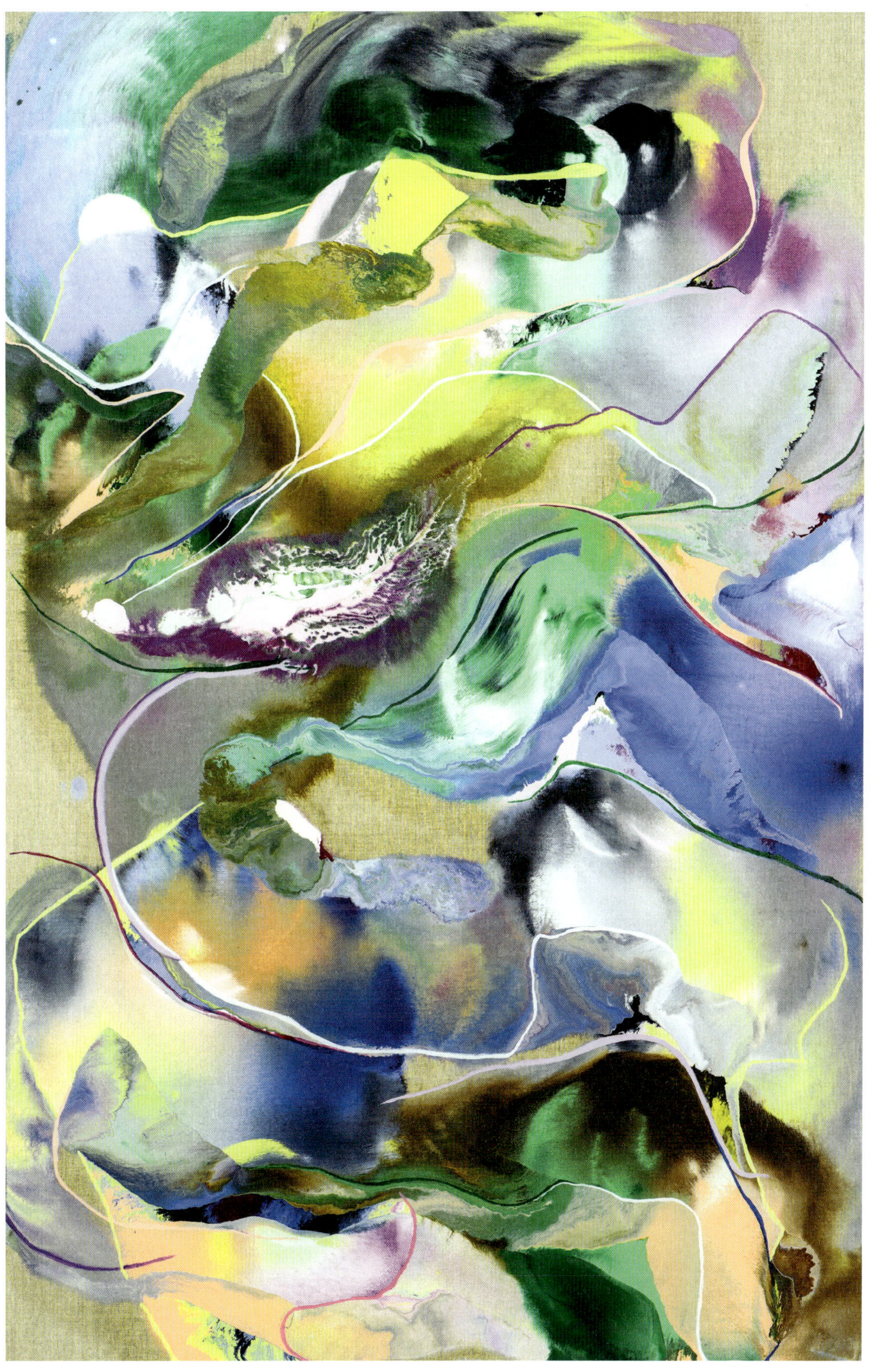

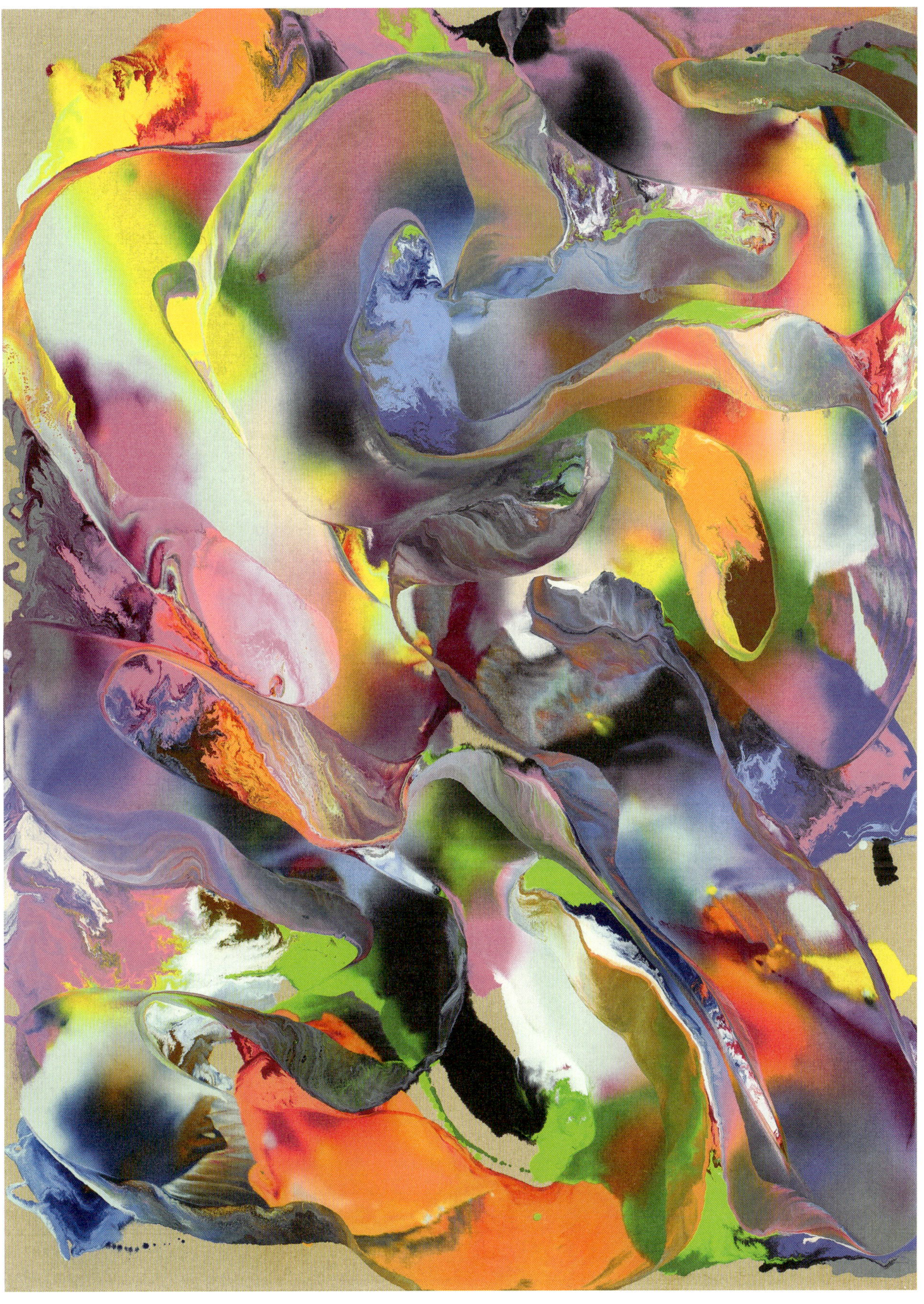

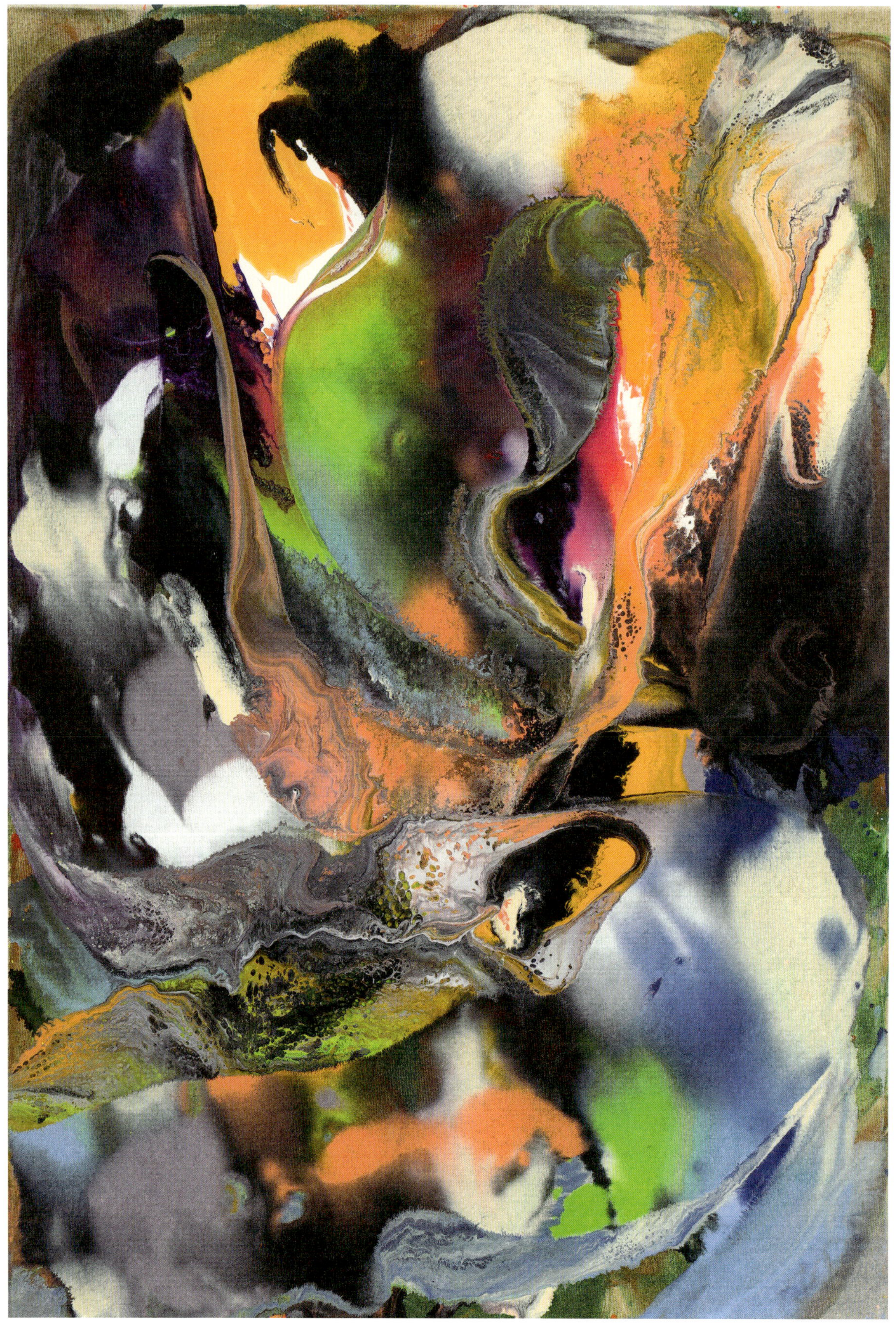

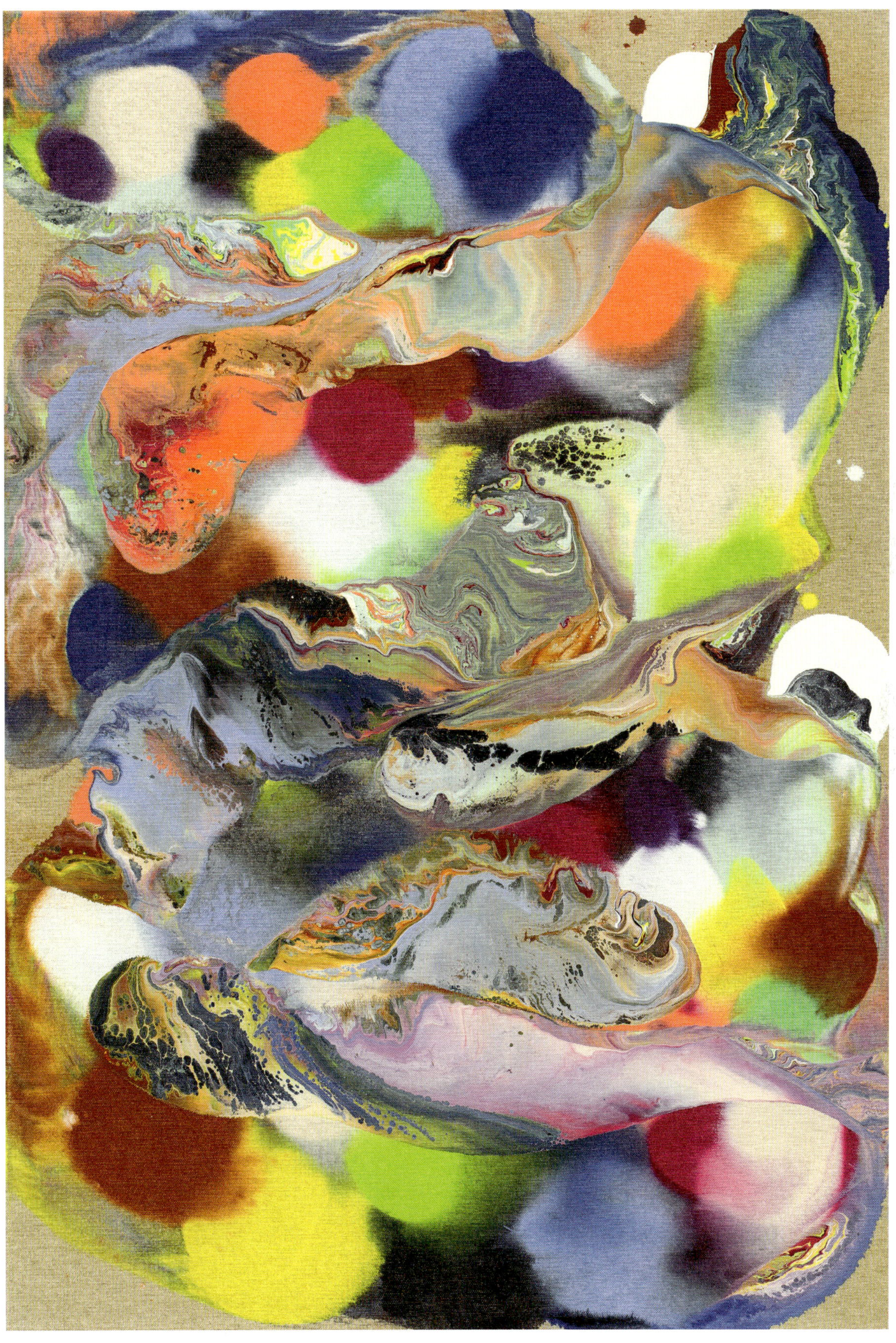

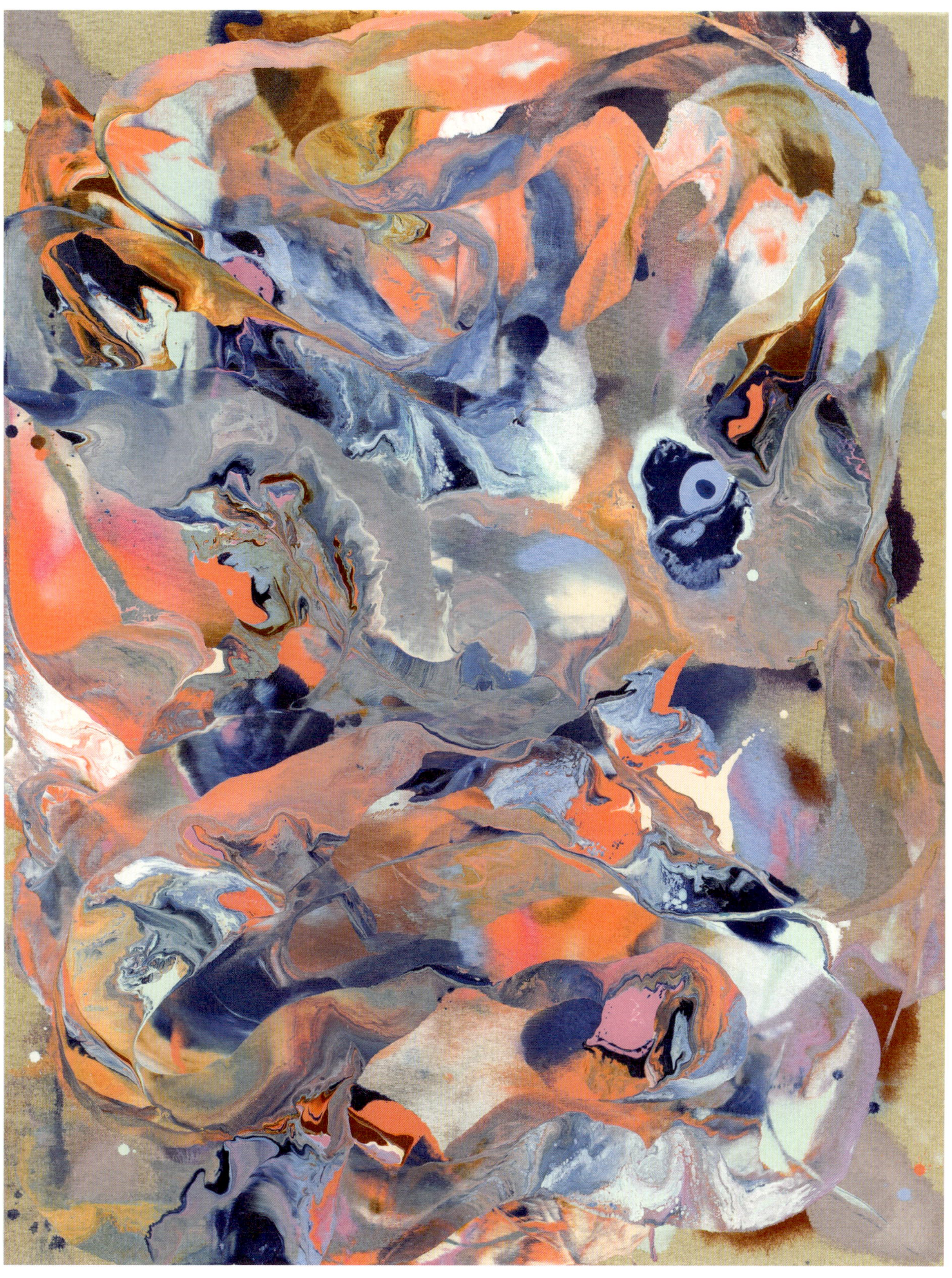

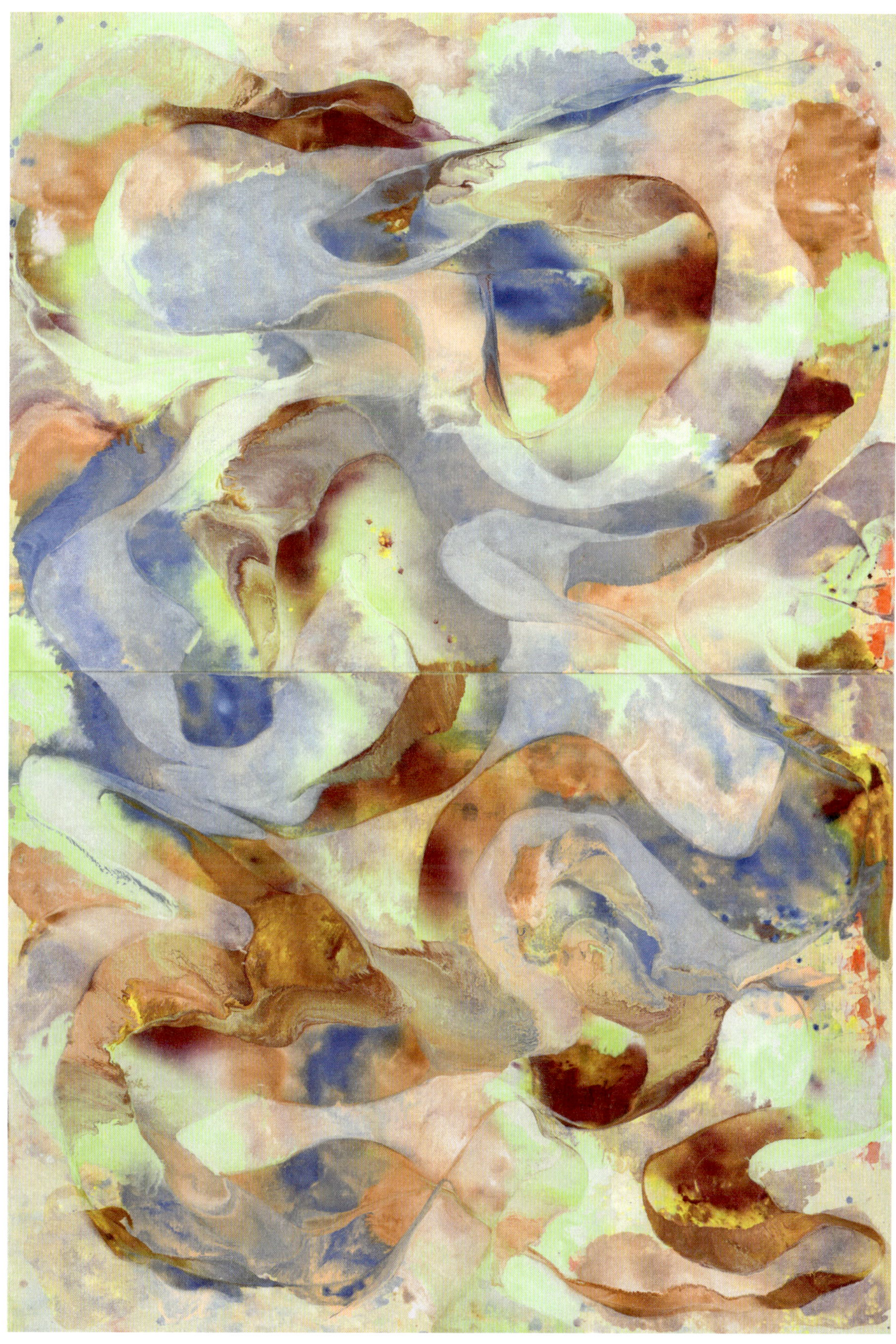

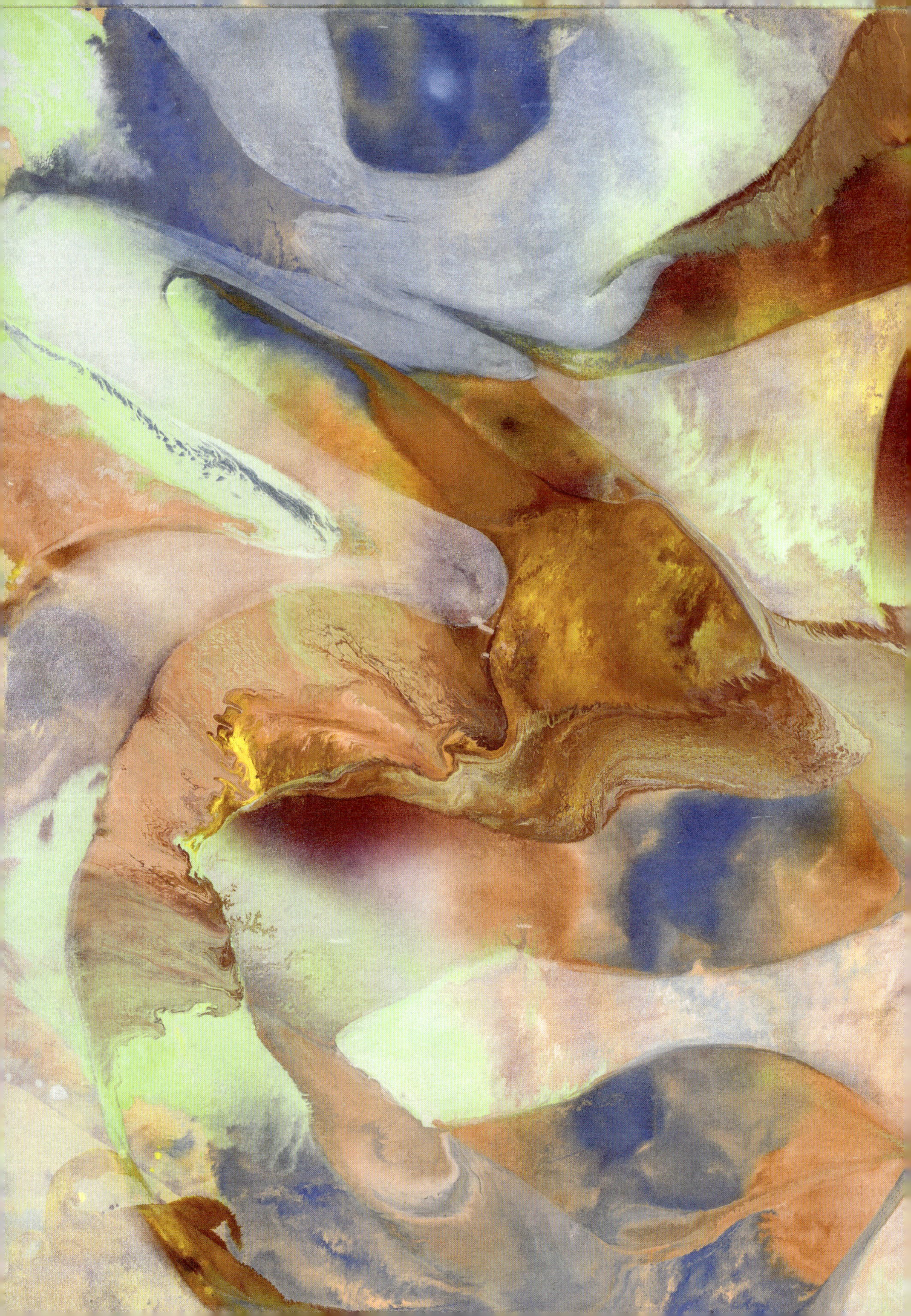

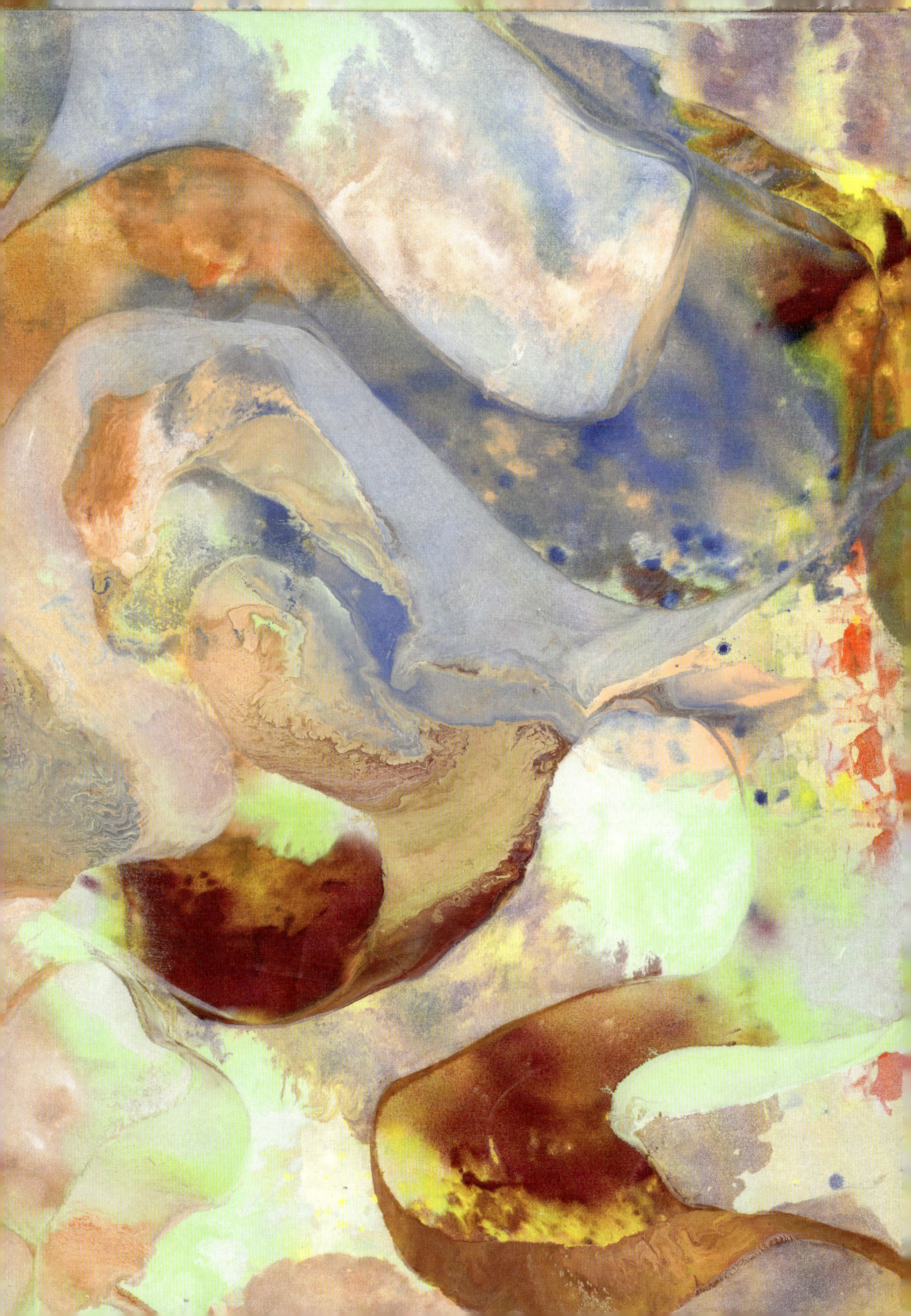

Should-Be Is Not a Color
Cooking Sections

"For now, the first timid pleasure that I feel is being able to say that I have lost my fear of the ugly. And that loss is a very great good. It is a delight."
—Hélène Cixous[1]

When one's urine is not the color it should be, it's ugly. It's ugly because *should-be* is not a color we easily recognize. It's ugly because we might not know what is happening inside our body. Ugly, *uglike* in Old English, comes from Norse *uggligr* (dreadful), *uggr* (fear), and maybe even *agg* (hate). Its meaning softened over the centuries to become "offensive or unpleasant to look at."

Some of the oldest European color charts, dating back to the Middle Ages, come from uroscopy—the visual examination of human urine to determine symptoms of metabolic diseases or other bodily disorders.[2] Hues ranging from healthy yellow to bloody dark red would help diagnose different ailments, which were often treated with the symptom itself: doctors would prescribe color in order to treat color. In the fourteenth century, it was not uncommon to treat patients with *mummia,* a powdered brown substance made of ground-up Egyptian mummies. Centuries later, when the demand for medicinal mummia declined, painters began using its umber hue as a base for Mummy Brown pigment. Interest in the color persisted, and it was not until 1964 that London's last Mummy Brown-manufacturer Roberson and Co. ran out of bodies to grind.[3] "We might have a few odd limbs lying around somewhere, but not enough to make any more paint. We sold our last complete mummy some years ago for, I think, £3," said Mr Roberson. "Perhaps we shouldn't have. We certainly can't get any more."

Mummy Brown was not the only pigment of "ugly" origin. The once popular Indian Yellow, made from powdered urine extracted from cows fed mango leaves, became another filter through which painters depicted their gut feelings in the colors that should be.

One understands the beauty of "ugly" colors when spending time with Tyra Tingleff, even if, she would tell you, "there is no such thing as an ugly color." That cheaply made object that you thought was ugly turns out to be beautiful. And that exquisite object you thought was precious turns out to be your ugliest possession. What's worse, it's out of place. It's not the right tone of should-be: "It doesn't challenge you enough." It has to reach a balance of beauty/ugliness, even if such binaries are ugly in themselves. They are not simple horizontal couplings, never the face-to-face of two terms, but a hierarchy and an order of subordination, showing the layering of time, transparencies, decay, and perhaps contamination.[4] No hue is right or wrong, and yet it has to embody a carefully crafted instability, a loving tension. But how to judge that subtle perception?! Tyra thought *Pastel me not* (2015) was one of her ugliest artworks, until viewers kept admiring its remarkable beauty.

After living in Berlin, Karl Rosenkranz wrote in 1853 that ugliness is not only an indispensable feature of its salient representation, but such salience can make an ugly work aesthetically valid, even beautiful.[5] Ugliness has often served as the all-purpose repository for everything that does not quite fit—disorder, dissonance, deformity, the marginal. In short, the Other.[6] It is a pejorative marker for bodies, things, and feelings that fall beyond or outside the limits of acceptability. Ugliness has long been used to mark, collect, and exclude the aesthetically intolerable, disgusting, dirty, monstrous, revolting, or grotesque; but it can also operate alongside identities, intimacies, practices, and spaces.[7] Tyra occasionally paints with brushes, but we are always more thrilled when she uses a mop. When her canvases turn taller than her ceiling, they go horizontal on the floor, at times elevated or rotated sideways, upside-downing the whole room. Unexpected tools squeeze the visual finesse from her out onto the canvas. For her, chromatic harmony is not pre-mixed. She paints temperamentally. She needs confrontation, disruption. She sees solid pigments as a mixture of dripping and slipping liquids, only possible to dominate sometimes with a scrub sponge from the pound shop.

Her exploration of solvents reminds us of the chemical experiments of Friedlieb Ferdinand Runge, also known to his German contemporaries as Dr. Poison. Fascinated with venomous plants, he would test substances on his own cat—belladonna, henbane, thorn apple, or caffeine—, examining how the cat's pupils would then remain wide open in the sunlight.[8] By reading its gaze, Runge determined which chemical produced its ecstasy. It didn't take him long to start experimenting with coal tar, the waste coal from booming industrial processes, on which he would pour quantities of "magic" substances to unpack their chemistry. Like his cat's pupil, each drop of chlorine led to a different reaction. Ultimately, Runge isolated blue cyanol: the first-ever synthetic color. This discovery set the foundations for *Der Bildungstrieb der Stoffe* (1855), his publication featuring thirty-two visual distillations mapping the presence of chemicals in coal tar and their unique colorful footprints.

In Runge's case, it was the blackness of coal tar, Esther Leslie notes, that allowed him to synthesize all the colors of the rainbow.[9] Pigments under "elective attraction" (*Wahlanziehung*) capture the moment when a seaweedy green turns into a reddish ocher or a bluish halo according to the different alcohols poured in the solution, which make them unusually *augenscheinlich* (apparent to the eye). This original decomposition of color (to understand color) makes one think of Tyra's work, and the analytical universe opening up a range of tones in one's pupils with every of her strokes.

Exploring the construction of color implies dealing with volatile toxicity. Before the world became accustomed to face masks, we thought Tyra would need her own to stop the accumulation of paint layers on the inside of her body. Odd exchanges between us also include a tube squeezer for Scandi "fish caviar" paste. Moving away from the tragedy of industrially farmed fish such as salmon, which are fed synthetic pink to dye their flesh, we genuinely saw it appropriate to repurpose the fake food squeezer for actual pigments; and for Tyra to create other-worldly, highly aesthetic appearances.

In Runge's *Letters on Household Economics* (1866), he reminds readers that chemical experiments are nothing extraordinary. They happen daily in any ordinary kitchen, disguised as evaporation, reduction, emulsion... Perhaps that is the connection that binds our practice with Tyra's. We've shared a roof in so many circumstances, arrangements, and geographies that we've learned how to see through each other's dilated pupils and color mixtures. In our world, spices are staggered in nameless jars such that one recognizes them by hue or smell. It may be cryptic for the other to navigate our kitchen—one might end up mistakenly brewing coffee out of sumac.

Tyra loves to buy cooking ingredients for us. On the kitchen worktop she arranges them as still life, because, she says, "My kitchen is my canvas." In her everyday alchemy, a strong sense of aesthetic presence is what dictates the right of a color to be. She will happily remind you to remove any food labels—logo stickers on fruit pieces just repeat they all belong to the same global distribution system. But items like wash soap may not need a label to communicate that it is soap to do the dishes. Its location—next to the kitchen sink—reveals its function, by being in the place where it should be.

Anthropologist Mary Douglas notes that dirt is simply matter out of place.[10] Being out of place comes with two conditions: a set of ordered relations, and a contravention of that order. For Douglas, dirt is never an isolated event, but the result of a classification system where some elements are rejected. Food is not dirty in itself, but it is dirty —ugly, we could even say—to leave cooking utensils in the bedroom. Tyra sees bananas and apples, lemons and tomatoes, and peppers and onions perfectly arranged on the kitchen counter; not as shapes but as a Baroque feast of hues without any branding noise that puts fruits out of place.

Her hand makes new distortions happen, for instance making some shades misfit everyday routine, like unusually colored bodily fluids. "One person's silence is someone else's noise," Tyra would tell you, "but in the end, they equalize each other." When Tyra wakes up and goes to buy red and yellow tulips, she might come back carrying the red-and-yellow items to rearrange apples and bananas in a certain new composition. You can tell which chromatic connections are crossing her mind that day. It's not just about ugliness; it's about shades and hues that constantly challenge her regarding how to co-exist with those visual inputs all around.

In her analysis of the general use of the notion of *use*, Sara Ahmed points out that use instructions are perhaps more likely to be made and enforced when incorrect uses make correct uses impossible.[11] That is the troublemaker *Geist* that floats in Tyra's vision of the world. Her sharp eye captures moments that might go unperceived by most. But by taking a picture of the performance of embarrassment, the use of the unusable gives the unusable its true use. Moments that a priori meant nothing can easily be turned into incredible ugliness when she spots the perfect misfit and frames exactly what is mismatching. And, as Ahmed says, the more a path is used, the more a path is used.

Like our attraction to desire paths that show signs of usage, our ability to fashion our appearance, whether to seduce mates or blend into the environment, is a matter of desire, and practice—an impulse of which we have made a formal art. During World War I, dazzle painting was developed to make war ships disappear on the horizon. Camouflage techniques were refined in the 1940s, when the British War Office established its dedicated Camouflage Centre.[12] The team was an unusually fantastic assortment: a magician famous for swallowing razor blades, a zoologist expert on animal coloration, and a Surrealist painter who enjoyed painting his naked lover green to blend with the lawn. They came up with an even more sophisticated technique of deception than dazzling. Their new art of camouflage transformed humans into colorful bushes, military vehicles into moving trees, and weapon factories into lush forests when seen from afar or above, turning imperceptibly ugly to the naked eye. For enemies to see through targets without seeing them, the latter needed to blend with the background. Similarly, the studio shots in this book showcase black-and-white images where Tyra camouflages in her own environment. She is not swallowing swords wearing camo, but she certainly blurs the line between the canvas and her chromosphere.

When Tyra frames a nonsensical scene with her camera, her special arrangement of people using useless things rather makes things start using people. In her photos, they will all be remembered in their constructed misfit, and *Will always be the opposite* (2018) no matter what. It is in those moments—when the performance of ugliness is at its best— that one remembers. "Don't worry, I'll keep those pictures for when you run for president," she'll say. No doubt she will.

Second-hand lingerie (2016) hangs in our living room. Well, actually not—that's the title of a different work by Tyra—but one sometimes wishes that her words could hang with you forever. "There is a lot of truth in a joke," Tyra loves reminding you, "the joker is the one who is allowed to tell the truth, but it's a joke, but it's also not." These poetic clashes, sometimes incongruent, are beautifully expressed in the bewitching names of her paintings. Her titles have the power to teleport you to a state of mind very dear to her. The colors of her life experiences are perhaps the vehicle to cross that portal.

Studying painting in London was a big learning curve in her career. Being embedded in a male-dominated environment certainly pushed her feminist statements. Not only technique, format, and chromatic choice, but titles played a major role in marking her presence. No chronological periods easily classify her work. Instead, her written reflections capture where she finds herself, sometimes tracing recurrent moments in life —*Of course I'm not sorry* (2018); *I want it all, but slowly* (2019); *I've been planning while you're playing* (2019); *Just when I discovered the meaning of life they changed it* (2019).

In 2016, Pantone 448C was appointed the ugliest color in the world, the non-color of the year. A shade between brown and green, it conjures disgust via sewage. The color has even been incorporated in cigarette packaging to put off smokers. Also known as Opaque Couché, the ugliest color may become desirable one day, perhaps in an act of *self-conscious sabotage* (2019). In the meantime, sewage, like urine, is nothing but an idea of a color looking back at us, forcing us to see what our cities and our bodies metabolize.

We should, but also should not, be afraid of the refuse flowing in our waterways. Sewage should not simply be something *not* to look at, rejected into the invisible world underneath our feet. When washed down the drain, many industrial and post-industrial substances eventually enter our bodies. Today, more and more noxious compounds are flowing through our guts and gutters. To such a scale that substances no longer flow through our bodies. Rather, as Hannah Landecker writes, our bodies have become postindustrial metabolisms that circulate through those substances.[13] This new amalgamation of refused toxins, hormones, microfibers and nanoplastics creates color turbulences that allow us to read (the rejects of) contemporary society. Juxtapositions, dissolutions, or emulsions of iridescent colors remind us of what we are flowing through. We should instead understand what is being refused and why, what layers scrape and wash off all kinds of substances that, as in Tyra's work, makes all levels transparent.

When one early Friday morning we took Tyra to London's wholesale flower market, we knew what we were getting into. She arrived, and she scanned. As she opened her eyes in awe, like Runge's cat, we could discern the levels of stimulation going on in her brain. Flowers are one of the most important parts of her visual life—she would even sometimes hide and sleep in the flower shop where she worked in her early days as a painting student in Copenhagen. Walking among the flower wholesalers, her unique gaze searched for combinations, rearrangements, tones that you would not expect together. There in the industrial warehouse she chose angelicas, bellflowers, and bluebells; then changed them for chamomiles, chives, chicories, poppies, and forget-me-nots in spontaneous bouquets made in passing. Moving them from arm to arm, from vase to vase,

she drove the flower sellers mad. But a few hours later, by the time
the market was about to close, all her flowers had found the right tone,
the colors that should be.

1   Hélène Cixous, *Coming to Writing and Other Essays* (Cambridge: Harvard University Press, 1991), 75.

2   Sarah Laskow, "What a Chart of Urine Tells Us about the History of Color Printing," *Atlas Obscura*, February 27, 2018, https://www.atlasobscura.com/articles/chart-urine-manuscript-medical-history

3   Cooking Sections, *Salmon: A Red Herring* (London: isolarii, 2020).

4   Jacques Derrida, *Margins of Philosophy* (Chicago: University of Chicago Press, 1982).

5   Karl Rosenkranz, *Aesthetics of Ugliness: A Critical Edition*, ed. and trans. Andrei Pop and Mechtild Widrich (London: Bloomsbury Academic, 2015), 4.

6   Nina Athanassoglou-Kallmyer, "Ugliness," in *Critical Terms for Art History*, ed. Robert S. Nelson and Richard Shiff (Chicago: University of Chicago Press, 2003), 281–95.

7   Ela Przybylo and Sara Rodrigues, eds., *On the Politics of Ugliness* (London and New York: Palgrave Macmillan, 2018), introduction.

8   Esther Leslie, *Synthetic Worlds: Nature, Art and the Chemical Industry* (London: Reaktion, 2005), 48–49.

9   Leslie, *Synthetic Worlds*, 48–49.

10   Mary Douglas, *Purity and Danger: An Analysis of the Concepts of Pollution and Taboo* (London: Routledge, 2002), 36.

11   Sara Ahmed, *What's the Use? On the Uses of Use* (Durham: Duke University Press, 2019), 29.

12   Michael Taussig, "Zoology, Magic, and Surrealism in the War on Terror," *Critical Inquiry* 34 (2008): 103.

13   Hannah Landecker, "Postindustrial Metabolism: Fat Knowledge," *Public Culture* 25, no. 3 (2013): 495–522.

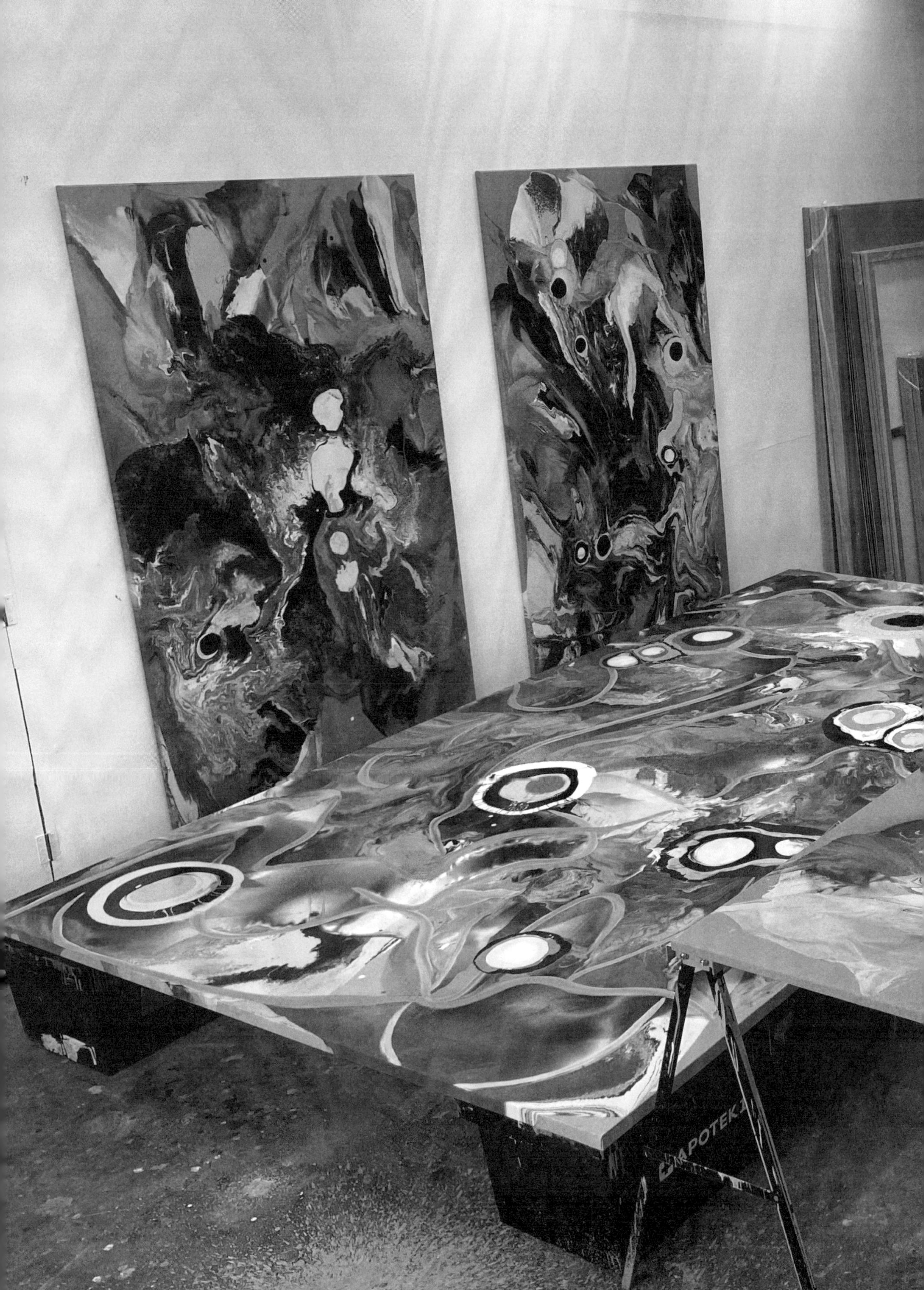

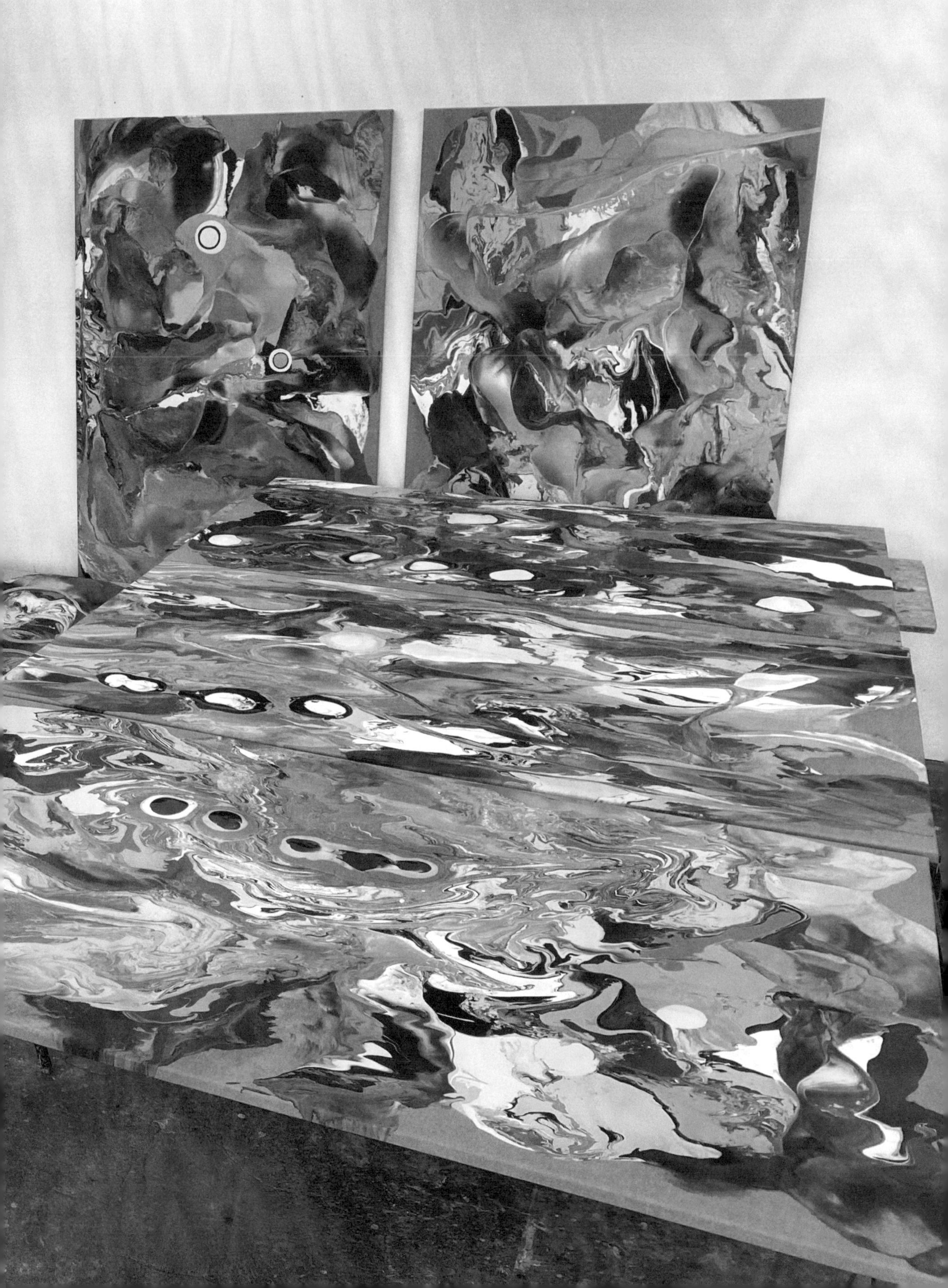

Travel North

Petter Snare

The painterly world of Tyra Tingleff—featuring abstract motifs achieved in a conversation, or maybe mediation, between thin layers of paint, the canvas, and the brush or swab—has no immediate sibling in the art history of Norway, although one can indeed find keys to understanding it in the chronology of Norwegian artists. The light up north is so fragile. It's given to us in abundance for a short while until winter approaches and it is taken from us, pitching us into monthslong darkness. The drama that unfolds between the sky and the landscape is essential to Norwegian painting. The northern lights and white nights, the delicate summer flowers making the most of a few weeks without frost, the glaciers and their unforgiving nature, all express a dynamism that is palpable in Tingleff's paintings.

The sublime is a bedrock in Norway's fairly young art history. Fearful nature, its power to produce "the strongest emotion," as Edward Burke describes it, has been an inspiration for countless artists. Consider, for example, Peder Balke's frightening waves washing over the shore at North Cape in his paintings from the 1850s, or J.C. Dahl's 1844 painting of the Nigard Glacier, a massive force overwhelming everything in its path. In a similar way, Tingleff's microcosms encapsulate us, demanding a near-physical reaction to their size, the colors fighting for space, the paint overtaking the canvas.

The seminal artist Harriet Backer, whose ability to capture light is still unmatched in Norwegian painting, was known for grappling with depicting reflected light in interiors. She described her self-doubt in this regard in a letter to a friend in 1909: "I can hardly judge if this is a good painting, here by myself, alone. . . . The room is filled with light, and everything I see is false." This painterly struggle is reflected in Tingleff's works, which seemingly emit light from an unseen source. The shades and hues reveal the artist's probing investigation of the consequences of each stroke.

Around the turn of the twentieth century, Nikolai Astrup was painting in his beloved Jølster, a fjord in western Norway. He painted the fjords, the mountains, and everyday life, capturing the ever-changing summer colors and light in a manner totally unique. His greens are never the same; likewise, the yellows change with every brushstroke. Tingleff's works also unpredictably explore the full range of colors. It is as if each individual painting is simultaneously a piece in, and the complete, jigsaw puzzle.

Tingleff's dissection of colors and movement inspires in the observer an effort to let go of prior convictions regarding painting. Just as we must yield to the immensity of nature, we must undergo disorientation and destabilization when encountering the works, in order to arrive at a sense of their meaning.

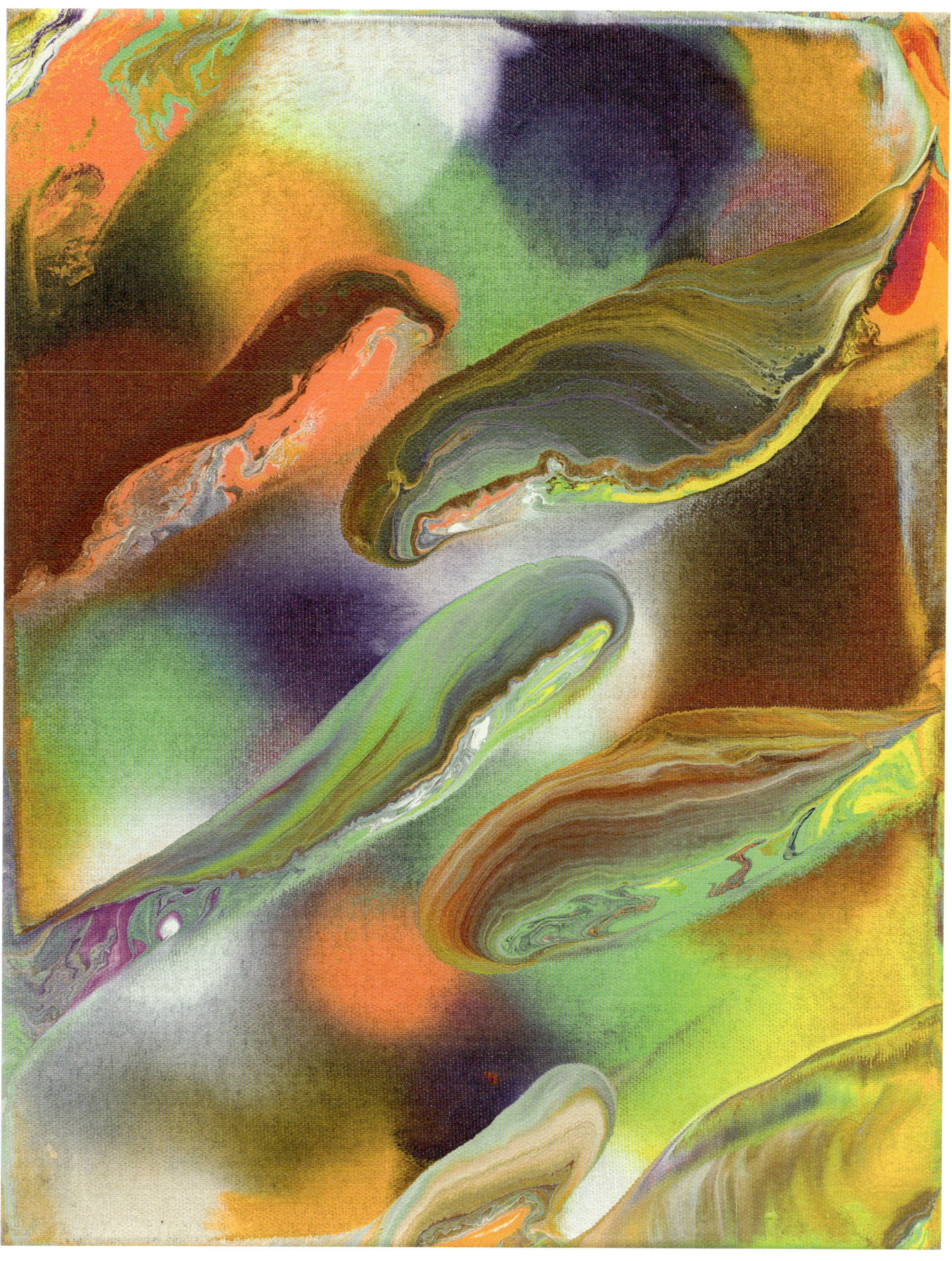

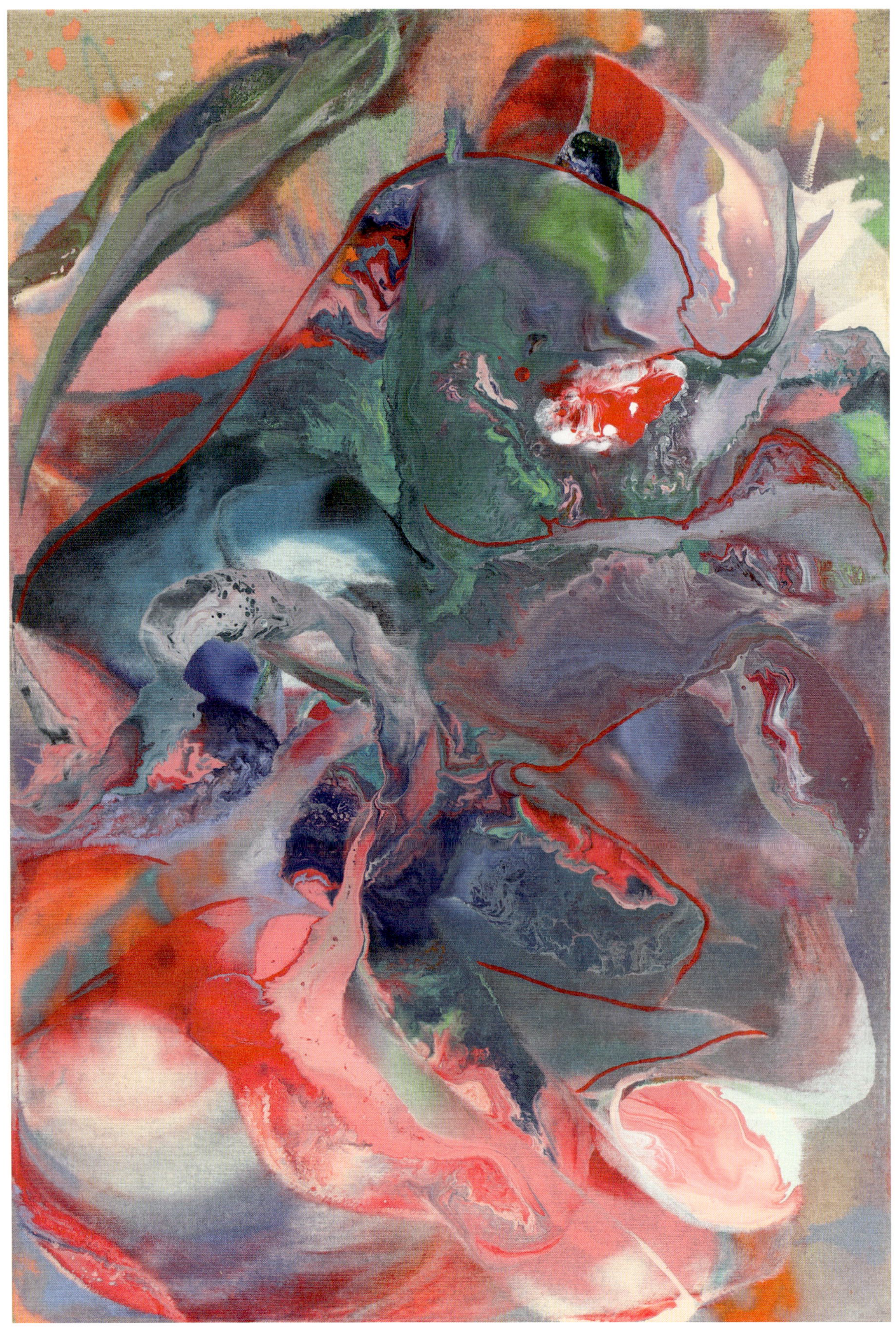

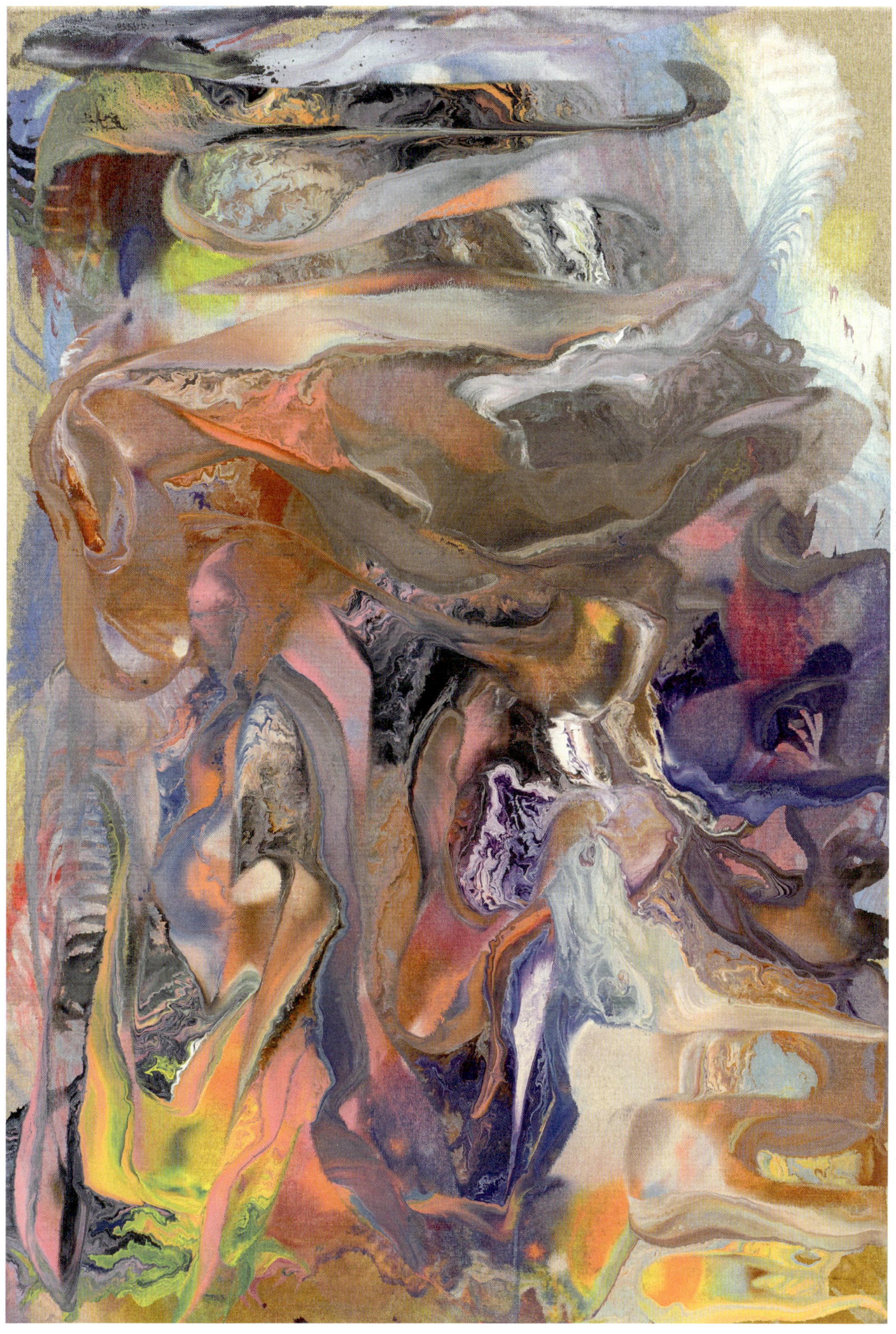

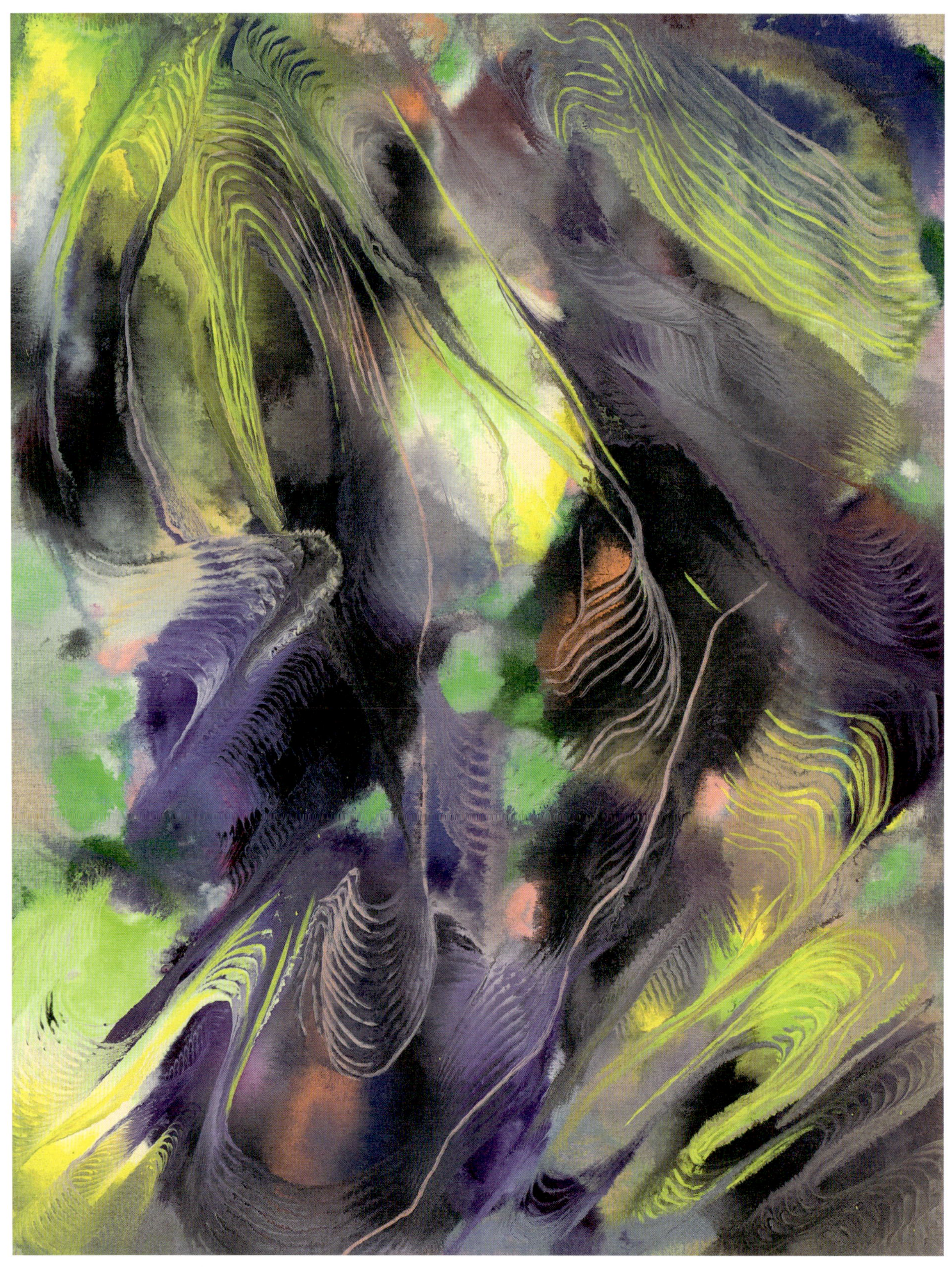

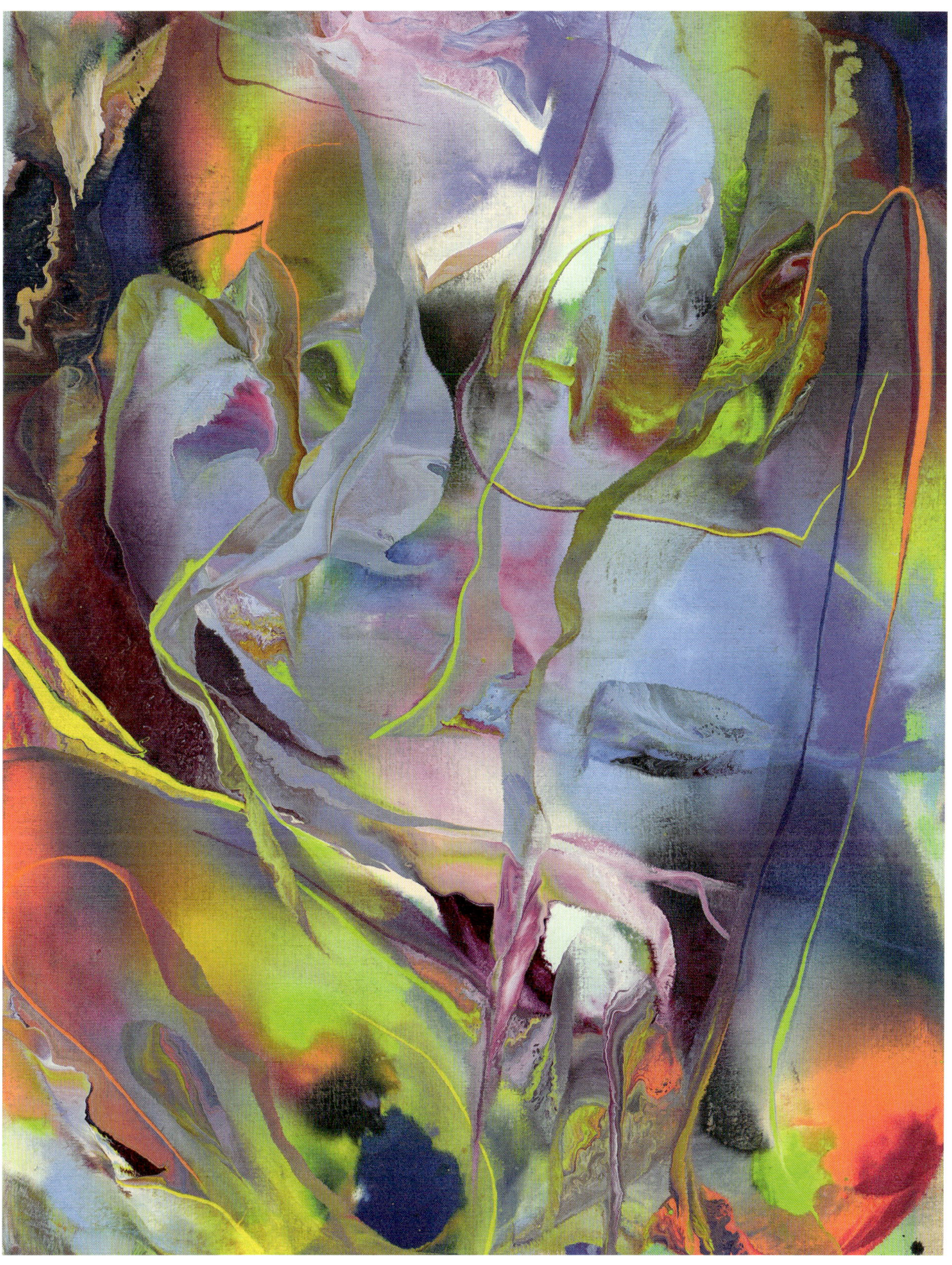

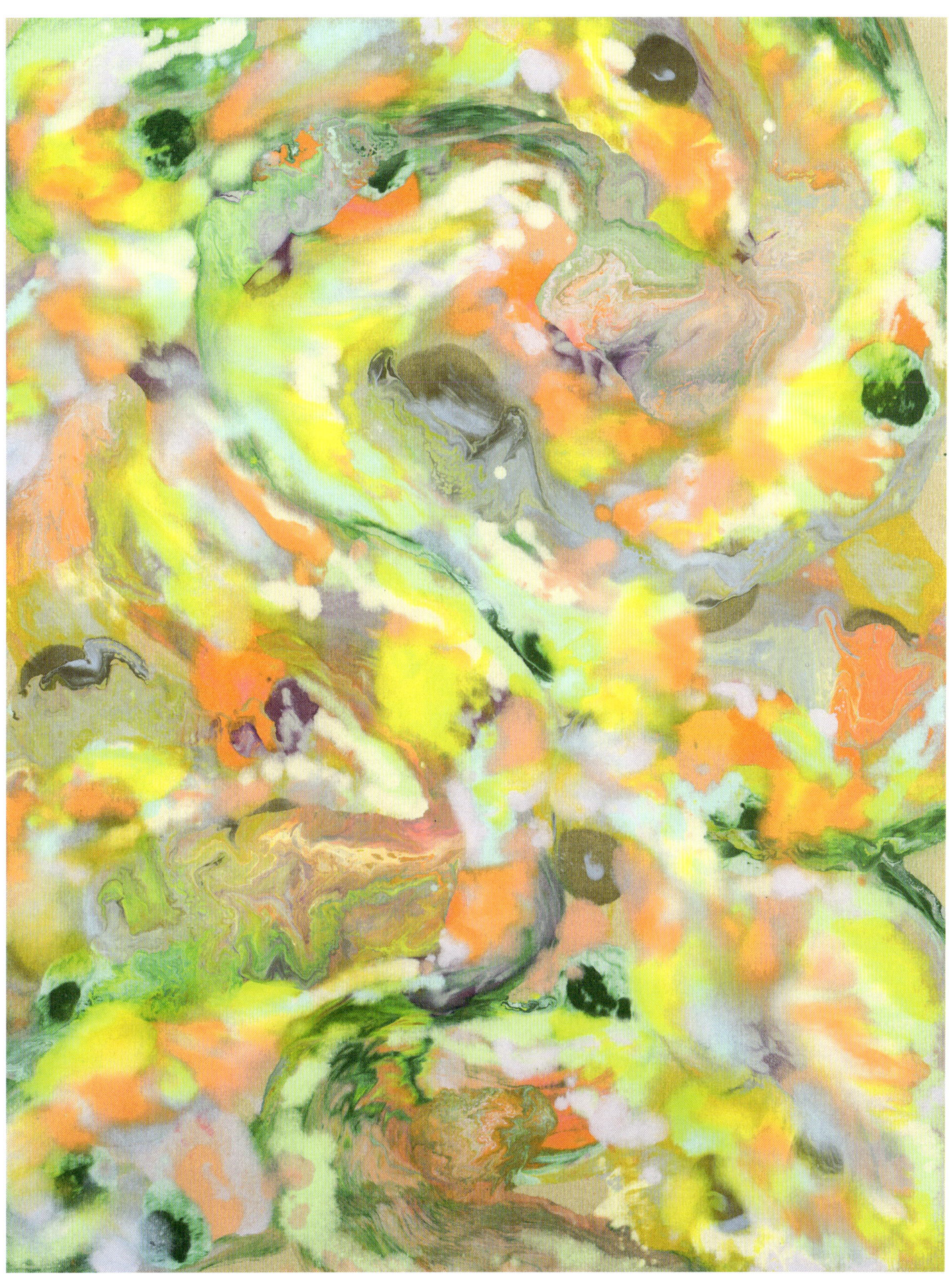

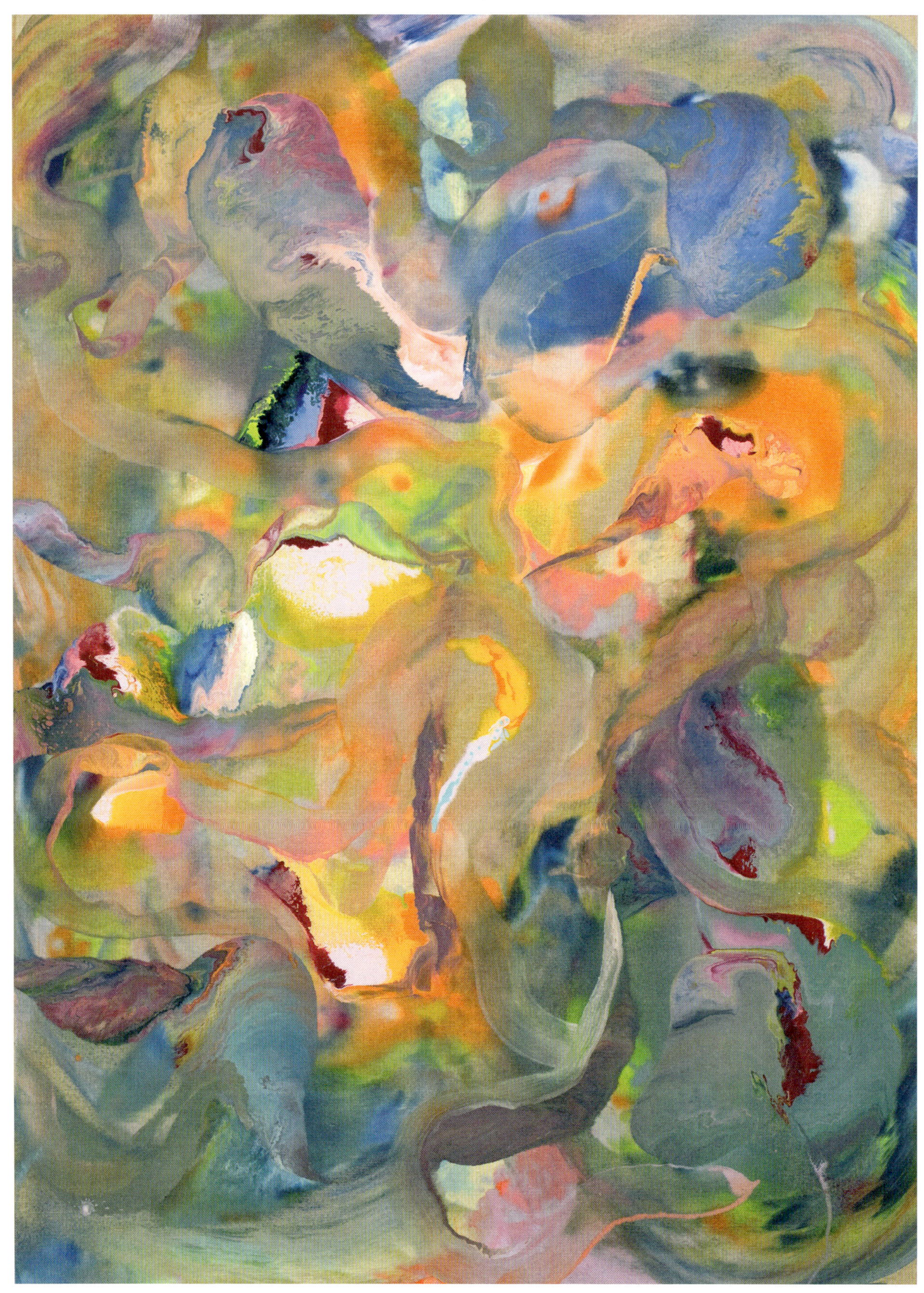

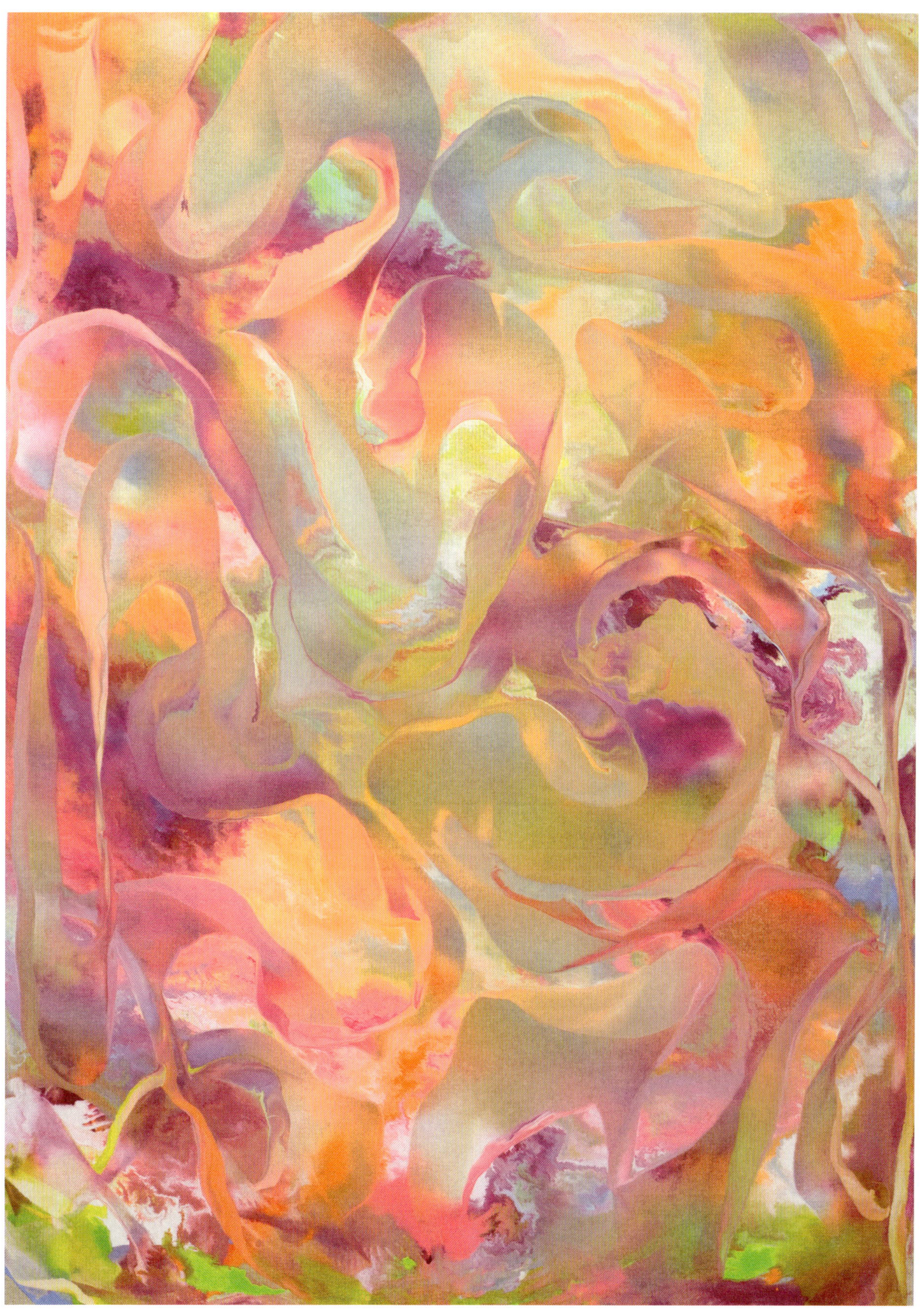

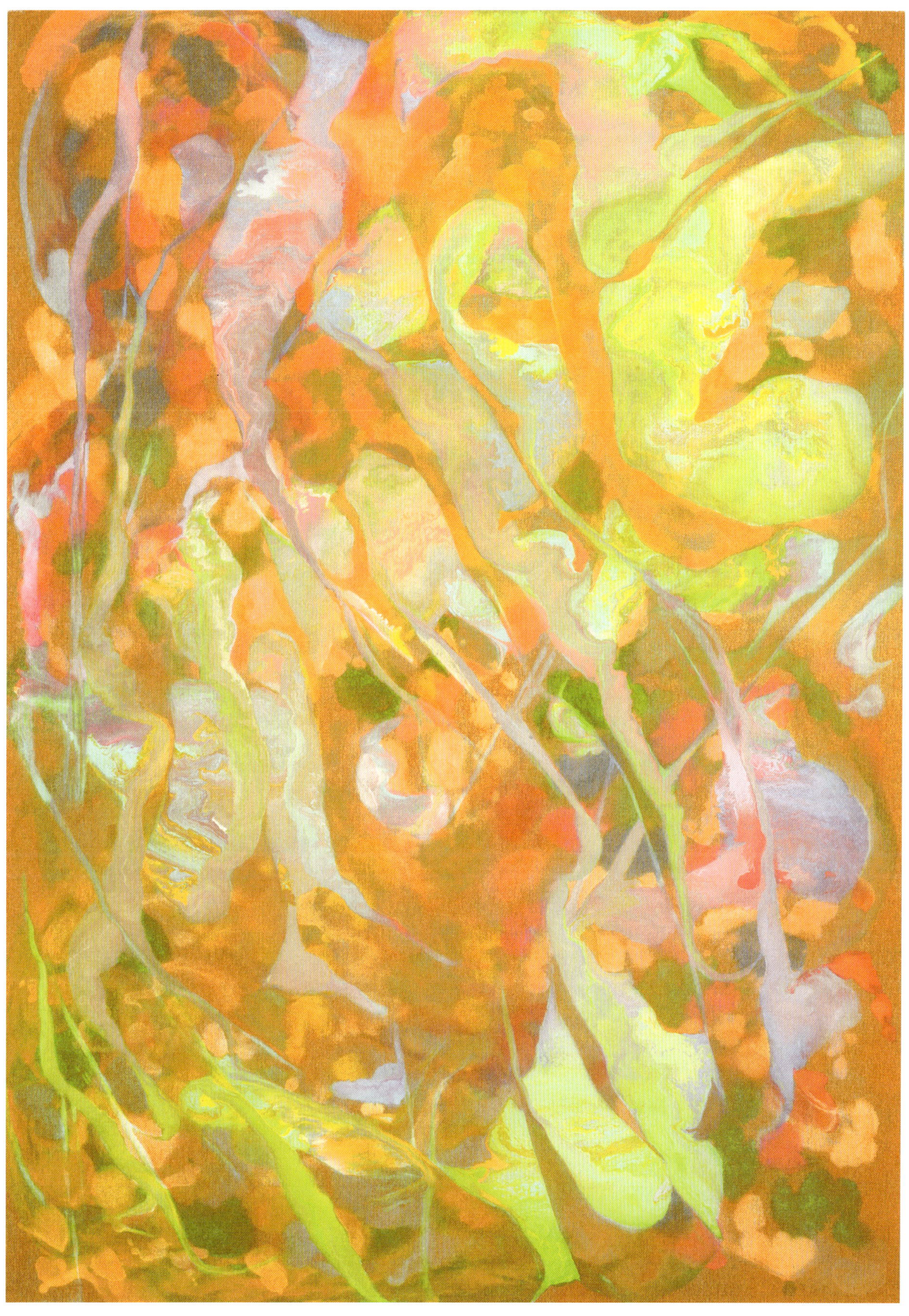

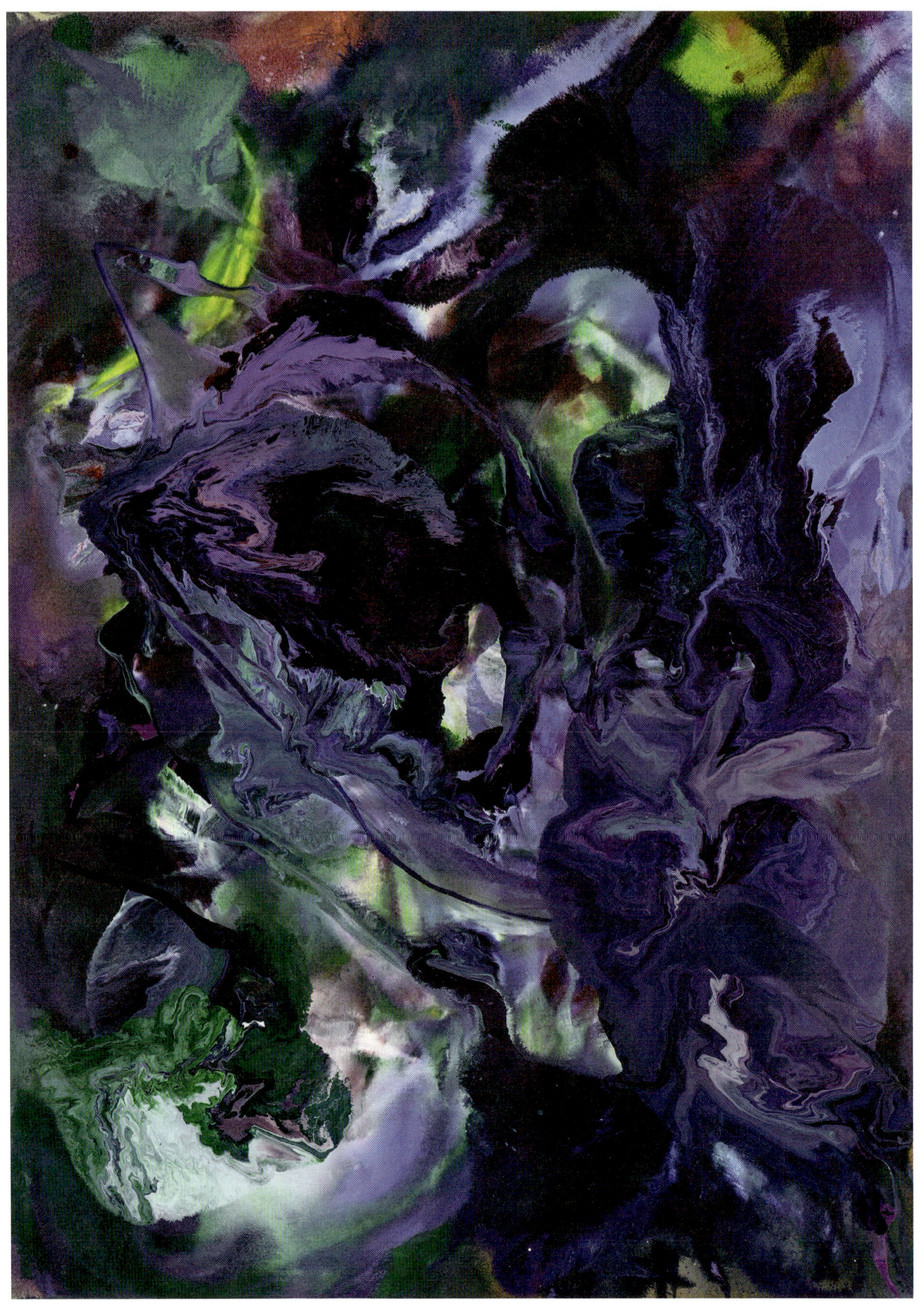

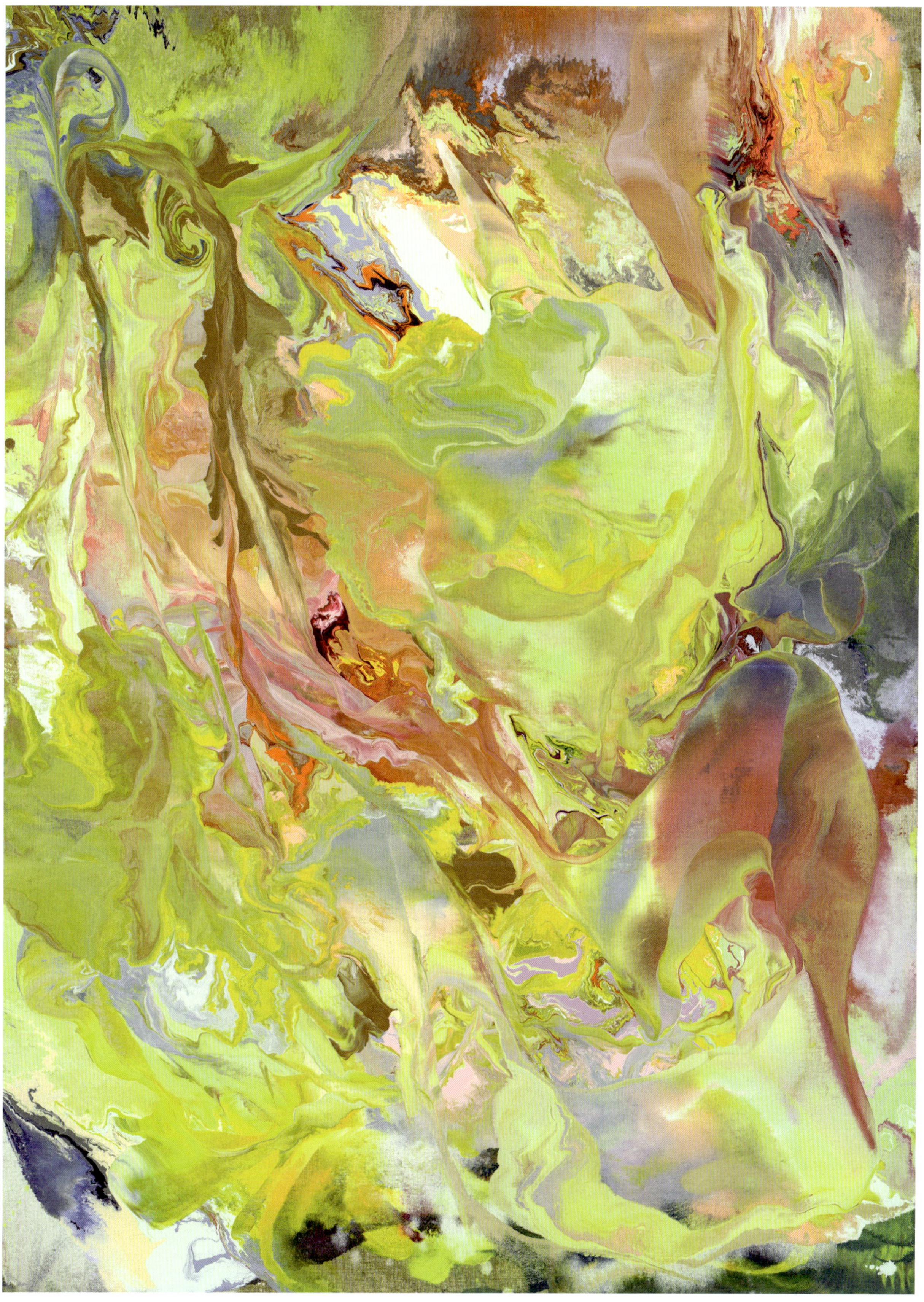

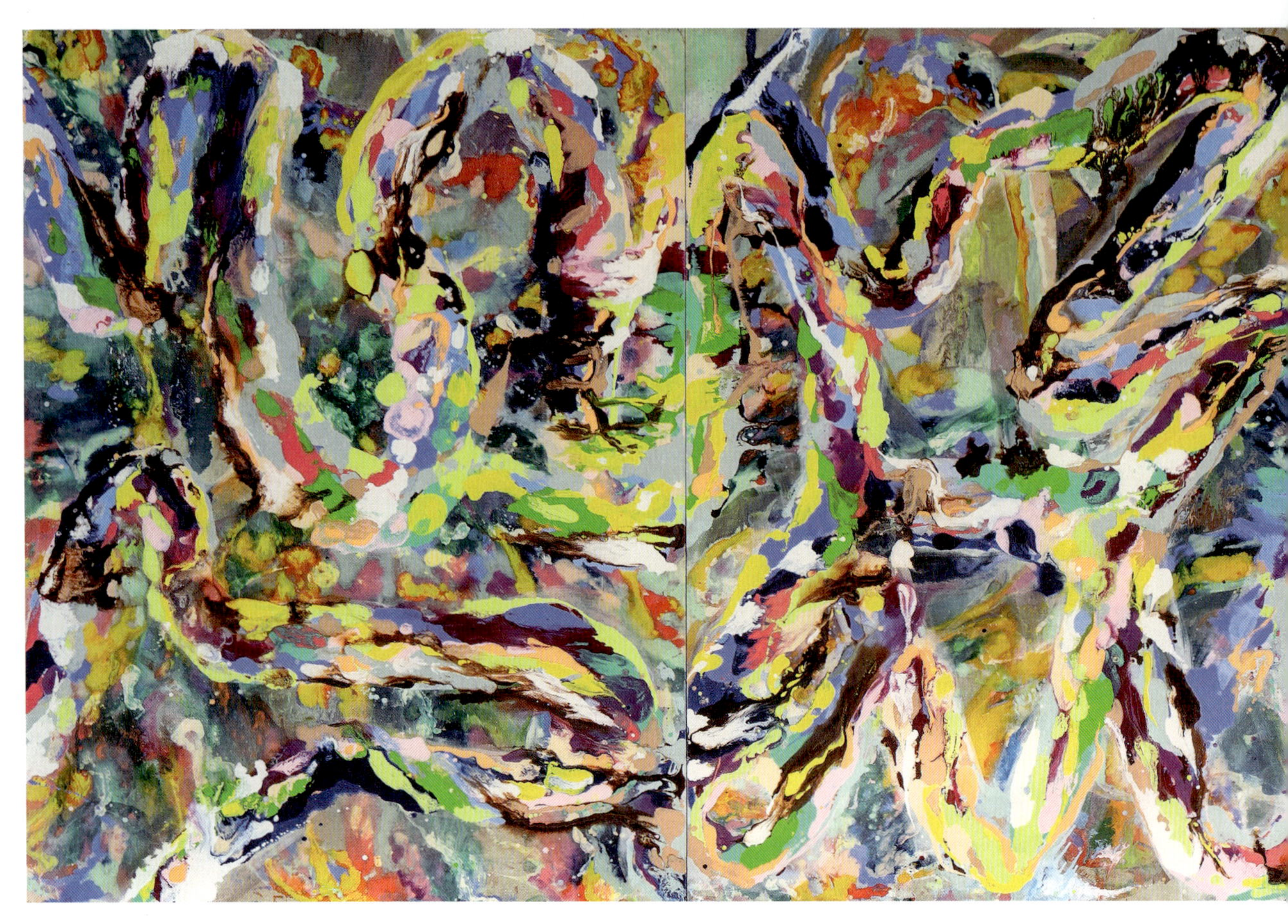

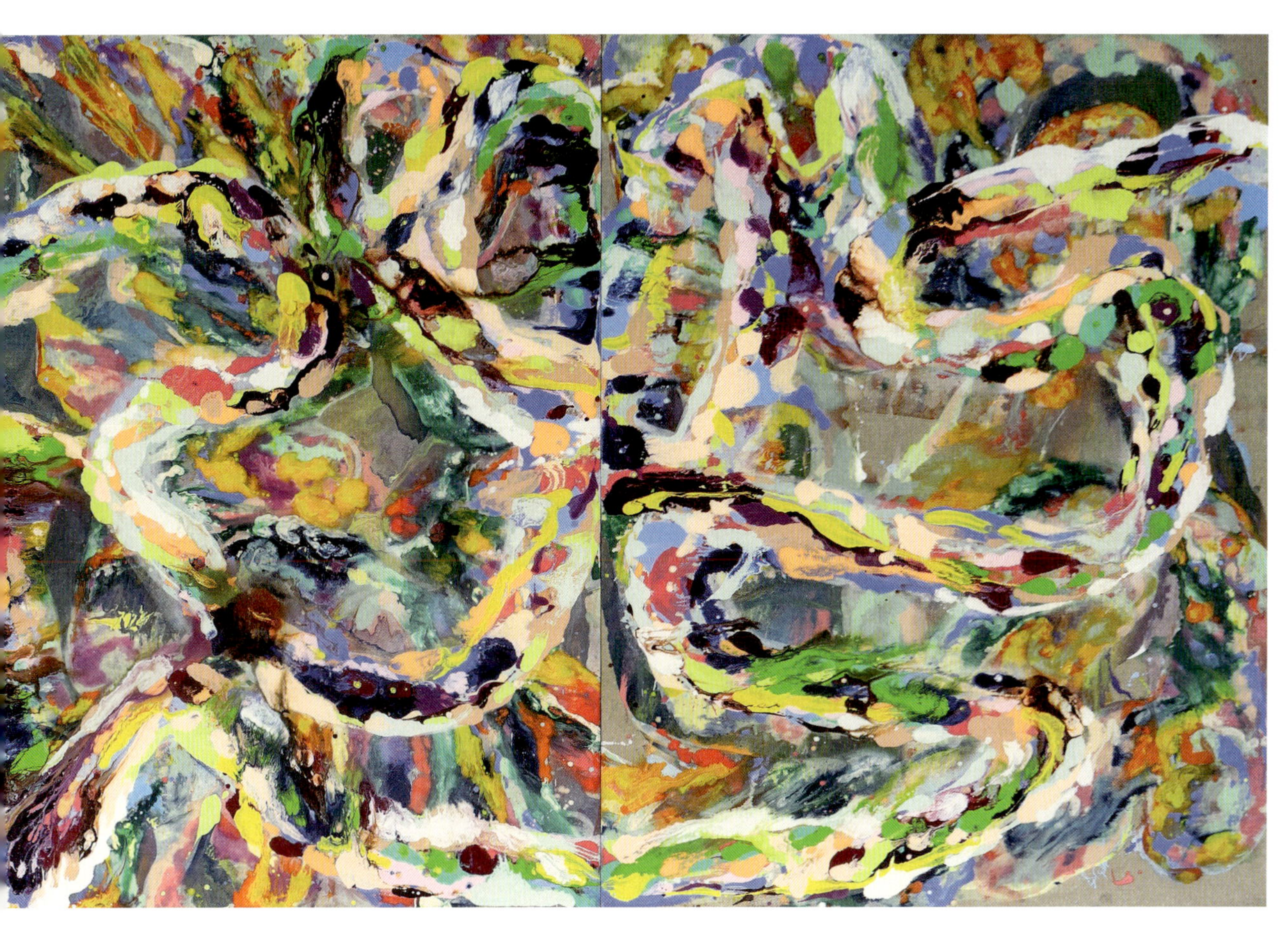

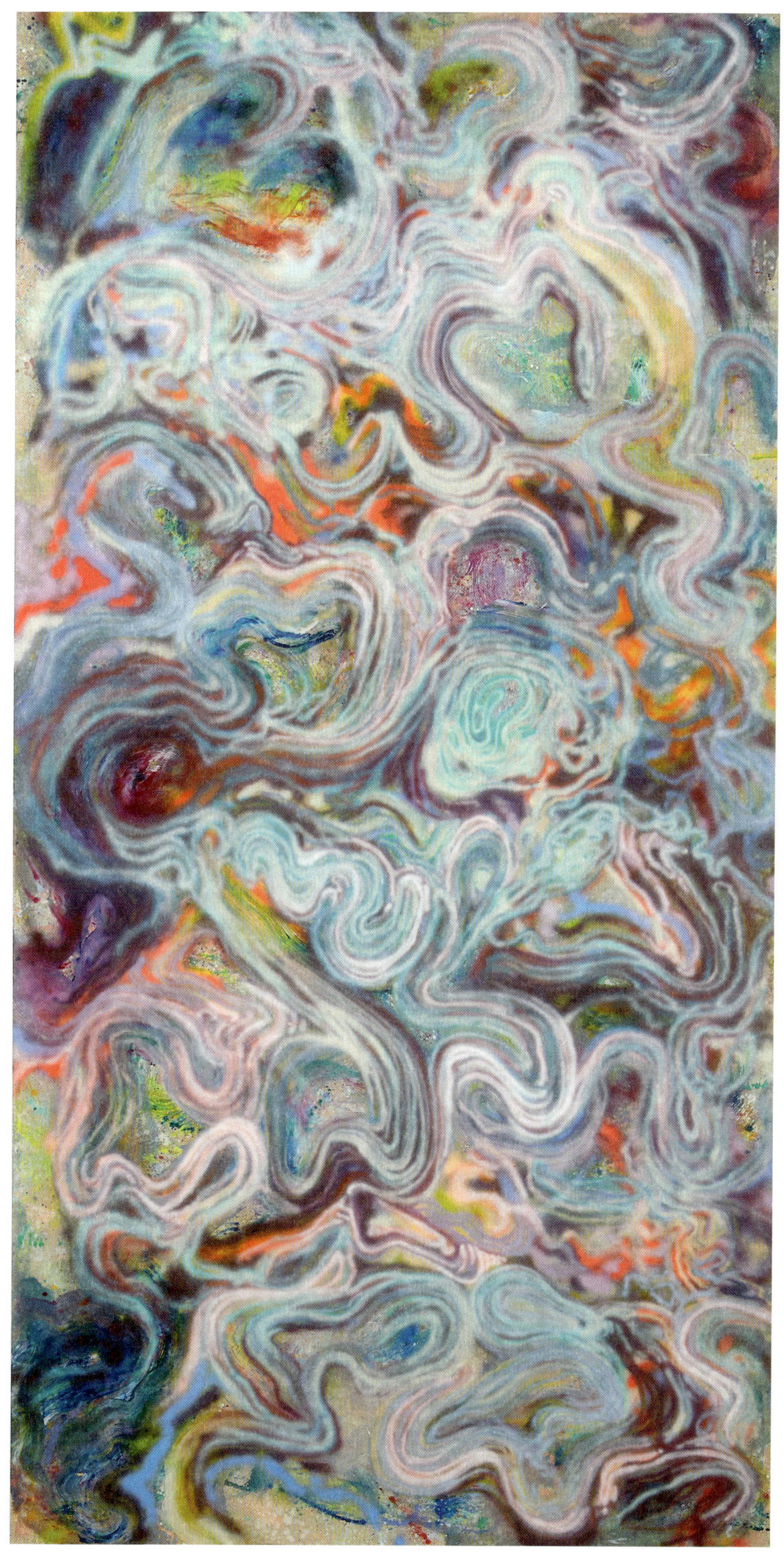

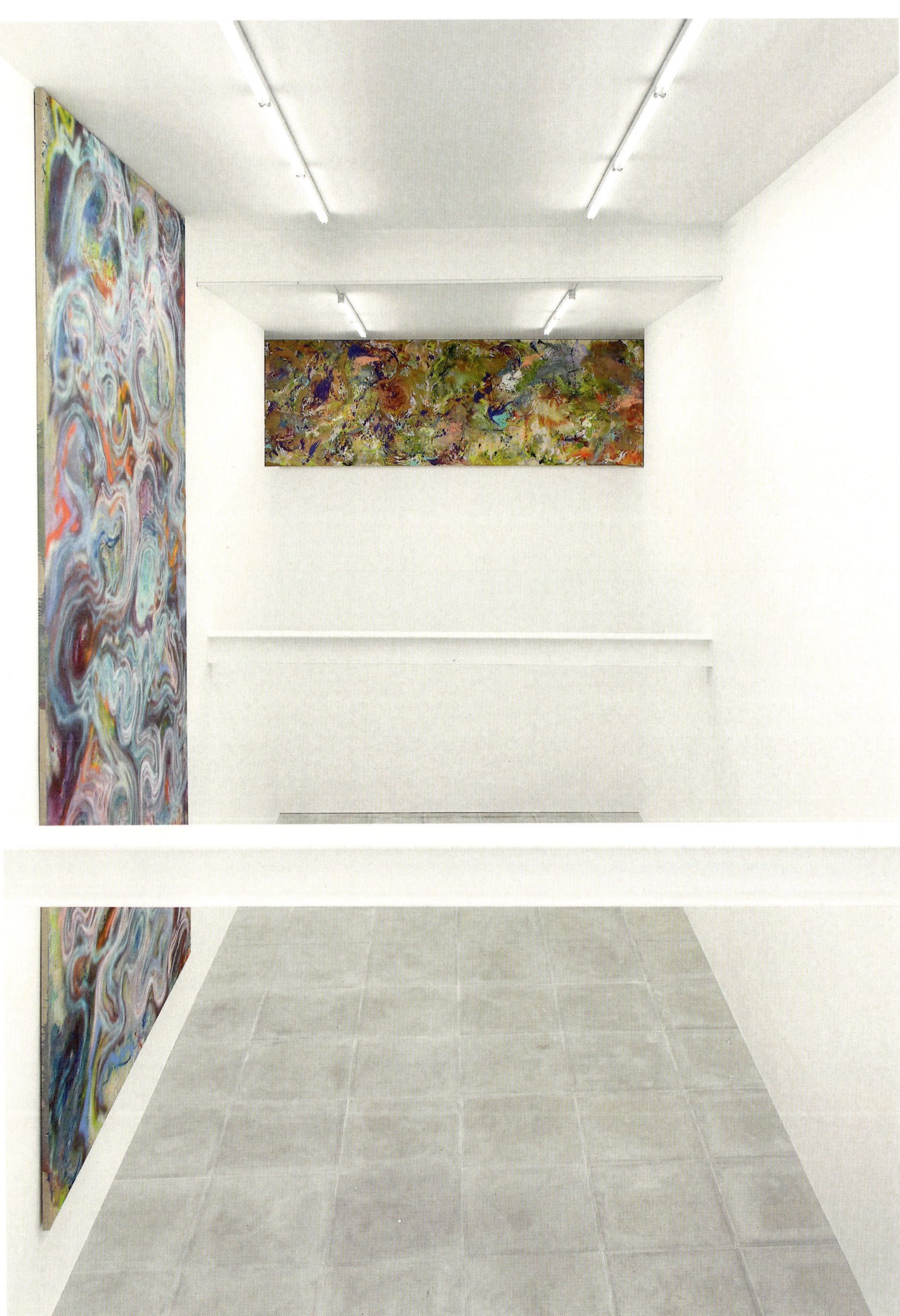

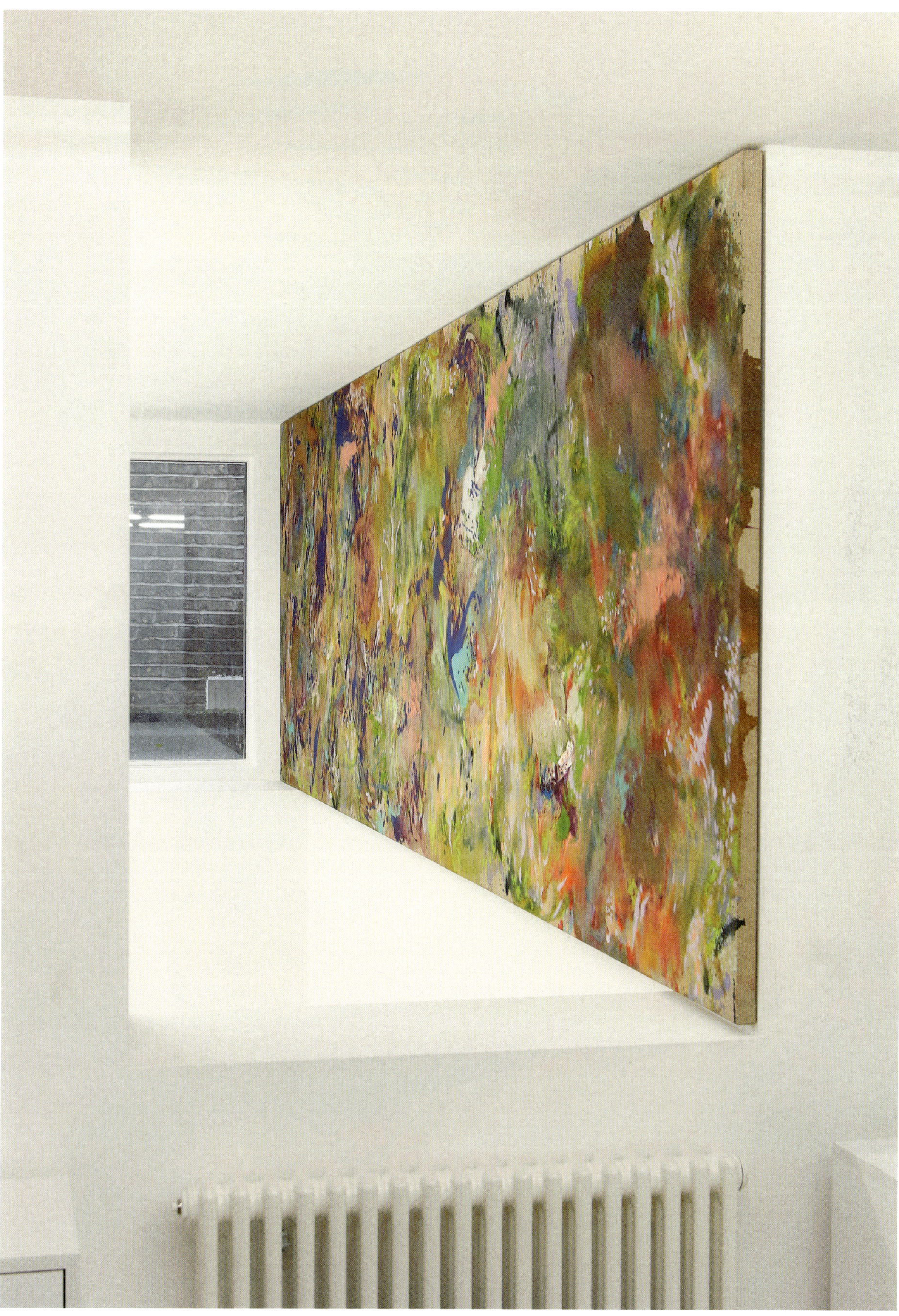

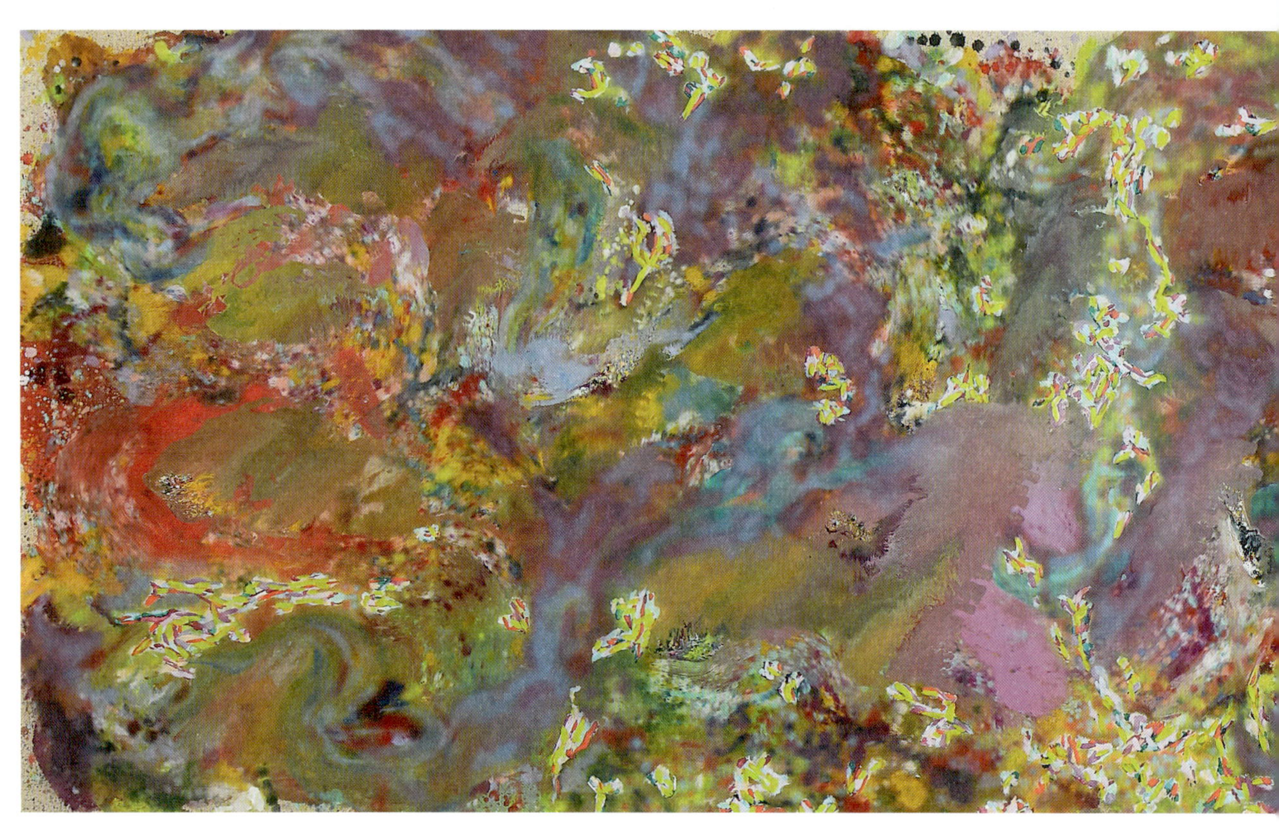

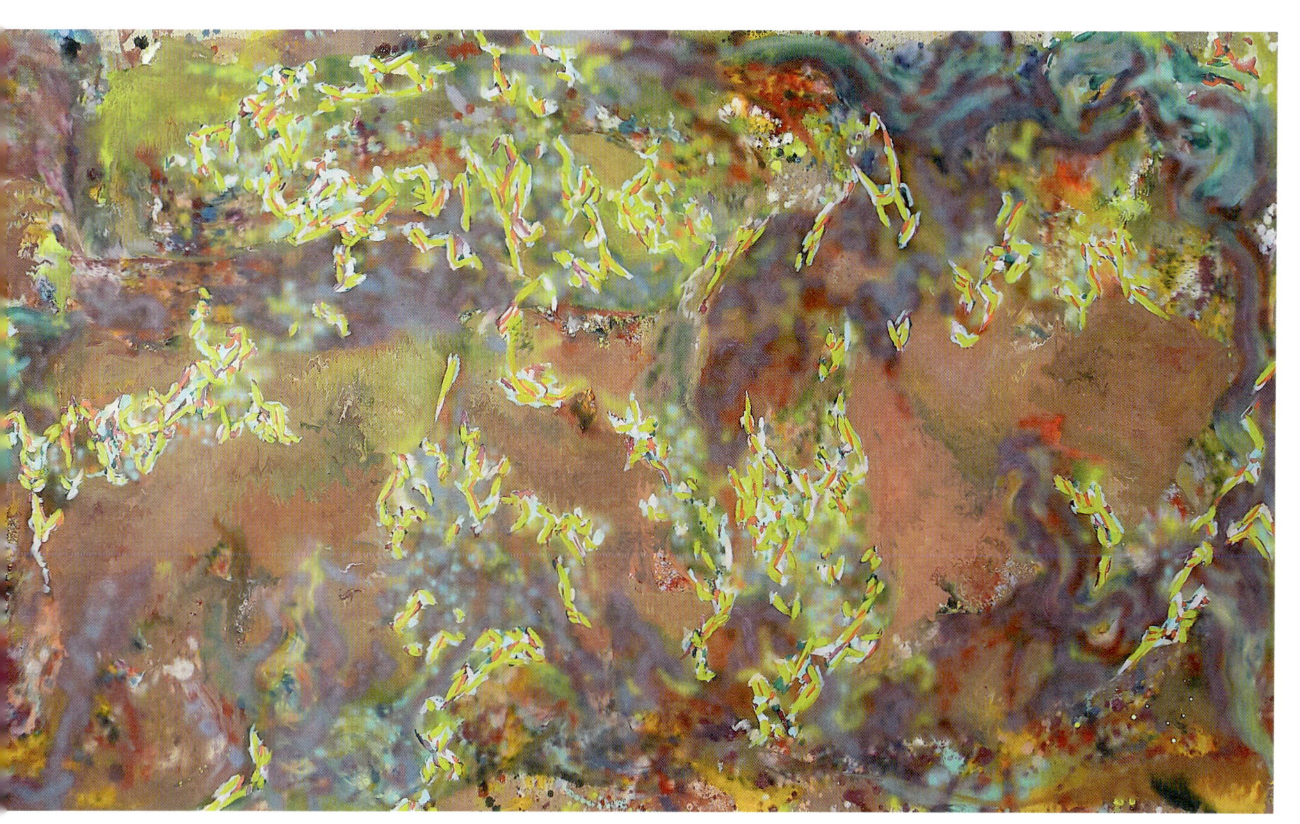

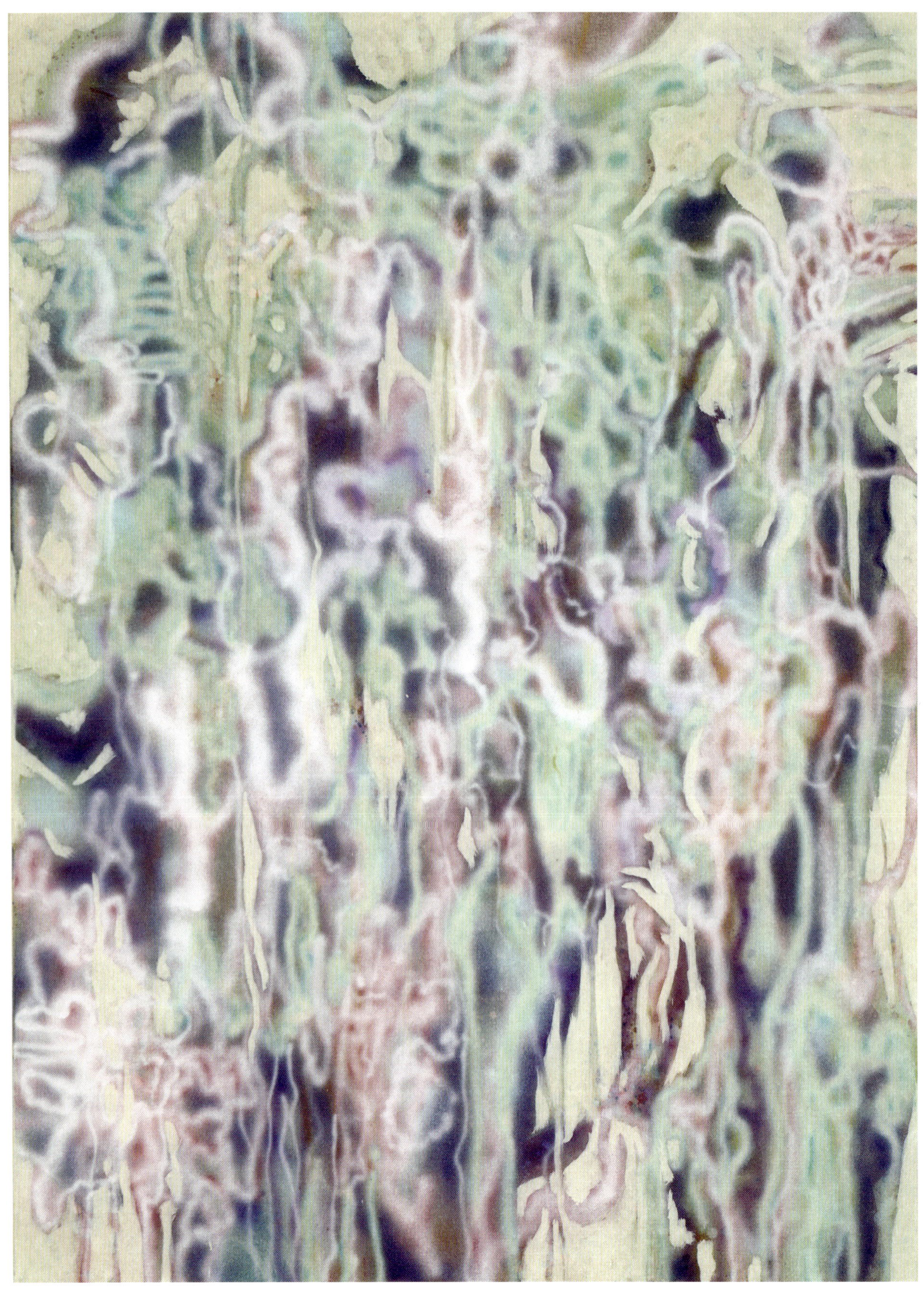

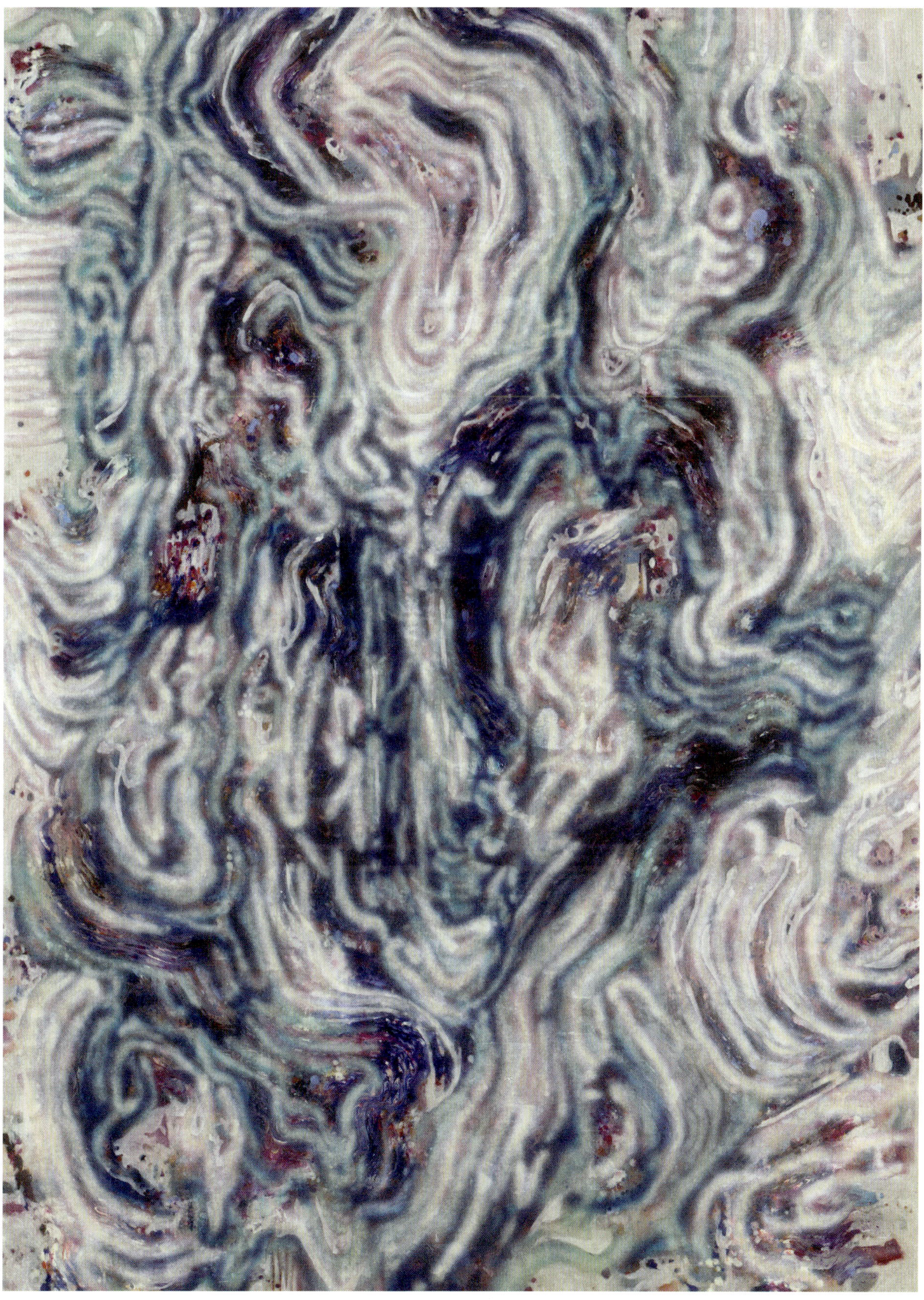

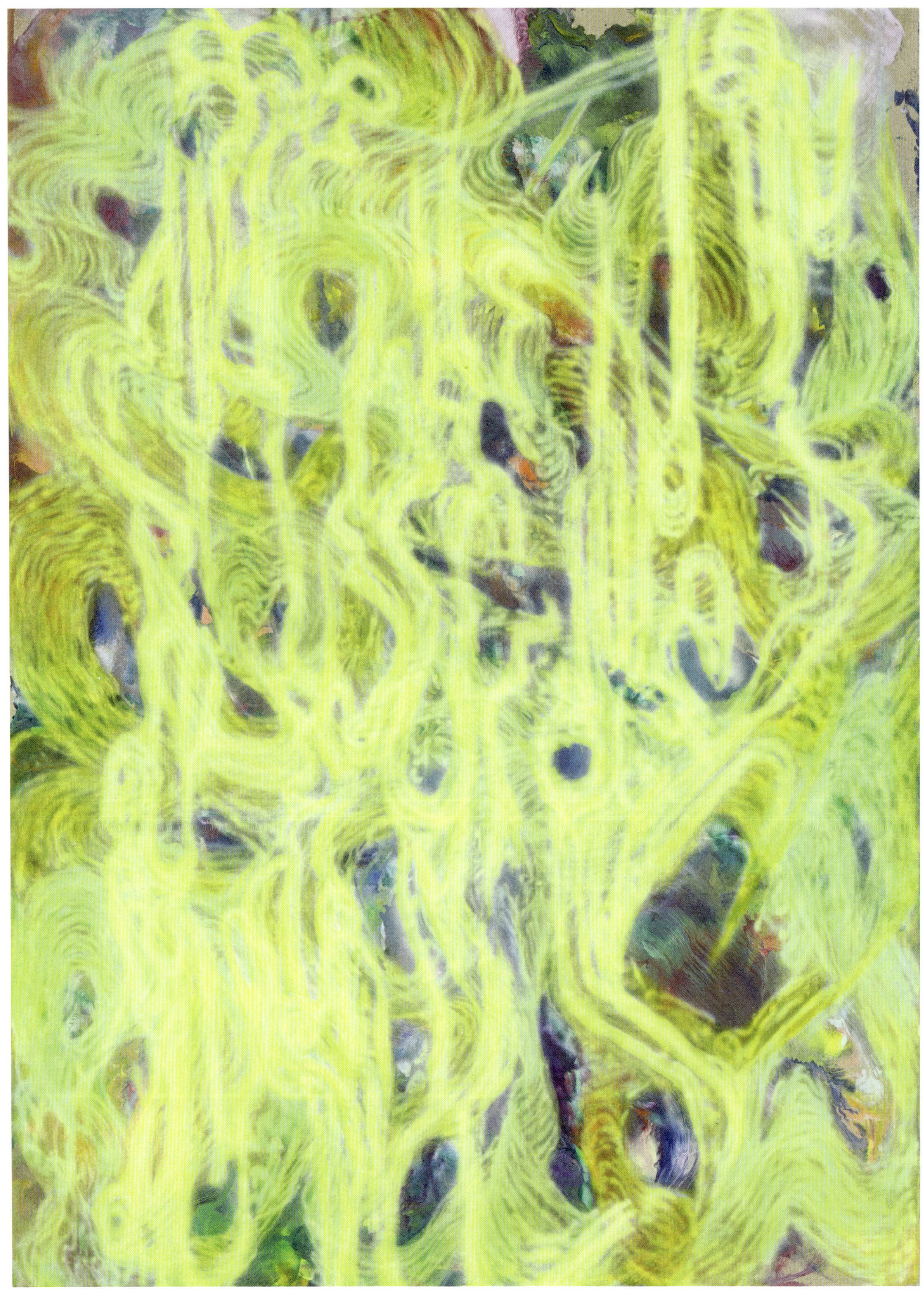

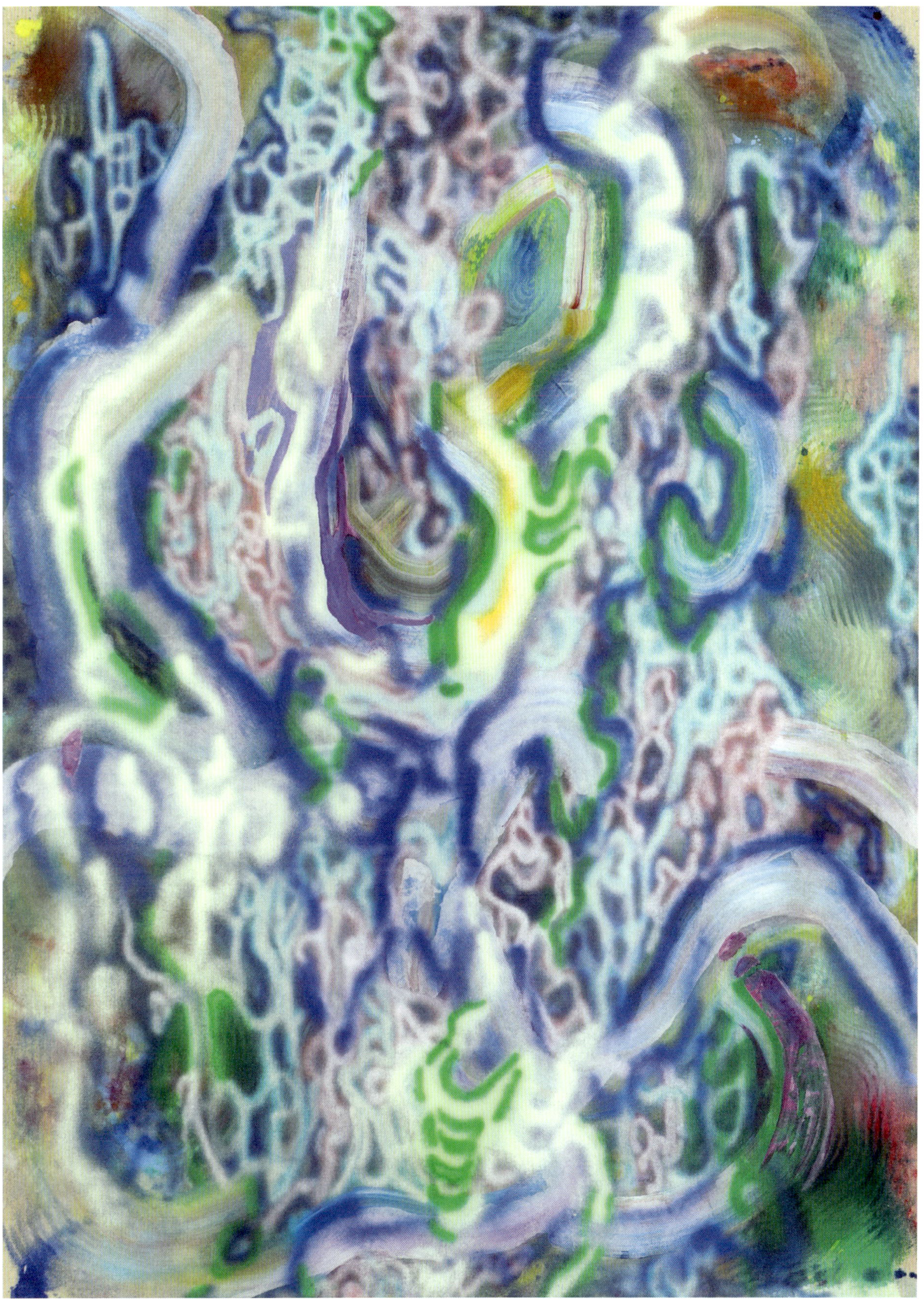

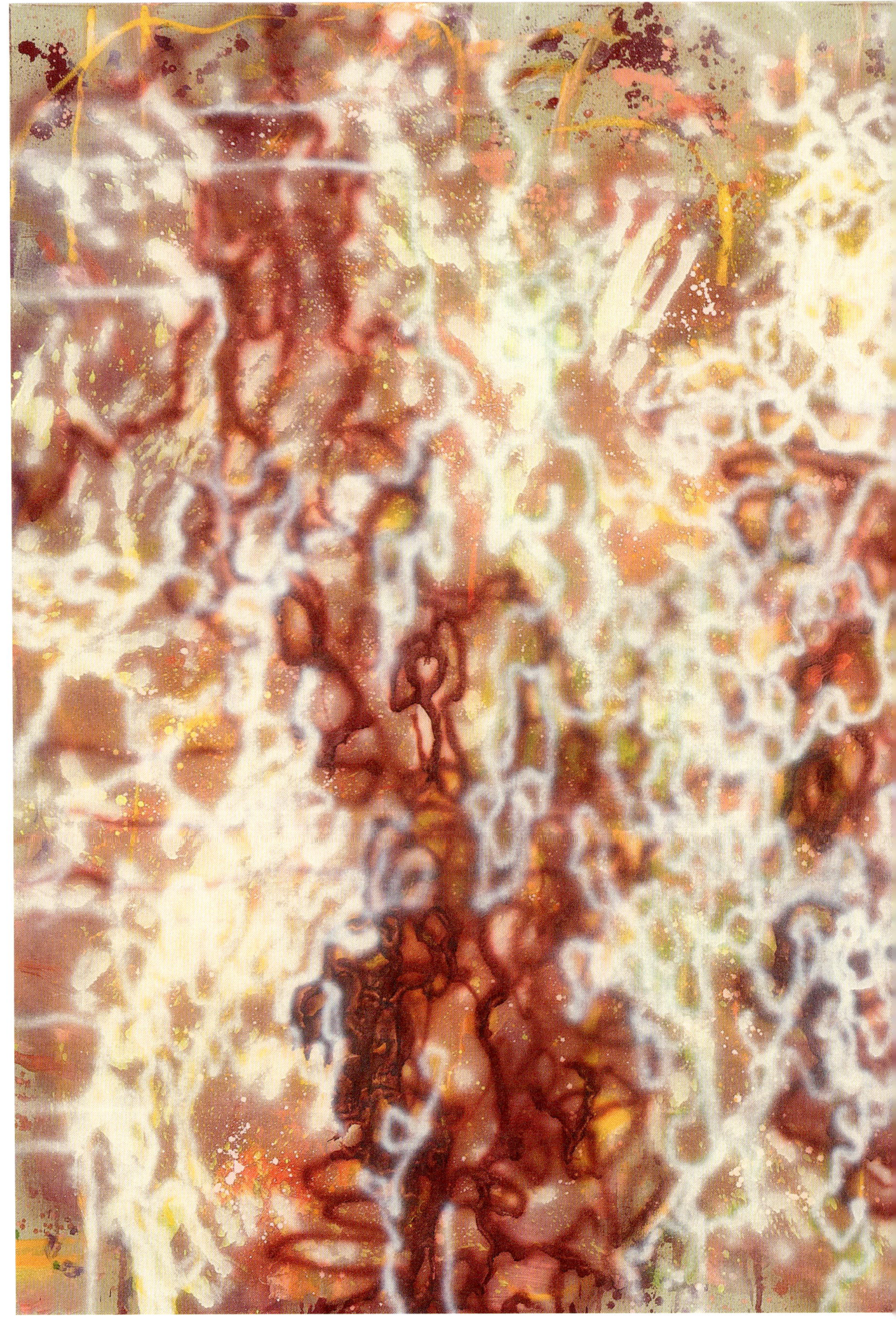

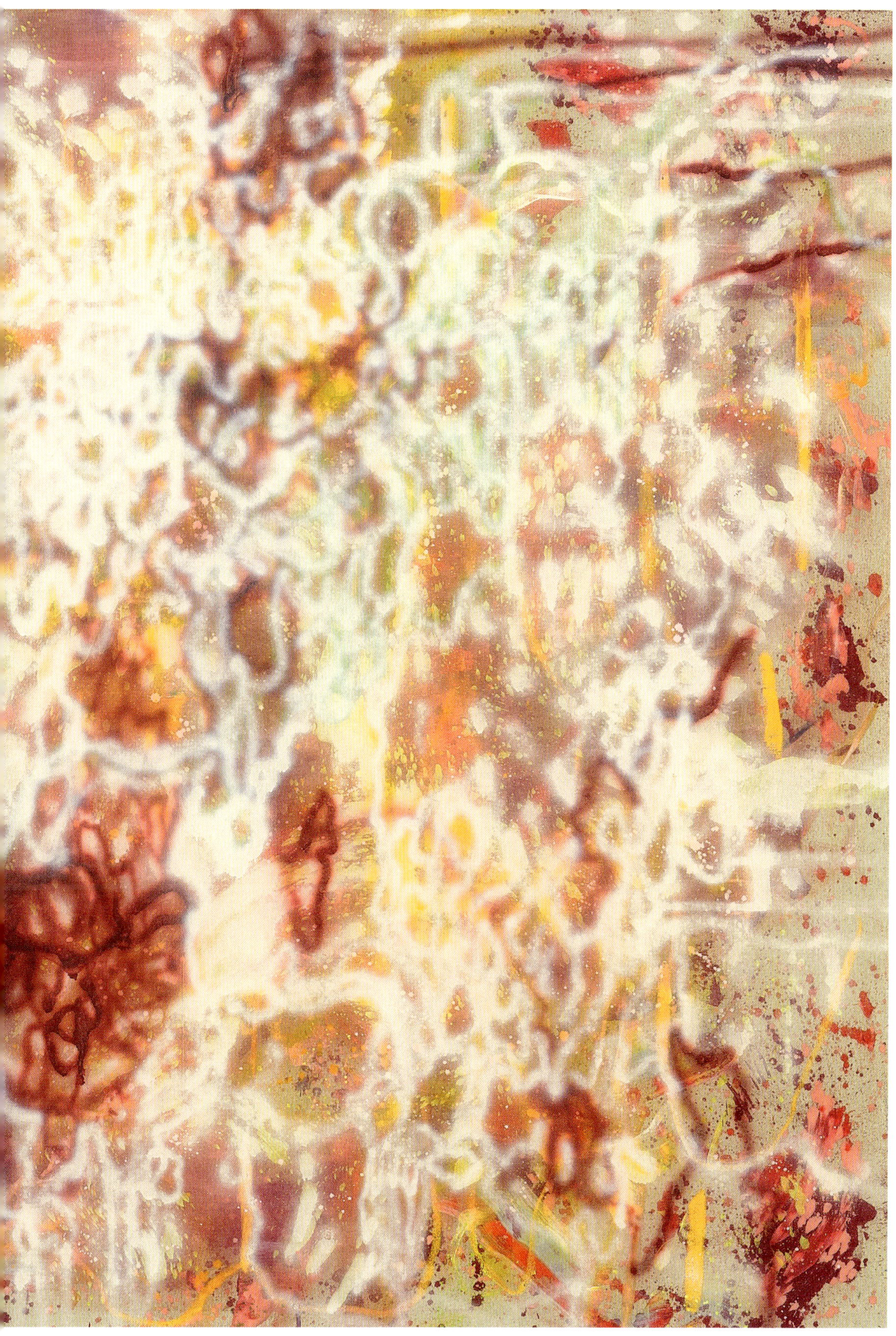

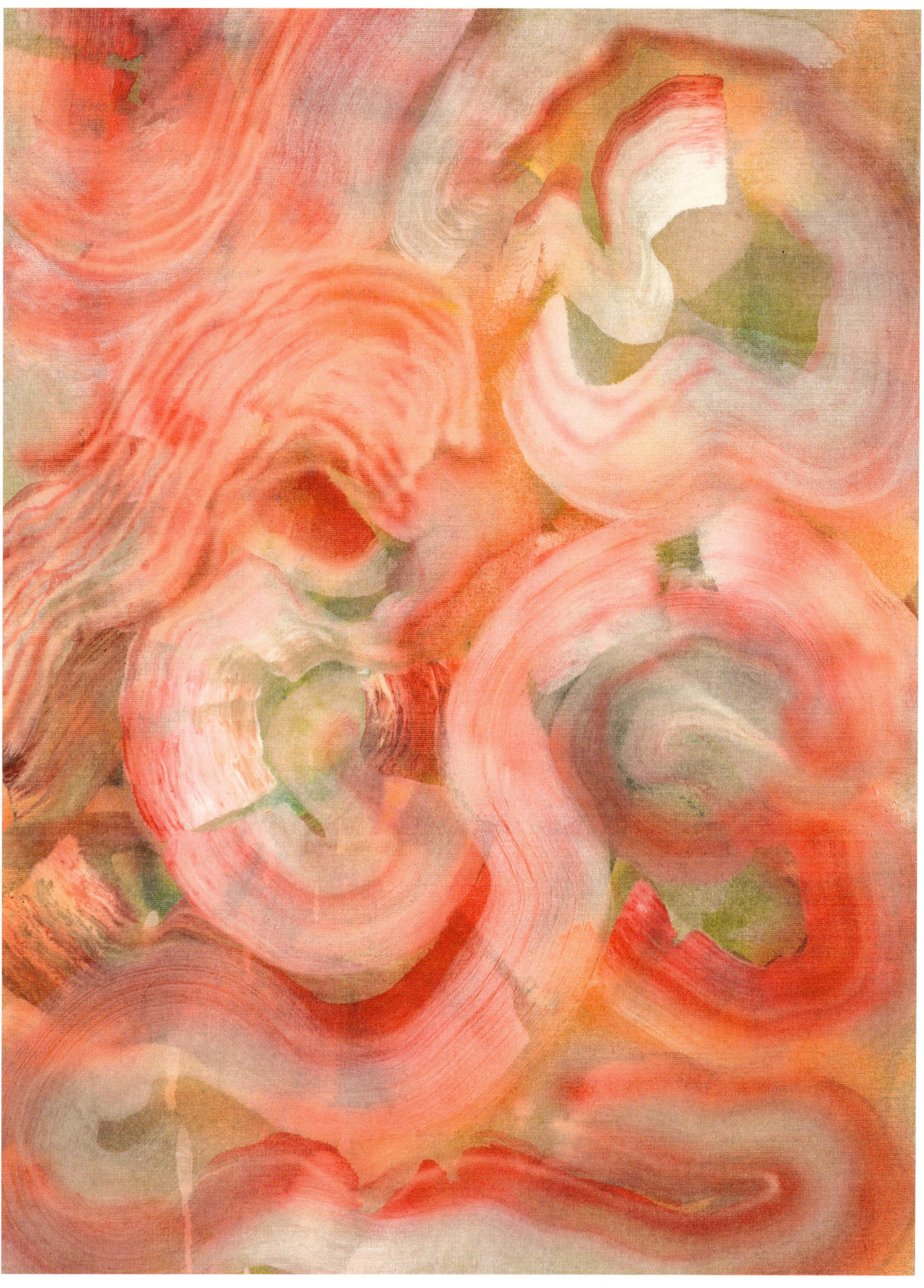

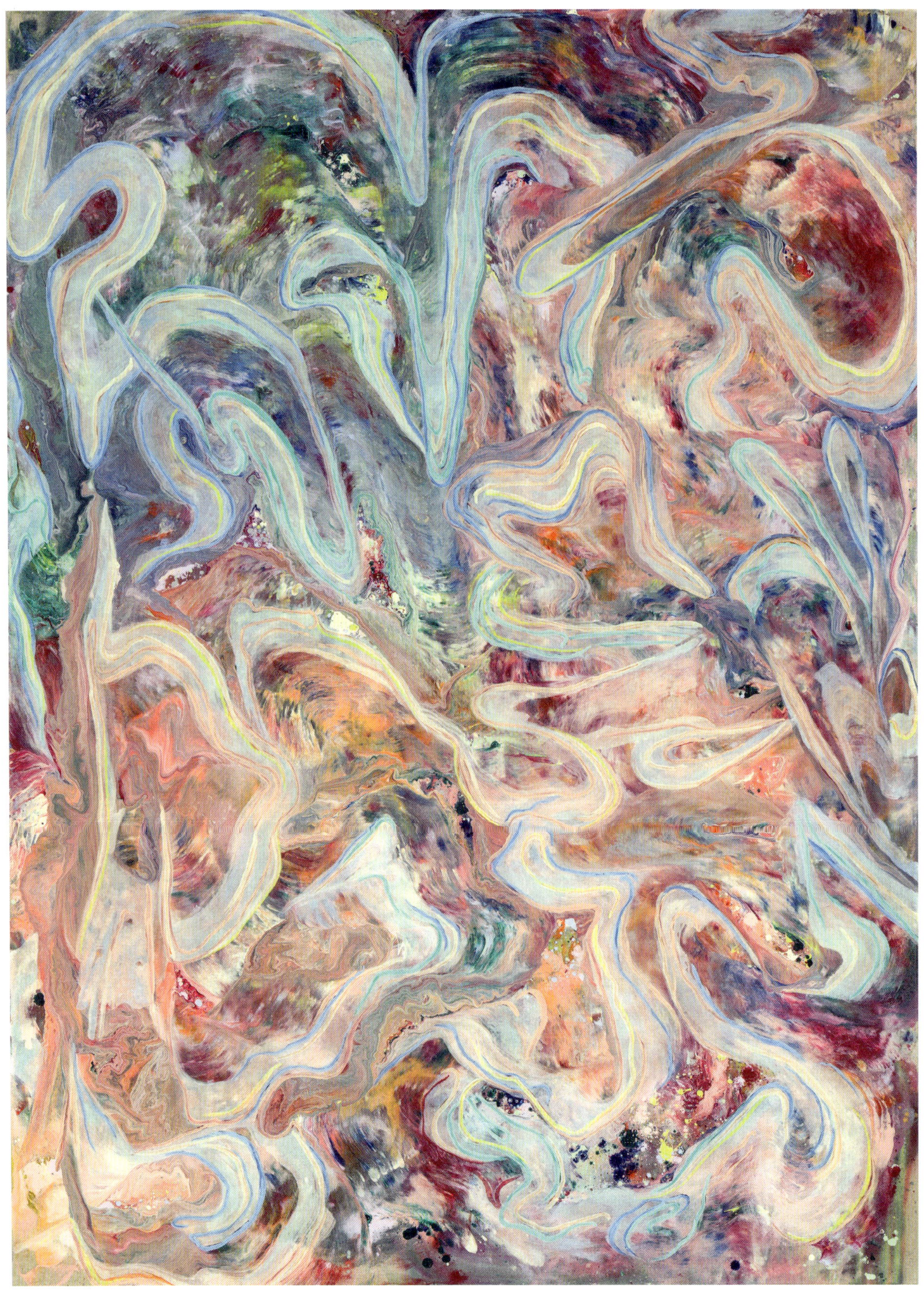

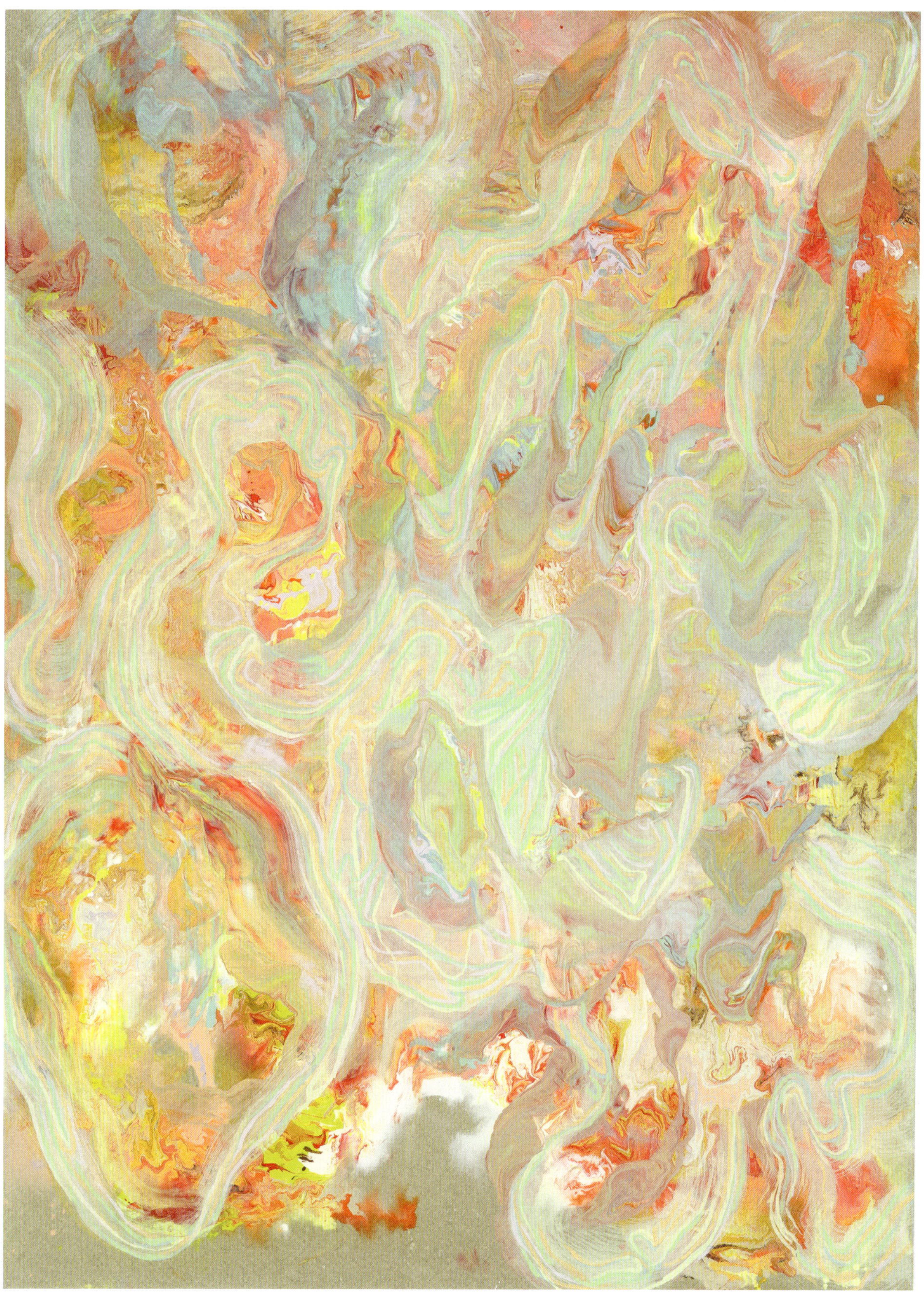

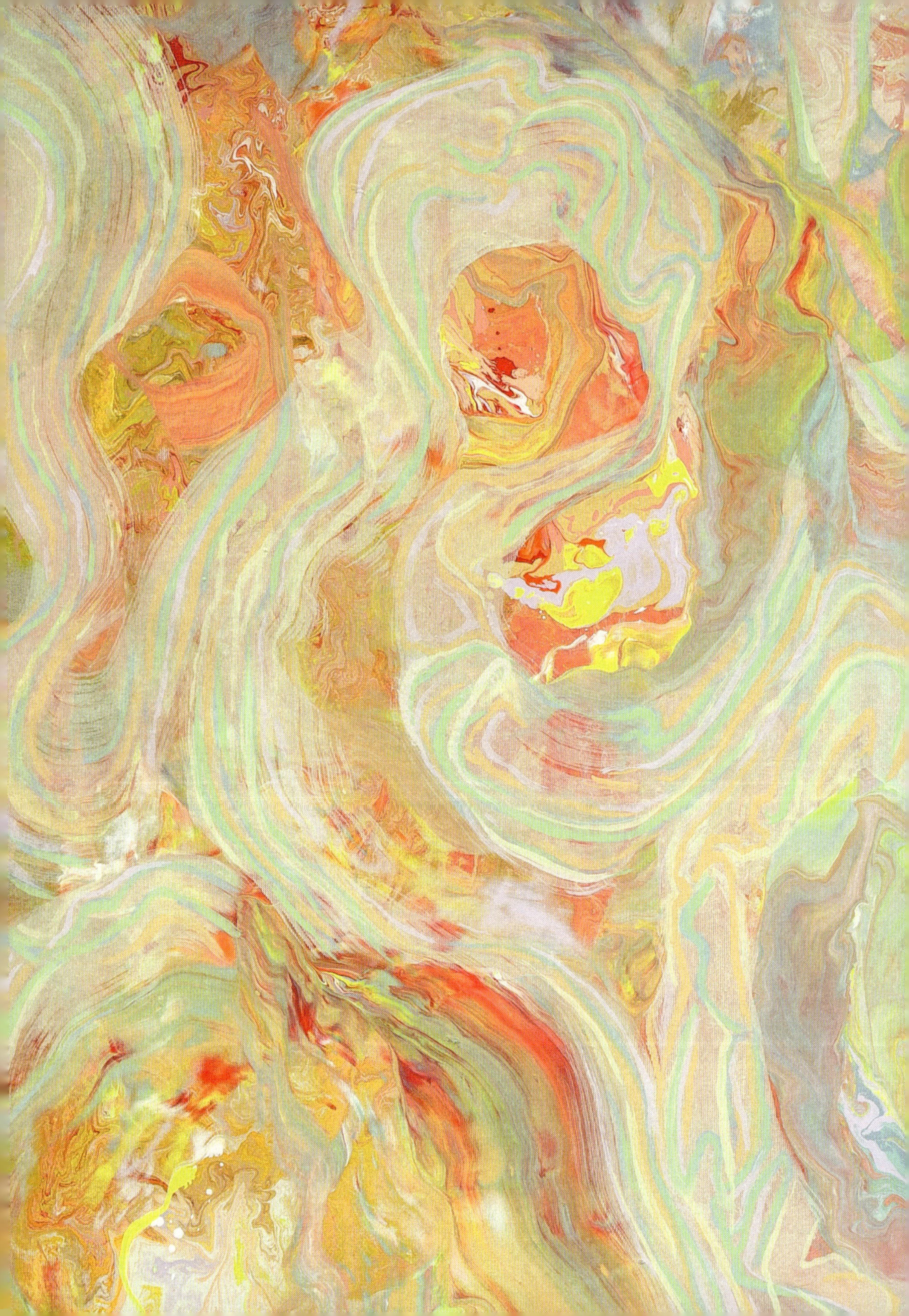

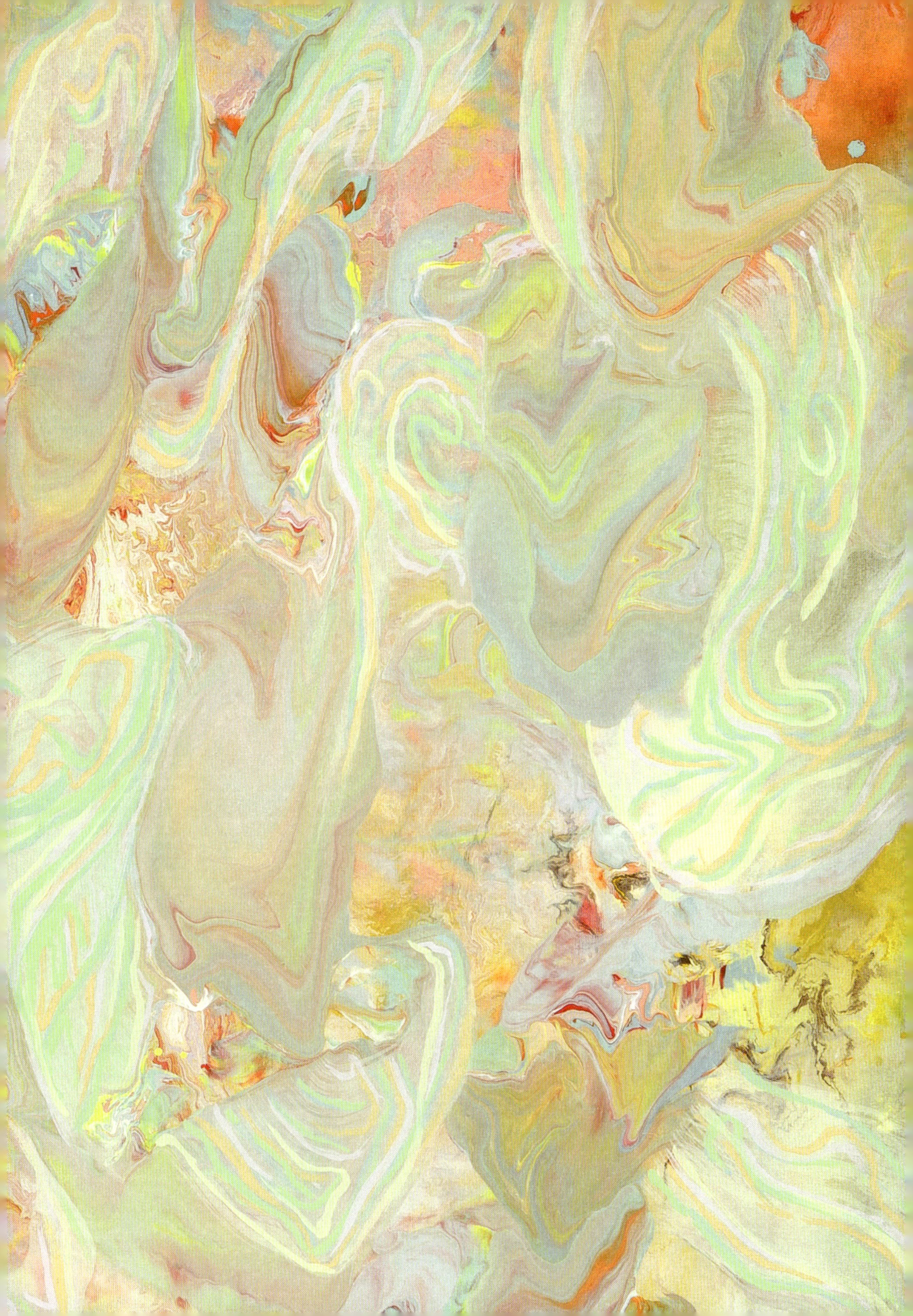

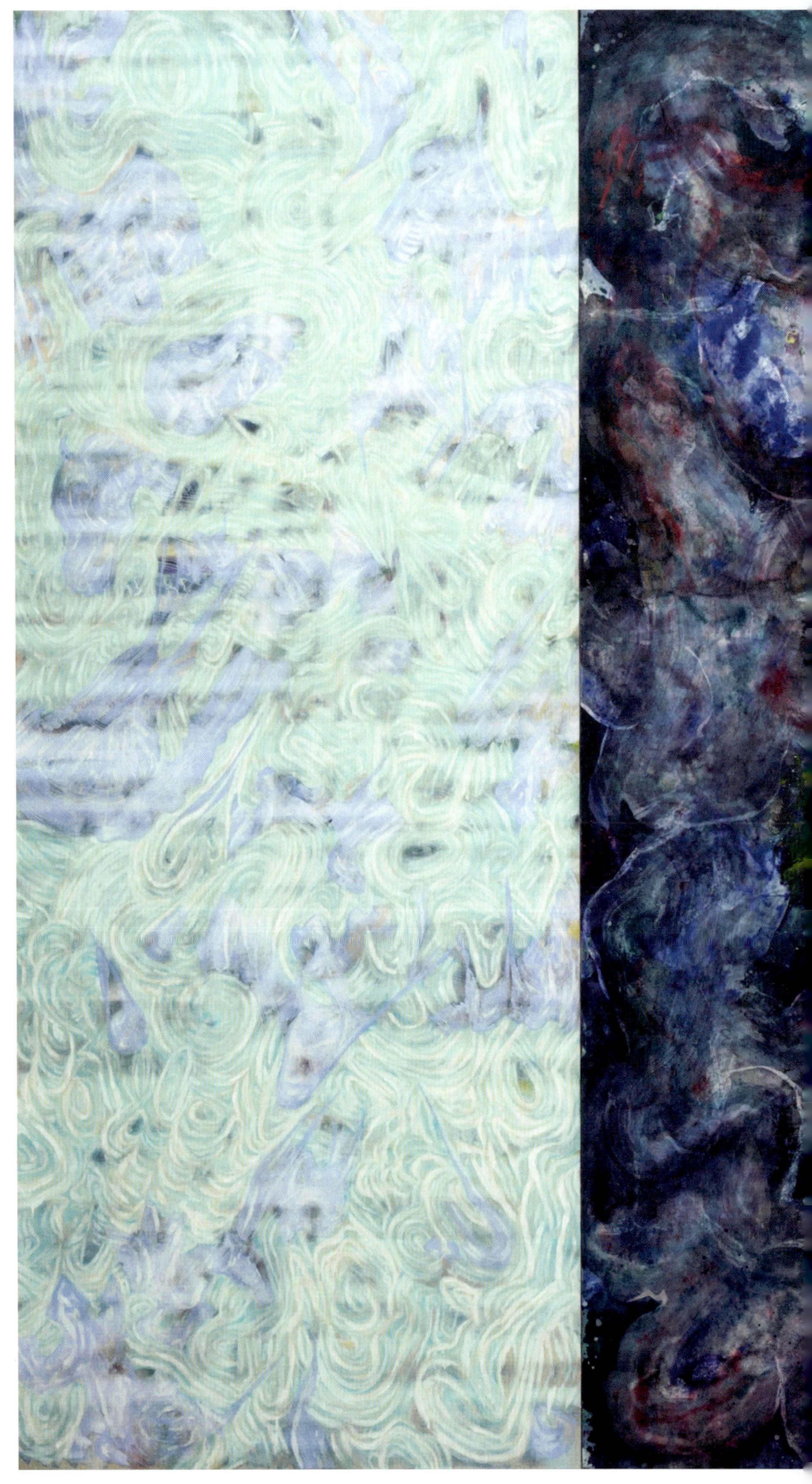

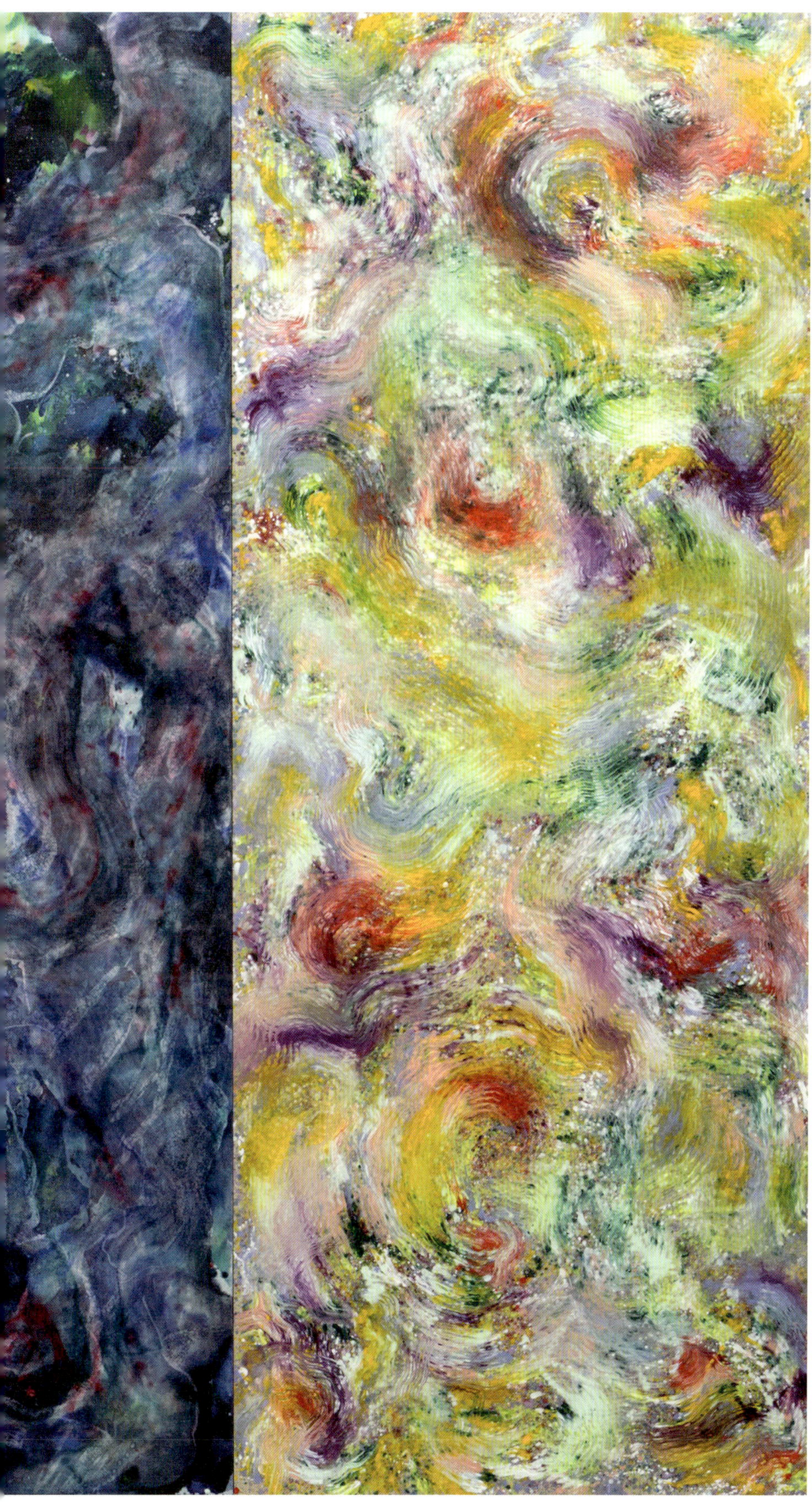

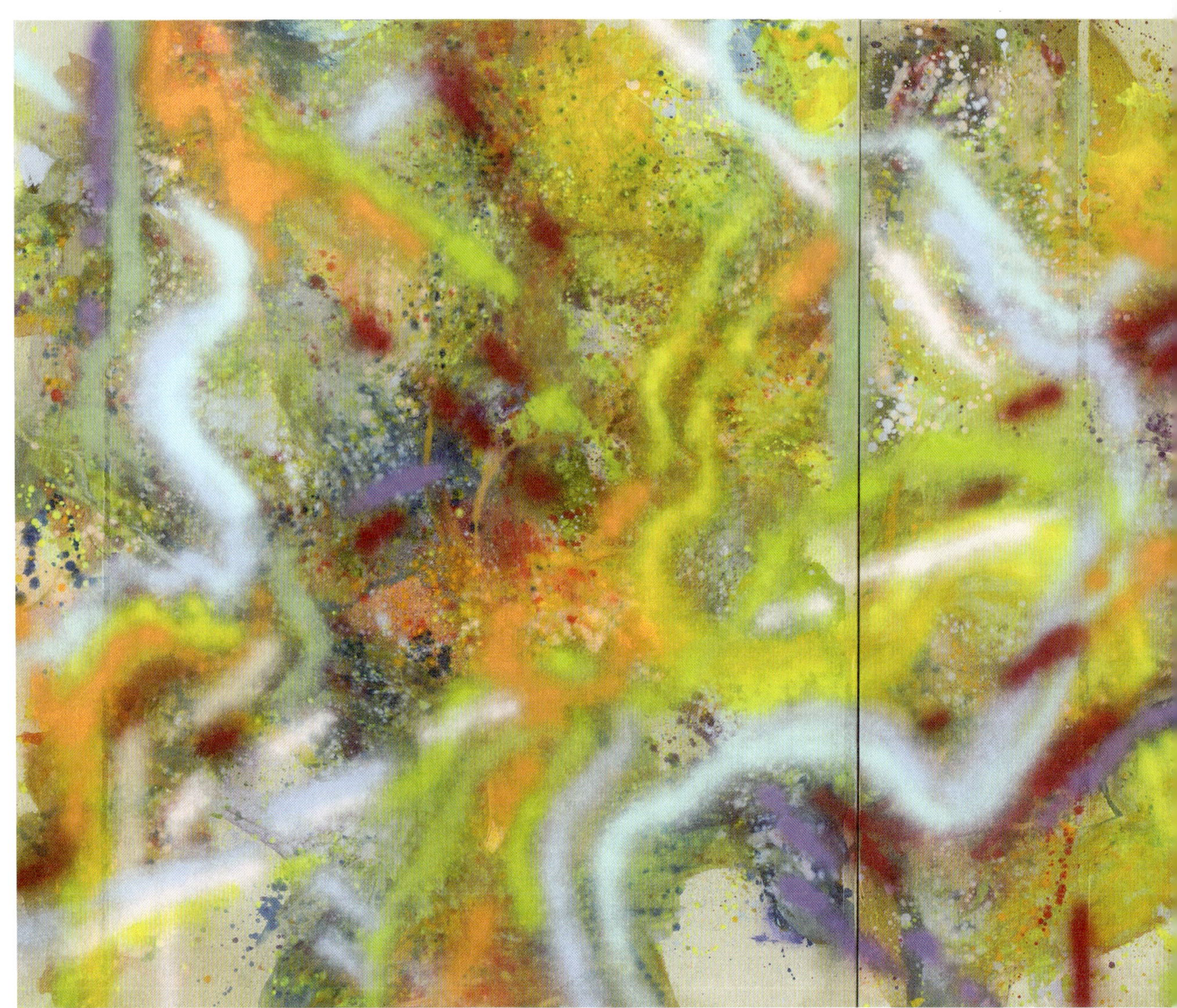

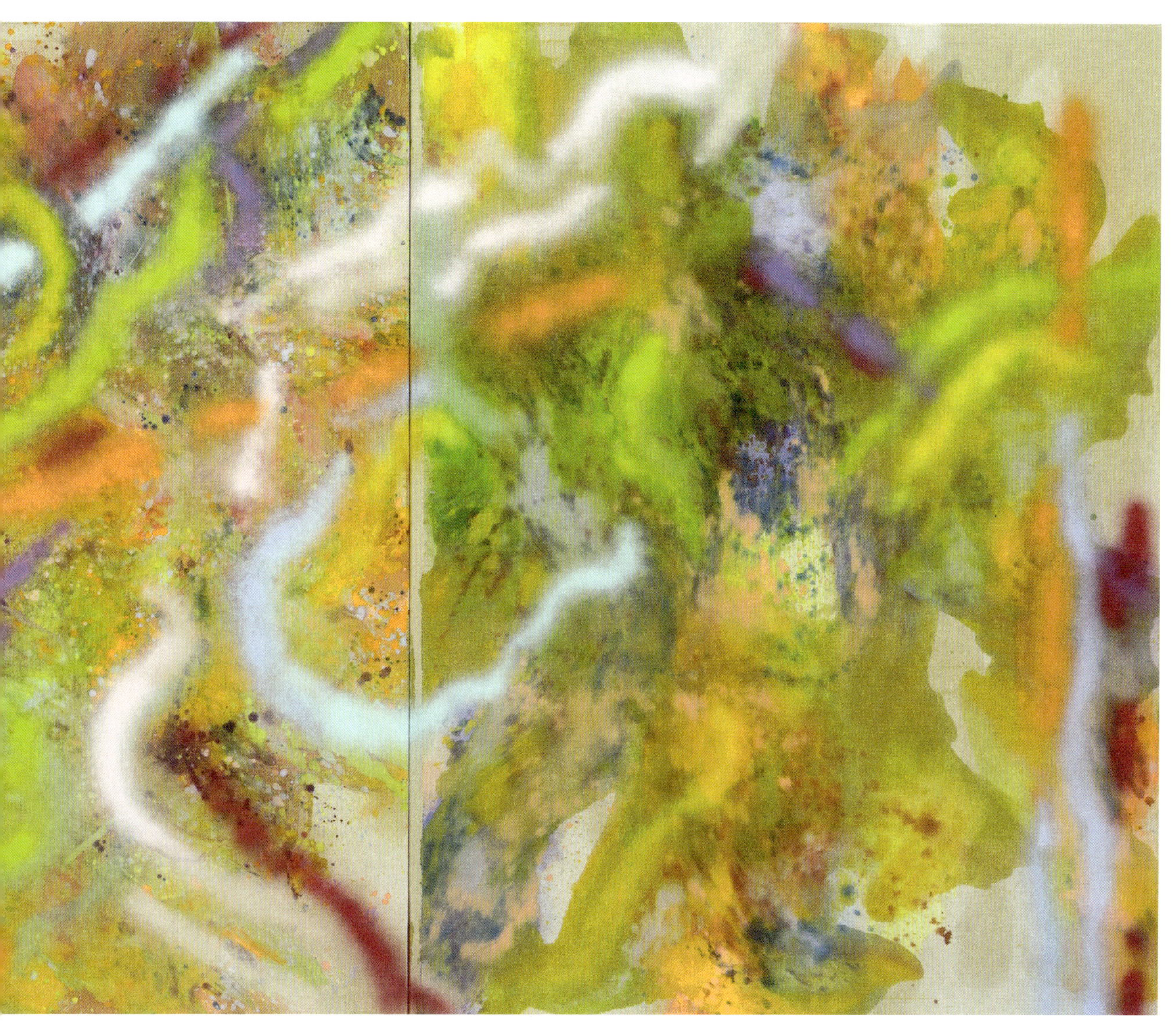

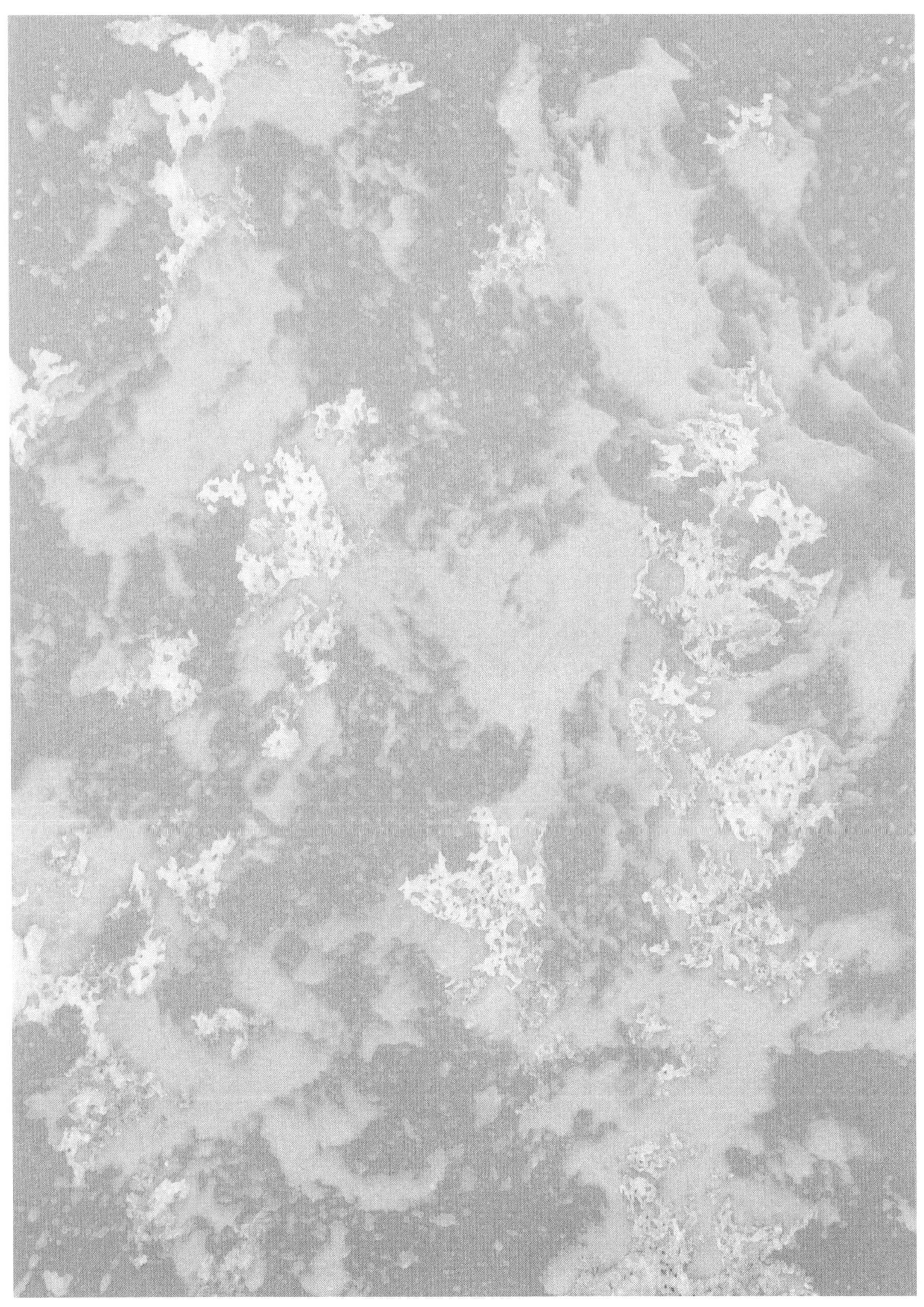

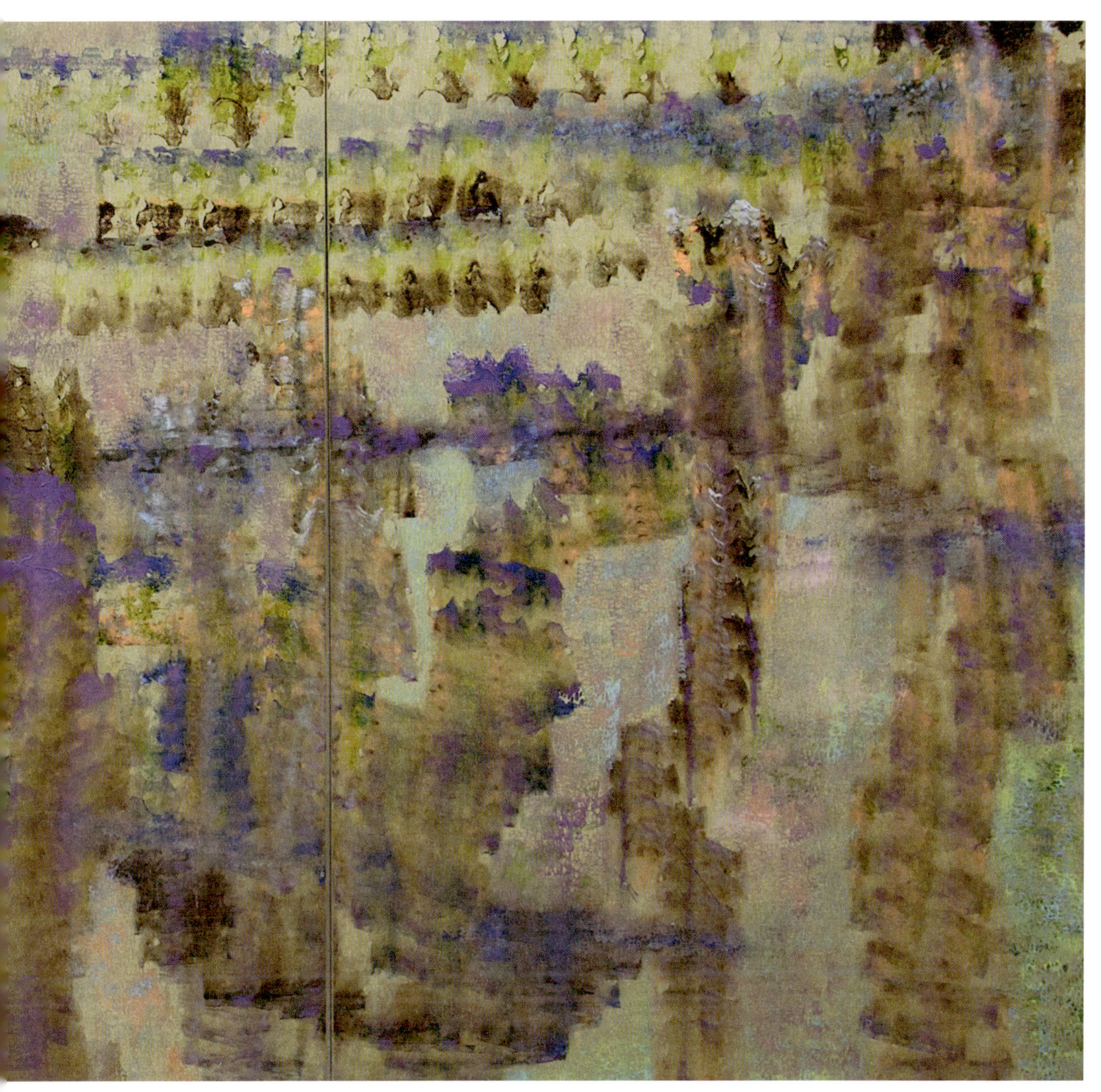

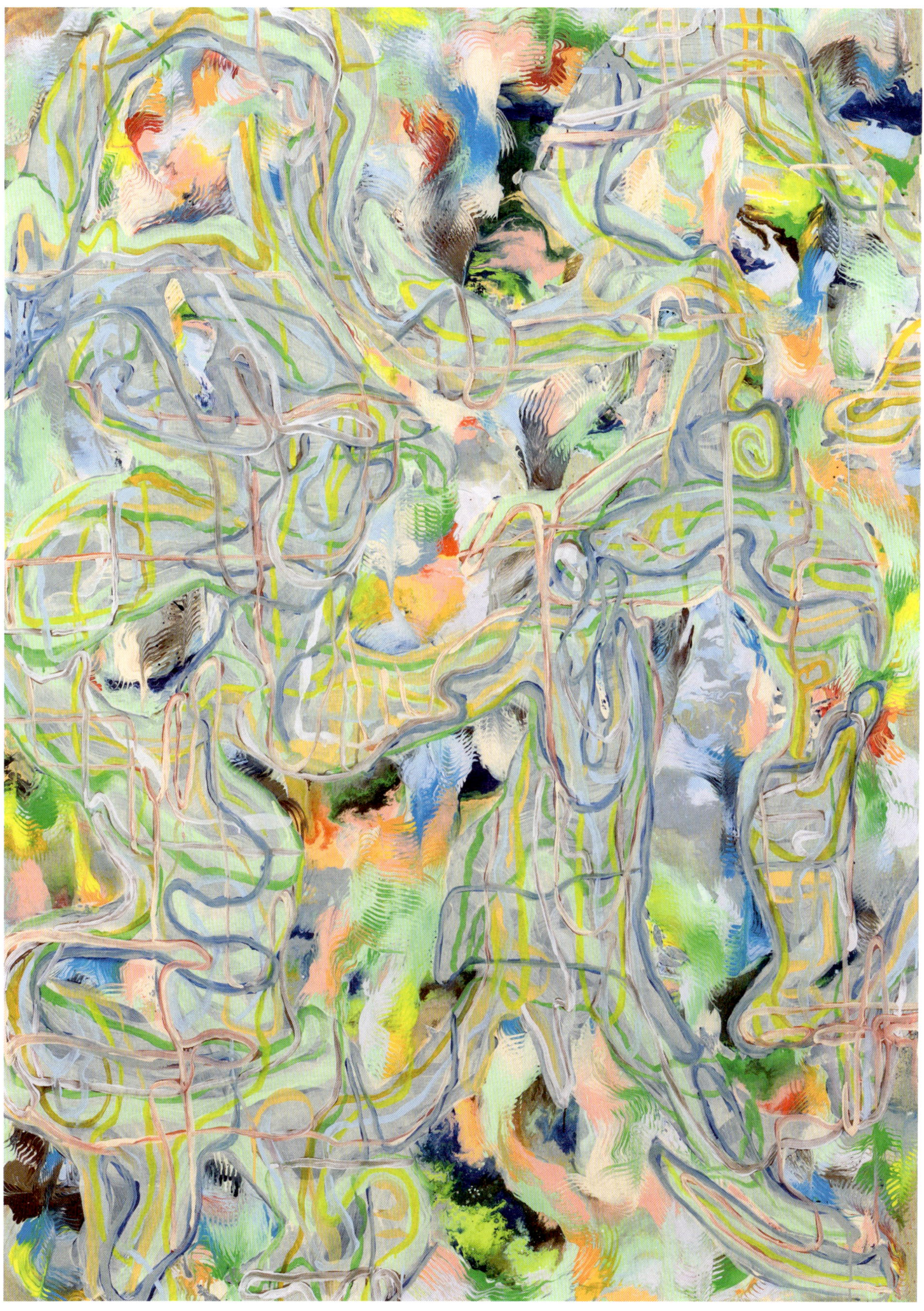

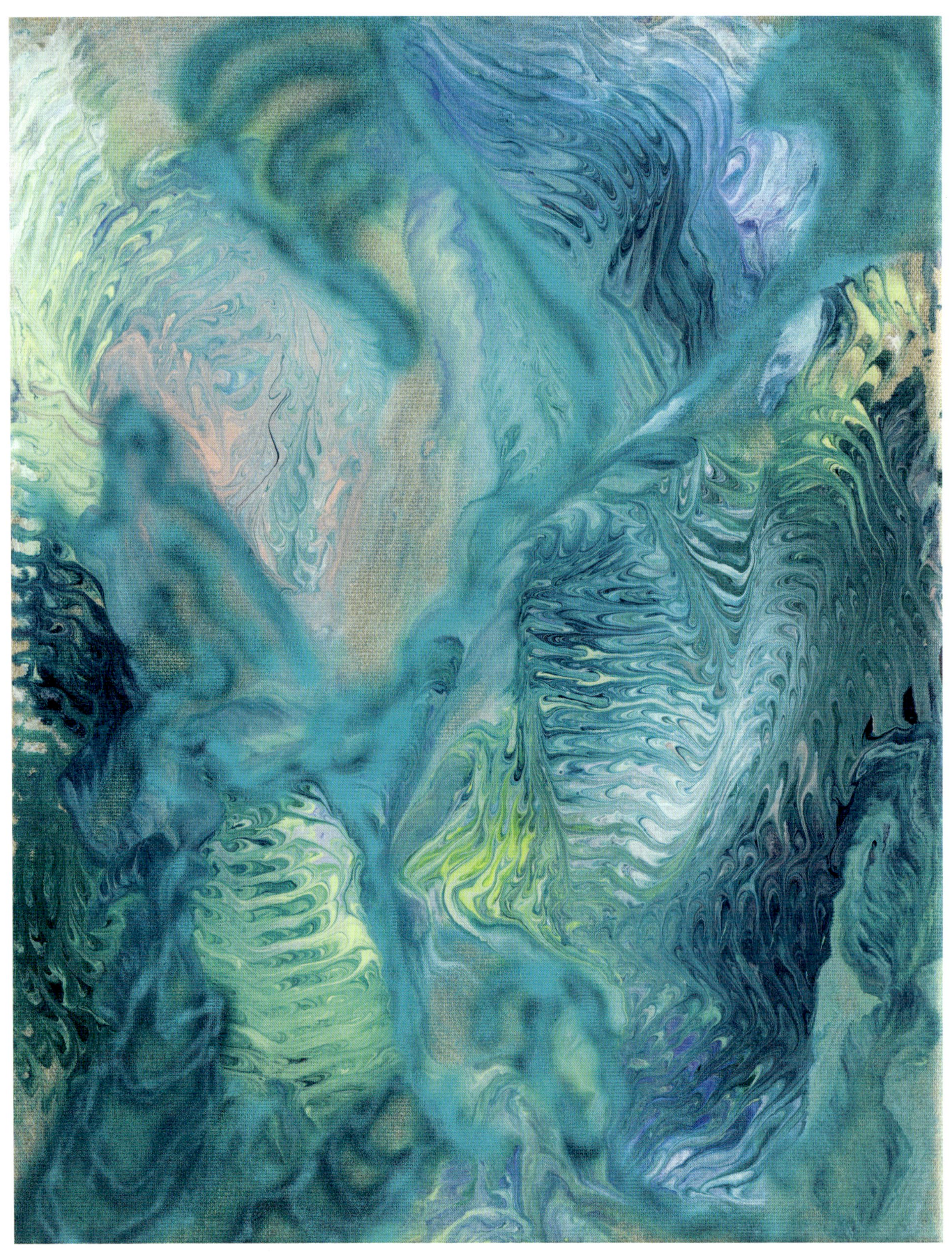

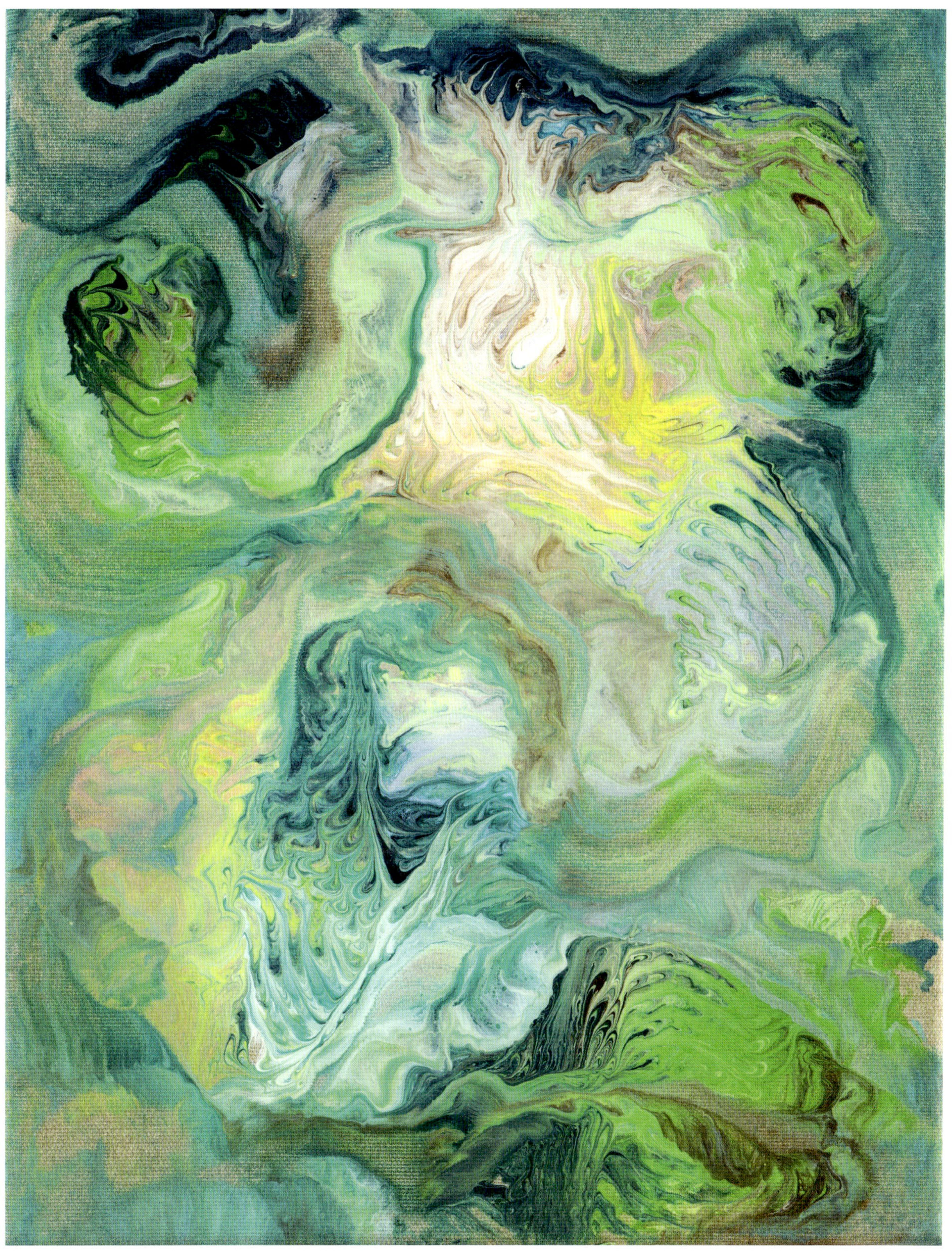

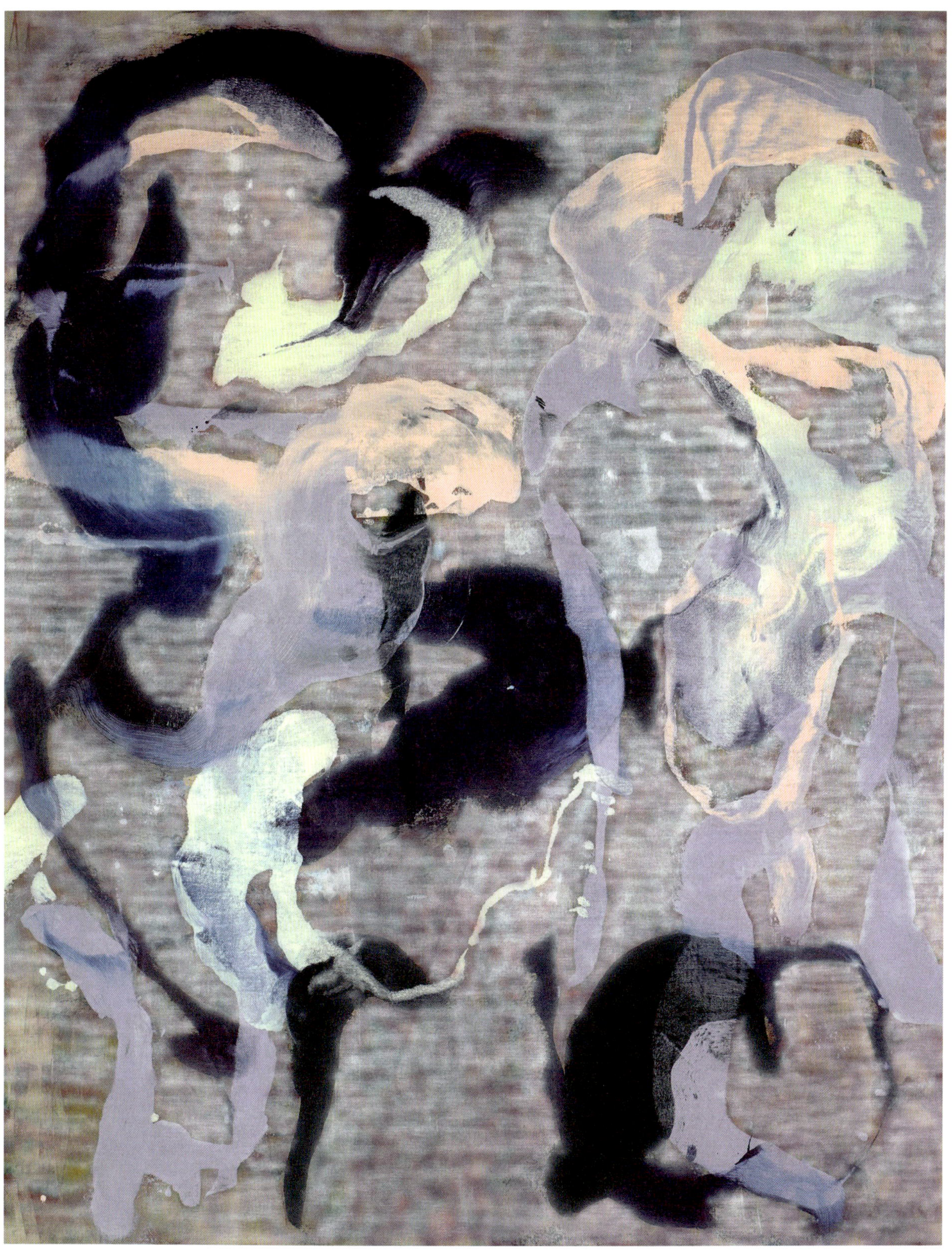

Tyra Tingleff
in conversation with

Amy Zion

Tyra Tingleff, from her studio in Berlin, and Amy Zion, from her home in
New York, spoke over Zoom in May 2021 about Tingleff's practice, her process,
and the wider concerns that haunt painting, specifically abstract painting, today.

AMY ZION

Last time we spoke, we discussed how hard it is to write about
abstract painting and the frequent impulse to find a life raft
in language. Often that can take the form of an art historical
narrative—fitting a practice into a historical arc—which is something that happens to painting more than any other medium.

TYRA TINGLEFF

Absolutely. These lifelines can provide a grounding in terms that
everyone already knows, but they can be very narrow.

A Z

Particularly the mention of figures like Jackson Pollock or Helen
Frankenthaler, that sometimes come up in reference to your work.
All American, and all of a very specific generation. One of the
biggest differences between today and, say, back when Pollock
and Frankenthaler were working is that so much painting is made
to be photographed and to circulate as photography, whereas
your work does not lend itself to that.

T T

My work has never been easy to photograph. The photographer's
eye never sees the same thing as when you see it in person, which
I think is a strength, but it's also difficult because it demands that
people actually see the thing. It's a dilemma of our time that you
need to have a photograph of a painting for more people to see it,
but what they are seeing is such a different thing. Even on this Zoom
call, I can see what you see through the camera, and it's not at all
the same as what I see here in the studio.

A Z

That's true. I am not actually seeing the work right now, and the work
I have seen in person is a couple of years old by now. Do you take
photos during your process so that you can look back at the progres-
sion of the work?

T T

I do, but I am very physical in the painting process, so I'm not looking at the photos. I don't use them as work tools, but only to review
the paintings' evolution. Sometimes I wish I was more patient.
But my temperament is too quick, so I'm already done before I stop
to look at images of the work in process.

A Z

Well, that makes sense, because it would take it into some other
language. I think that's a really difficult but interesting thing about

work like yours, namely that so much translation is required—for this book, for instance, or for the translation of your work online, which has now become inextricable from exhibiting art. But the logic of the production of your work has not used or incorporated that technology. It is not translating back and forth from computer or digital renderings or even photographs. Would it be correct to say that you have an almost stubborn commitment to an older, somewhat romantic mode of a fight with the self in the studio, unhindered?

> T T
>
> Yes and no. It's a cliché, it's old-school and romantic, but I think it's also a kind of dedication to the work process in the studio, which is still a contemporary question. That's something I'm stubborn about. Also, when it comes to this question of when a painting is better on Instagram than it is in real life. I'm stubborn about the idea that the artist's labor and what we get out into the world needs to be the thing that we talk about.

A Z

I think that's why so many painters are feeling the need to incorporate some kind of technological element into their work, or have some dialogue with technology, or show technological shifts impacting their work.

> T T
>
> To make it contemporary, yes. It can be an excuse, in the sense of wanting to be part of our time. I have some confidence in myself, likely in part because I was brought up by two very serious artist parents. I was raised to believe that art was the most important thing in your life. So that's in my bones, in the sense that I think this is extremely important, extremely serious. Of course, I am insecure about my practice from time to time—whether or not it has relevance, or whether a painting is good enough—so I'm not arrogant about it.

A Z

Not to fixate on the question of technology, but you're making me realize that the pull to even have a discussion about technology and painting hews to the idea of a teleology, of needing to situate oneself in line after well-known artists. When really, the work should be free to be about something else. It's not about building on something we all know or extending a linear narrative that comes out of New York, but rather leaving space for the possibility that there's something else happening. I keep wanting to say that your works are almost like inner landscapes that you're pulling out and allowing yourself to deal with. They aren't ahistorical—certainly not— but they aren't fitting into what I already understand or what's within my reach.

T T

The canon is something you need to go through when you're younger, as a student: you need to be aware of the references, but then you also have to let them go and have the confidence as an adult to be your-self. So, like you said, I'm confident that this is my story and my landscape. And then it's more the concern of making a good painting or not within that. I'm not concerned about whether it looks like a Pollock or a Frankenthaler; I don't feel I need to excuse it or that I need to make things "contemporary" by referring to digital culture.

A Z

When you say your main concern is making a good painting, what does that mean?

T T

When something goes out the door, I want to feel that I've worked through it enough for it to stand on its own. And that process can be so different in each case, because actual, physical paintings take so much time. A lot of the time, it's just looking. Looking, looking, looking. There's no getting around that you must take the time to look at your work. It's extremely important, because you see some-thing new every time you come into the studio. My first reaction is often negative. And then I go home and come back the next day, and the more I look, I see great things or weird things…

A Z

When does it end? When do you let it go out the door?

T T

At some point, you have to accept the weirdness of it. And find what the strength is or determine that it's just not working. Is it dysfunc-tional? Is it ugly? Ugly can also be great. Is it *too* beautiful? Beautiful can also sometimes be great. Often, it's this mix of the two, such that the brain has to be high alert all the time. And then I also have to be very aware of destruction, the possibility of destruction in any moment, because when I know a painting really well, I can end up destroying the whole thing. So, then there's this almost sorrowful process to undertake. A good painting needs to leave the studio very raw. But then it's also very scary—meaning, the idea that I didn't work enough on it. It's a constant mind game.

A Z

Do you ever gray up a painting to the point where you don't feel like you can bring it back?

T T

No, I haven't done that in recent years. I always work on the paintings until they leave the studio, so I don't destroy them or stow them in the back because I care too much about them. I need to somehow bring them somewhere. When your career takes off, it can create a pressure of production [*snap, snap, snap*]. I think it's a very big responsibility to also keep some things back, not give too much out. When you become known for a certain kind of painting or technique, and it sells, there can be pressure to overproduce to cater to the market's demands.

Because I know, as a painter, how to make something that looks seductive quite fast. The challenge to go beyond that is to change before you end up with something too decorative instead of something that engages you mentally. That line is so fragile; a painting can very easily become just a product. That's my responsibility to maintain that struggle within the work.

A Z

I almost imagine you on your board over the top of a painting you're working on.[1] How do you navigate that balancing act so that what's beneath you doesn't fall into decor, making the work merely a commodity?

T T

For example, I was working on a big painting that was in a very sexy stage. The marbling effect looked gorgeous and I could have stopped there. Maybe I should have stopped there to just let it breathe a little bit, but my brain was working so fast. I thought, no, this is too decorative: but people will say, "Ah, beautiful!" It's not at a point where I can let go of it and put it out into the world. But now it's a mess. Maybe I took it too far. The destruction mode is very close, all the time.

A Z

Having studied painting briefly, I can appreciate how hard it is to make the work you do. I appreciate your work, and the labor that goes into it, and the technique. But when I first saw it in 2018, I wasn't at a moment in my life where I could appreciate the production in a way that I do now. I needed some time to understand the importance of holding open this space that art needs to hold open, so as not to be propaganda, not be socially overt all the time, but allow people to go out to sea with you into this abstract, mental landscape. The value of that has become more apparent as this cultural moment continues, not as anything reactionary or conservative, but a kind of "in addition to" all the overtly socially engaged art that came out in the past four or five years.

T T

Definitely. I've been aware of that since very early on. Many of my friends are artists doing work that has political content or trying to act on the world in a different way, but I've always fought hard to not have this clear statement because that's not my voice. That's not my contribution to bigger political issues. We also need a break. That pause is important, especially in the world right now.

It is important to take a pause for yourself to even understand what's
going on inside of you. It reminds me of what you once explained
to me about a musical experience with your friend: you were sitting
and listening and got very emotional because you were thinking
through all the things that were happening to you. Music is the highest
form of art in that sense. It touches your emotions immediately
because you sense it so directly. Brushstrokes in painting are not
doing that as fast as music does.

But if you can allow yourself that space to go into a work, then I think
you can get something out of it. And that's the mix of seduction
of beauty and ugliness. That's very much in my life as a painter in
my studio. Of course, I can't see that *for* the viewer, but that's what
I'm trying to allow for. And when we talk about the canon, that's
perhaps why I am inspired by people like Agnes Martin or Joan
Mitchell. Their commitment to being in the studio is something
that I can relate to.

A Z

Speaking of Martin in relation to this moment of considering
abstract art, it's just become a different thing today when it's so hard
to escape being plugged into technology all the time, as opposed
to how people experienced life when she was painting. I'm tempted
to say we have to use art as a space to get away from capitalist mediums
and create space to emotionally process our own experiences of
the world, which I don't know that you can do when you're activating
the sorts of brain waves that are stimulated when you look at a
screen. You were referring to a story I told you about listening to
Glenn Gould's version of the *Goldberg Variations* with my friend who
was a classical soprano. It provided me a space to just be touched
by something. And I think if you're primed for it, and you're willing
to "go there" when you stand in front of a canvas that doesn't
demand anything of you in a strictly intellectual sense, but just be
with it, but at the same time, on some level, be connected to a much
longer history (like Glenn Gould with Bach), that's a virtue of
abstraction that has become more apparent to me in the past year.
And so, with your work, somehow, I just needed time to meet you
there. Obviously, your work has historical resonance, but the problem
is that reaching for the best-known references can be a way to intel-
lectualize one's experience and avoid having that more difficult,
more complicated experience.

Can I ask you about how you title the works?

T T

My awkward titles are meant to be kind of nonsensical. To go with
your metaphor of being out at sea, the paintings are so much
about being out at sea, like in the studio, you go on a journey into

something where you're literally in the middle of this storm that you
work on and work through. And then to me, the titles come when
the storm dies down. . . You offer something concrete, not something
obvious, but something—

A Z

I guess I'm wondering how you title the works or why you don't just
say *Untitled Number 525* or something like that.

T T

No, that would definitely refer back to the male history or old canon.
In my work, the title is like a punch line, because of course, painting
for me is the most serious thing I can do. But also, I see the irony
in taking something so seriously. The titles are almost like the joker
at court—the most honest person, in a way. The one who is able to
say something political, sensitive, or otherwise very serious because
it is within the joke, addressed to the people. I have a list of potential
titles that I keep in my phone. It is a huge list.

A Z

Where do these lines come from?

T T

From different sources. If I overhear something, I write it down.
Or it could be from a song or a movie or something someone tells me.
I always like some small sentence that sticks or something that
I come up with when the work is on the wall, but it can be kind of
a silly thing. As we're making this book, we're also seeing how
the titles have changed. It reflects on where I am in my personal life.
I thought that, in the book, there should be one page just with
the titles. It looks like a very fucked-up haiku when you put them
together. But I take the titles very seriously. I've come to form a big
relationship with them. And I'll admit, it's funny when someone at
the gallery will say, "I just saw *my nipples are freer than yours.*" [*laughs*]

A Z

That's really funny. I look at your practice and think about how
it must be difficult, in this day and age, to defend the kind of work
you're doing and have people understand the importance of it.
The requirement to go into your studio every day and work.
Even someone like me needs several years to understand that,
which must be hard.

T T

It's been hard. But I also think that my conviction comes from my
upbringing. I have a security in myself: I know that the work is worth
something, and it gets easier and easier. The older I get, the less
I care, in a way, and the more respect I feel I gain. . .
I was very lucky to sign with my London gallery early after finishing
my MA at the RCA. The gallerists are the same age as me, so I feel

we kind of "grew up together." The same with my gallerists here
in Berlin, who are very close friends of mine and business partners.
This "family" connection is very important to me. But it has definitely been hard now and then to keep the motivation up. I have been
working hard for many years in different conditions and circumstances, but I continued to do the work, continued to be stubborn.
I think this stubbornness is also what makes the work valued,
and makes it involved and develop because it needs so much time.
Some people ask me, "Why are you just painting? Don't you have
the need to do sculpture or express yourself through another
medium?" and I think to myself, "Do you have any idea how much
time it takes to paint?" Fuck me! I haven't figured it out. This is
a life project. There's so much to do!

1   The artist works on the paintings on the floor, and uses a board positioned over the canvas when
     working on larger pieces.

Biographies

Cooking Sections
examines the systems that organize the world through food. Established in London in 2013 by Daniel Fernández Pascual and Alon Schwabe, they use site-responsive installation, performance, and video to explore the overlapping boundaries between art, architecture, ecology, and geopolitics. They have worked on multiple iterations of the long-term *CLIMAVORE* project (2015–ongoing), exploring how to eat as humans change climates. Cooking Sections has exhibited at Tate Britain; SALT Beyoğlu, Istanbul; the 12th Taipei Biennial; the 58th Venice Biennale; the 13th Sharjah Biennial; Performa 17; Manifesta 12, Palermo; Atlas Arts, Skye, Scotland; and Serpentine Galleries, London, among others. Cooking Sections is nominated for the 2021 Turner Prize.

Petter Snare
is the director of KODE Art Museums and Composer Homes in Bergen, Norway, one of the largest museums for art, craft, design, and music in the Nordic countries. Snare has extensive experience in all realms of the visual art field as an art book publisher, art gallery founder, and avid collector. Snare frequently serves on selection committees, and holds degrees in economics and business administration.

Amy Sherlock
is a writer and editor based in London. She is the deputy editor of *frieze*, the international arts and culture publication, where has worked since 2012. She is the curator of the annual Frieze Art & Architecture Conference, which takes place in London every October and has featured speakers including David Adjaye, Shigeru Ban, and David Chipperfield. In addition to *frieze*, her writings have been published in numerous academic journals, arts publications, and national newspapers. She was one of the directors and curators of Open Source, a free, artist-initiated contemporary arts festival, which took place in East London between 2014 and 16.

Amy Zion
is an independent curator and writer. She has curated exhibitions at the Queens Museum, New York; the Hessel Museum of Art, Annandale-on-Hudson, New York; the Museum für Gegenwartskunst, Basel, Switzerland; and other venues internationally. Since 2018, Zion has organized the Talks Program for Frieze NY, and from 2016 to 2021 she was faculty at the Center for Curatorial Studies, Bard College. As of fall 2021 she will be based in Paris.

List of Works

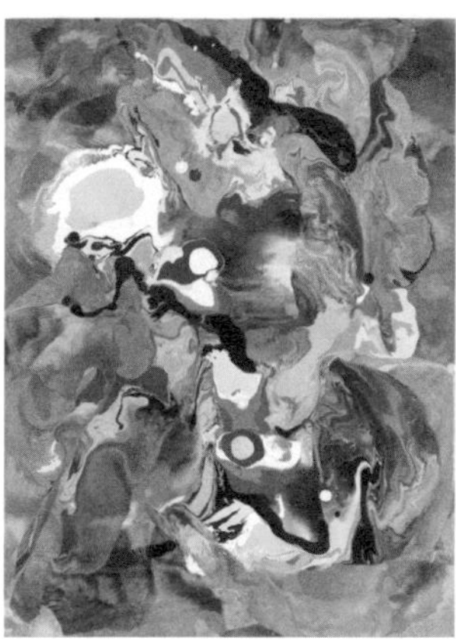

p. 17
On I go, 2021
oil on raw linen
90 × 65 cm

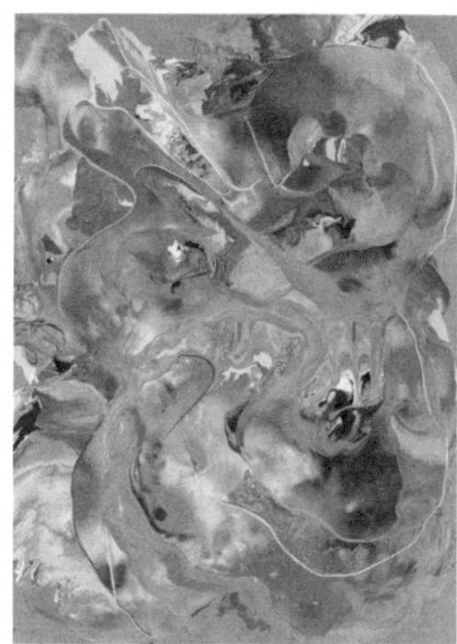

p. 18
I remember love, but I can't remember you, 2021
oil on raw linen
170 × 120 cm

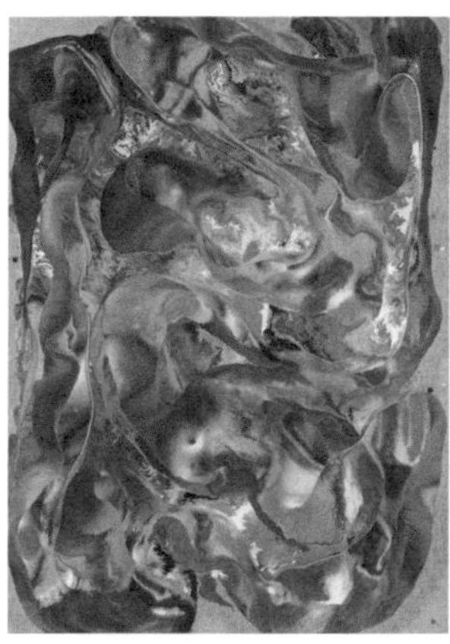

p. 19
My love life definitely skews towards crimson, 2021
oil on raw linen
170 × 120 cm

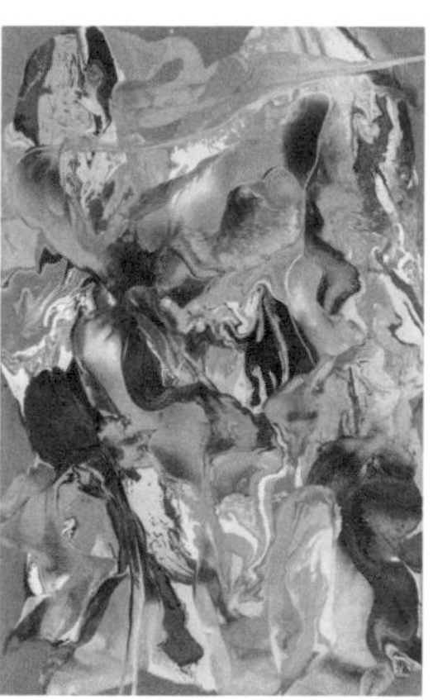

p. 21
The intimidation of sexual wealth, 2021
oil on raw linen
190 × 120 cm

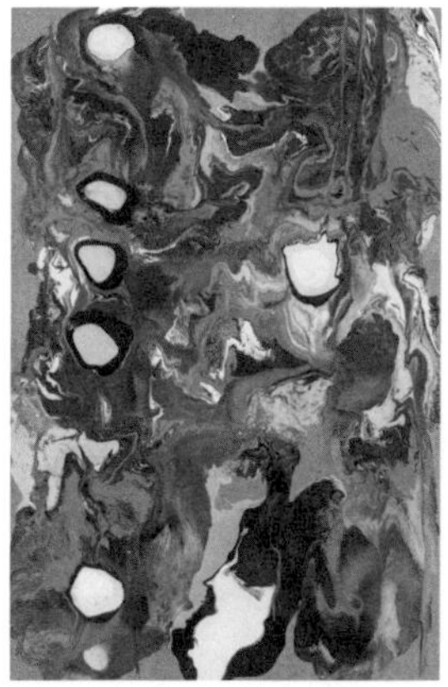

p. 22
The day I met you never ended for me, 2021
oil on raw linen
190 × 120 cm

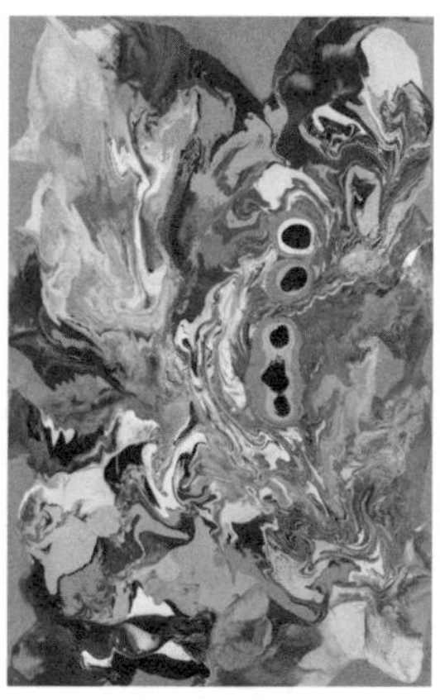

p. 23
It's curiously beautiful, like a loyalty we do not share, 2021
oil on raw linen
190 × 120 cm

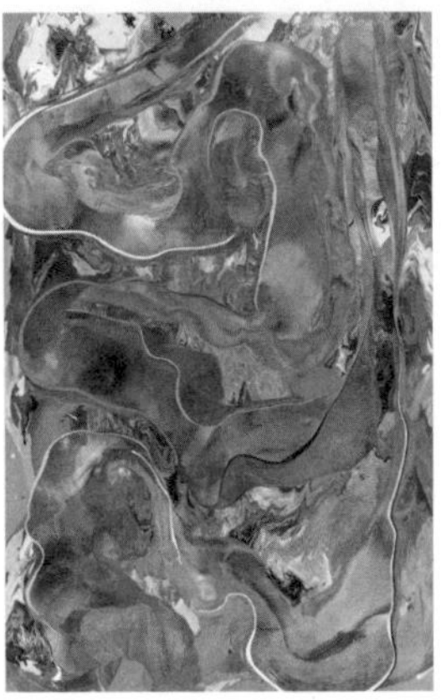

p. 25
It's deeper than you think, 2021
oil on raw linen
190 × 120 cm
Private Collection, Italy

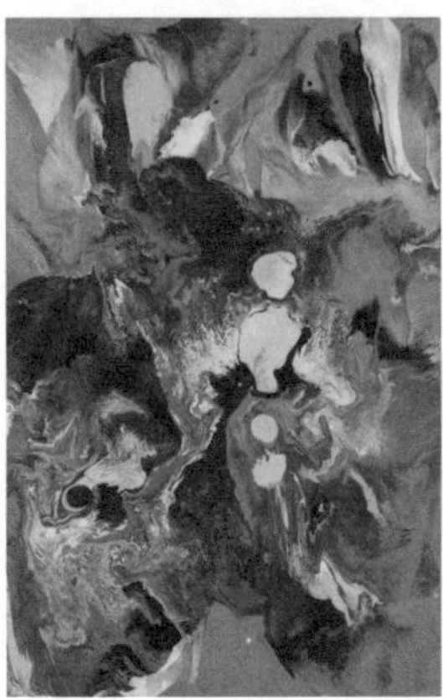

p. 26
How to cope inside of it, 2021
oil on raw linen
190 × 120 cm
Collection of Drammen Art Museum, Norway

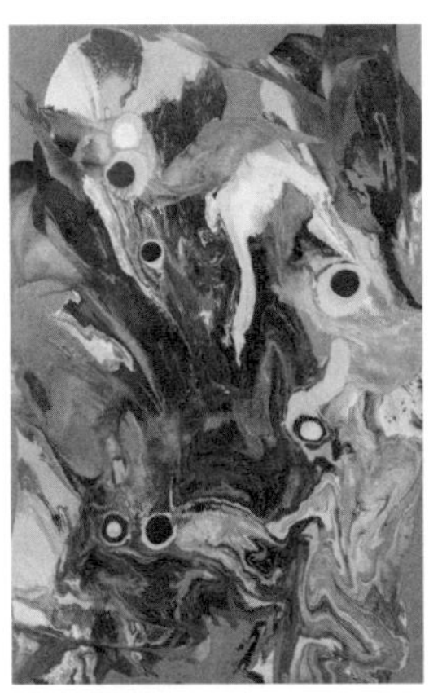

p. 27
I will never be satisfied with just one part of you. . ., 2021
oil on raw linen
190 × 120 cm
Private collection, Oslo, Norway

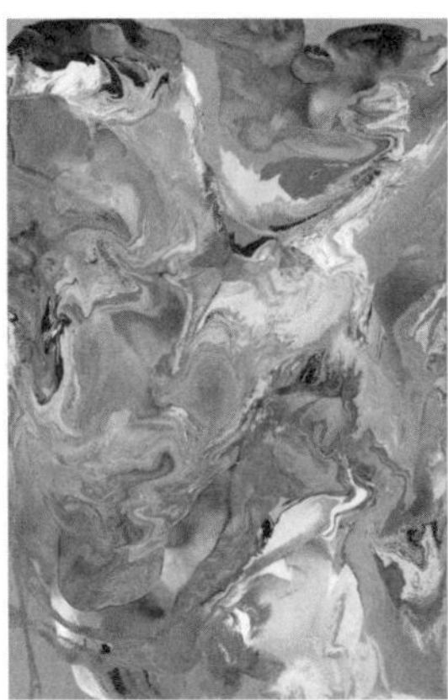

p. 29
You truly are awash of good ideas, 2021
oil on raw linen,
190 × 120 cm
Private Collection, UK

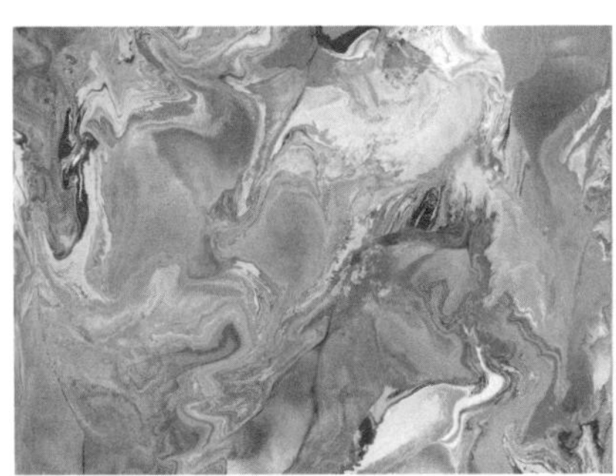

p. 30–31
You truly are awash of good ideas (detail), 2021

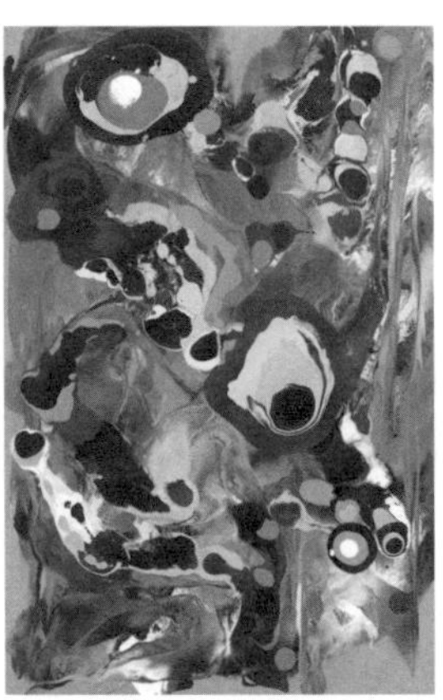

p. 33
I got a lot of space in my brain for you, 2021
oil on raw linen
190 × 120 cm
Private Collection, New York

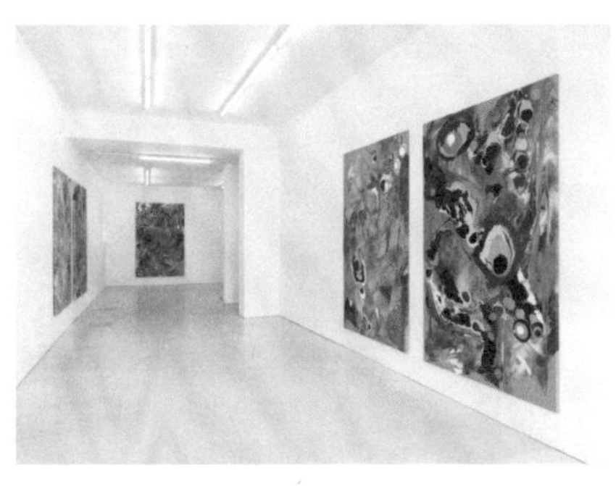

p. 34–35
Smile now, cry later, 2021
installation view
The Sunday Painter

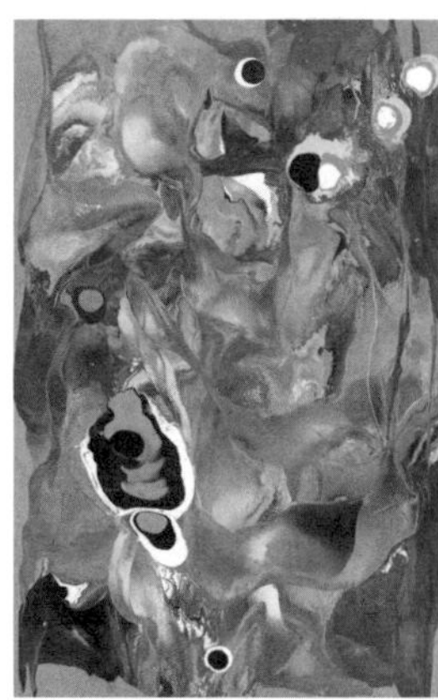

p. 37
Nothing to prove, move to move, 2021
oil on raw linen
190 × 120 cm
Private Collection, Italy

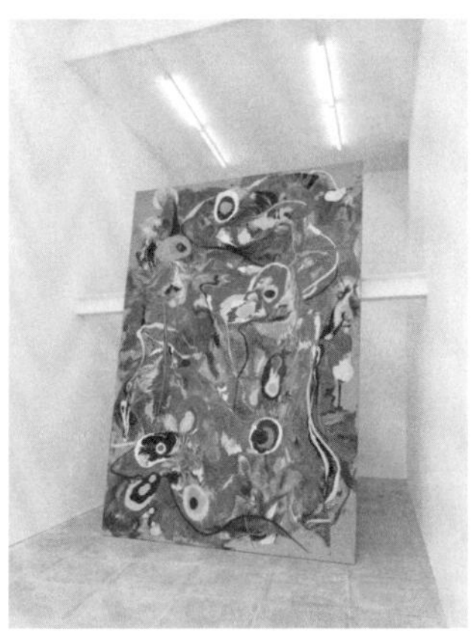

p. 38
Don't breathe out (but I know you will), 2021
oil on raw linen
380 × 250 cm

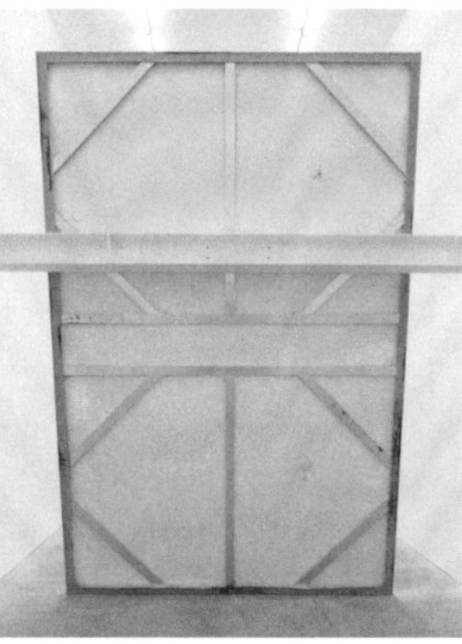

p. 39
Don't breathe out (but I know you will), 2021
installation view
The Sunday Painter

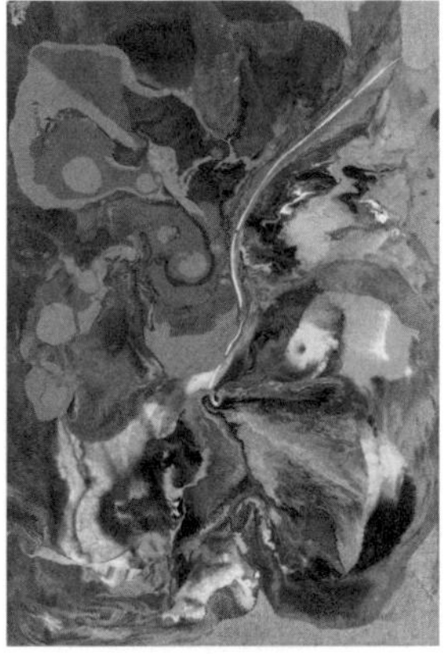

p. 41
I like to see how red the flag can get. . ., 2021
oil on raw linen
90 × 60 cm
Private Collection, Oslo

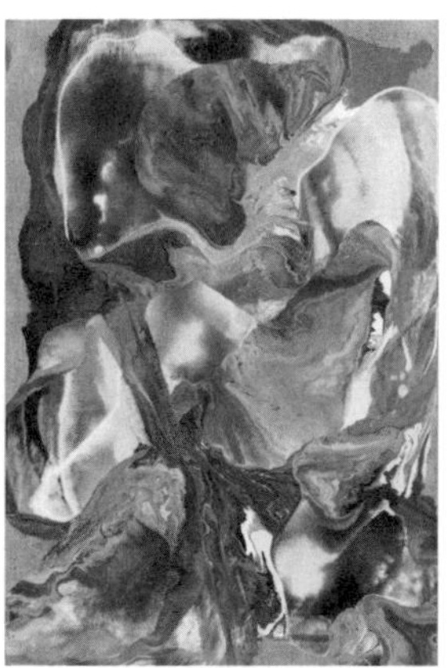

p. 42
Brush past me, 2021
oil on raw linen
90 × 60 cm
The Anthony Shaw Collection l York Museums Trust,
London/York

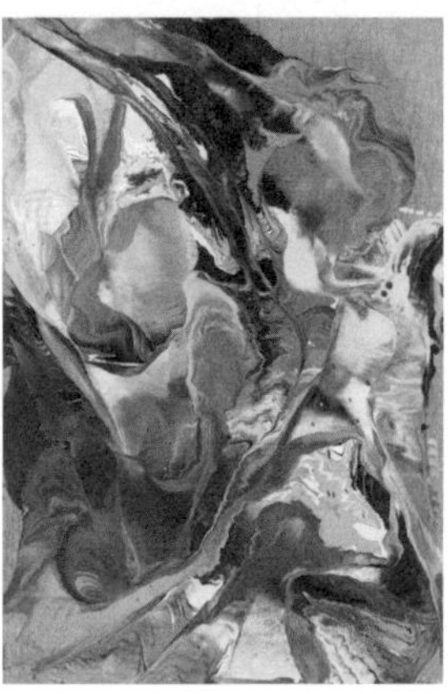

p. 43
Why do you mostly speak in quotations?, 2021
oil on raw linen
90 × 60 cm

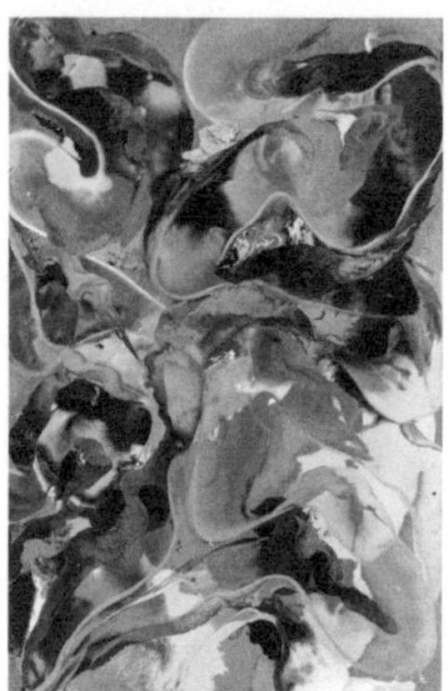

p. 45
I don't want the trouble, but the trouble wants me, 2021
oil on raw linen
190 × 120 cm
MMAT Mauro Mattei Art Trust Collection, London

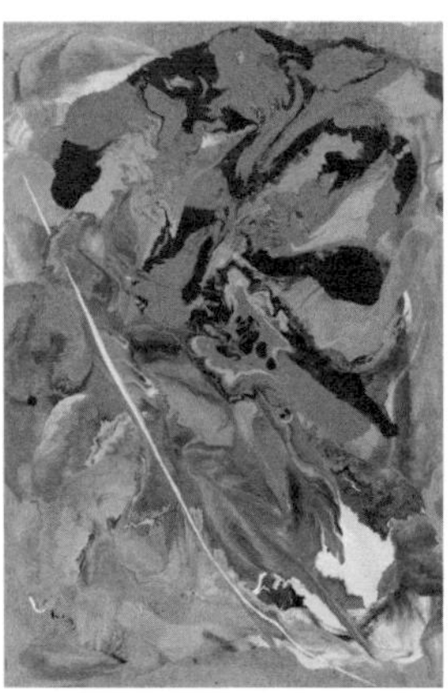

p. 46
Shovels of coals (I no longer feel the shovel. . .), 2021
oil on raw linen
90 × 60 cm

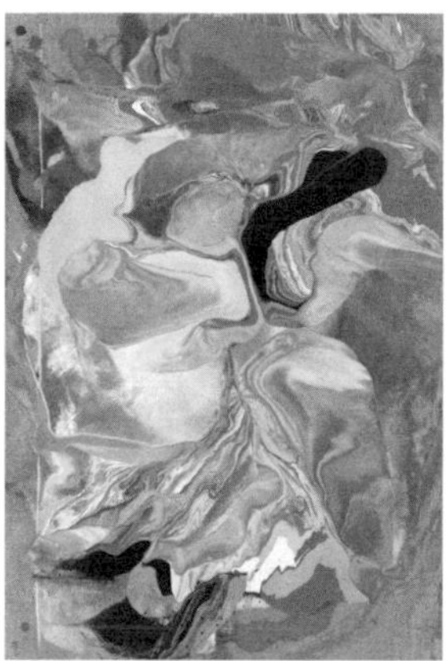

p. 47
PMS is my definition of time, 2021
oil on raw linen
90 × 60 cm

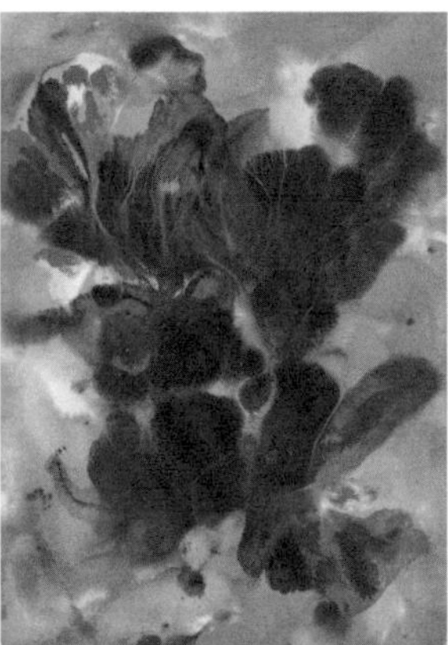

p. 49
I slept where you slept so I slept with you, 2020
oil on raw linen
170 × 120 cm
Formuesforvaltning Art Collection, Norway

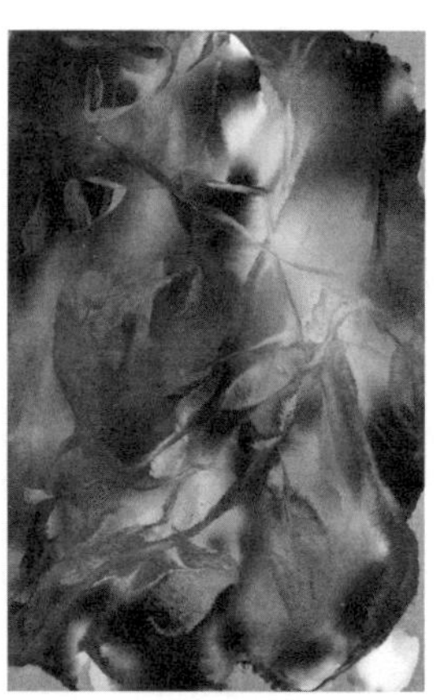

p. 51
I am now the one looking, 2021
oil on raw linen
190 × 120 cm
Private Collection, Berlin

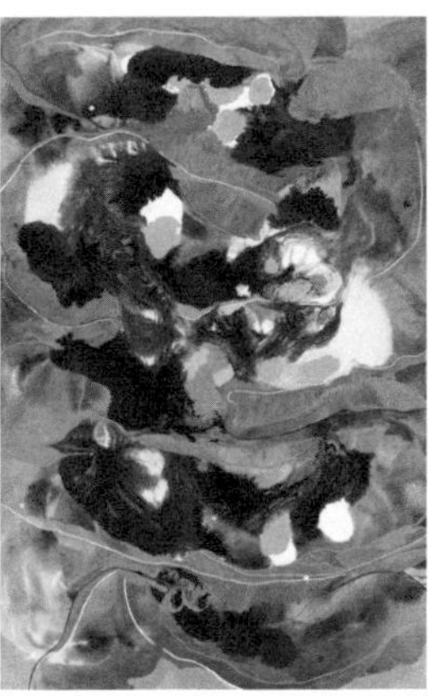

p. 52
Dear blue I am just like you, 2021
oil on raw linen
190 × 120 cm

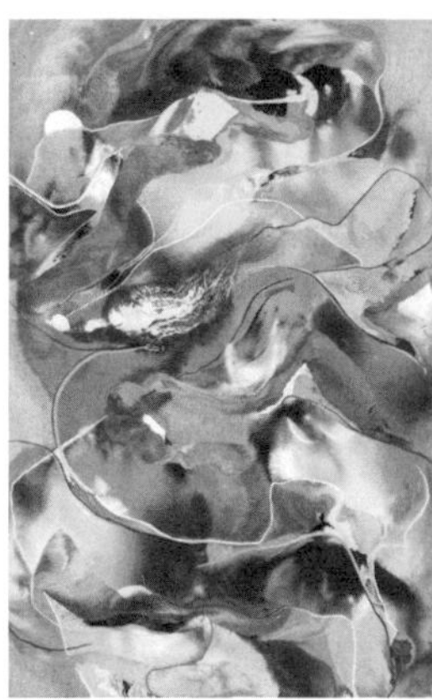

p. 53
Total existence needs meaning and myth, 2021
oil on raw linen
190 × 120 cm
Gleneagles Collection, Scotland

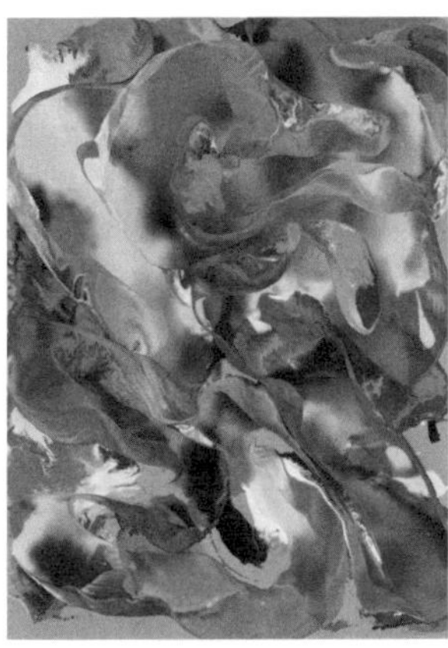

p. 55
Due to not wanting to, I will not, 2020
oil on raw linen
170 × 120 cm
Private Collection, Dubai

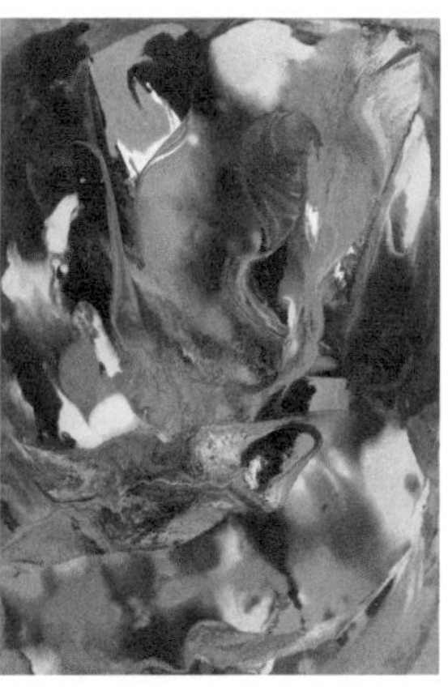

p. 56
French-kiss in chaos, 2020
oil on raw linen
90 × 60 cm

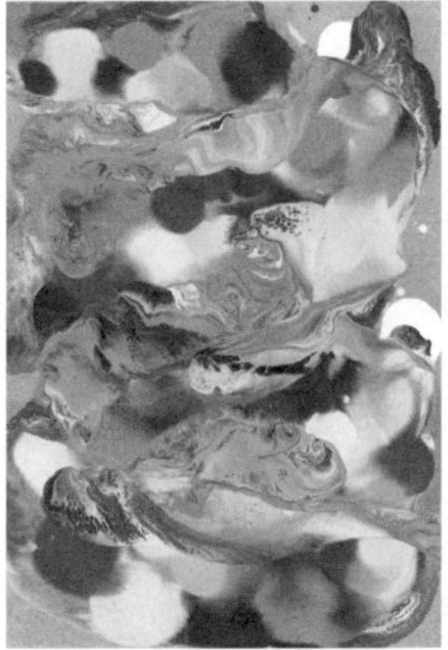

p. 57
Babe I'm poetry, just read between the lines. . ., 2020
oil on raw linen
90 × 60 cm
Private Collection, Bath

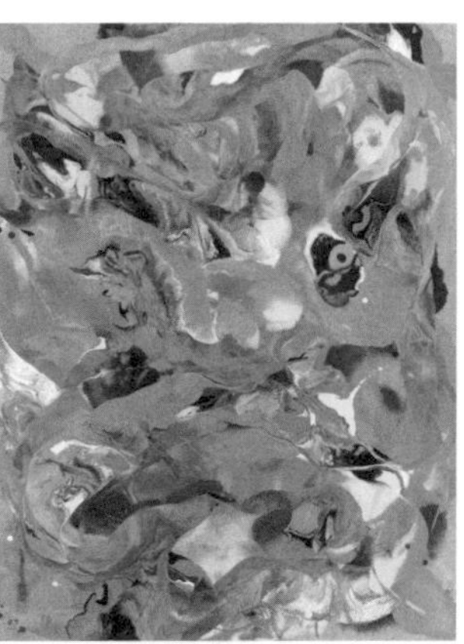

p. 59
How brave is your brain?, 2020
oil on raw linen
120 × 90 cm
Private Collection, Olso

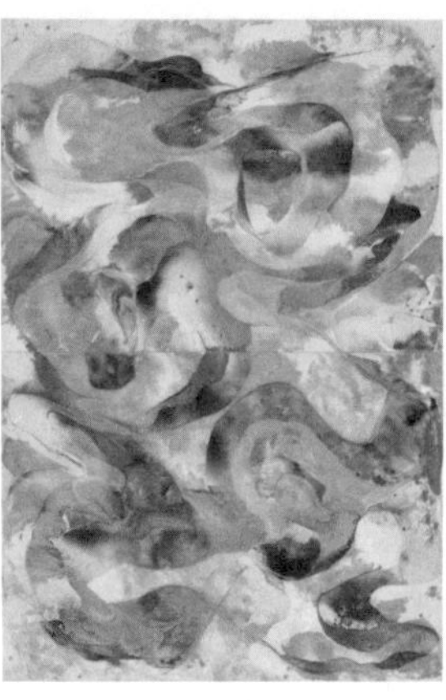

p. 61
Smile now, cry later, 2020
oil on raw linen
300 × 200 cm
Lani Invest Art Collection

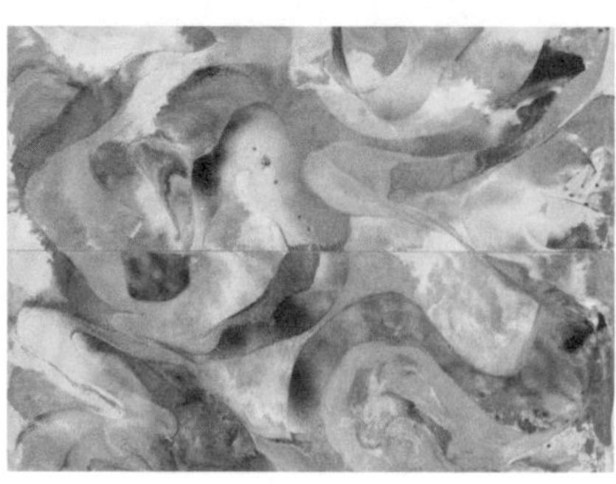

p. 62–63
Smile now, cry later (detail), 2020
Lani Invest Art Collection

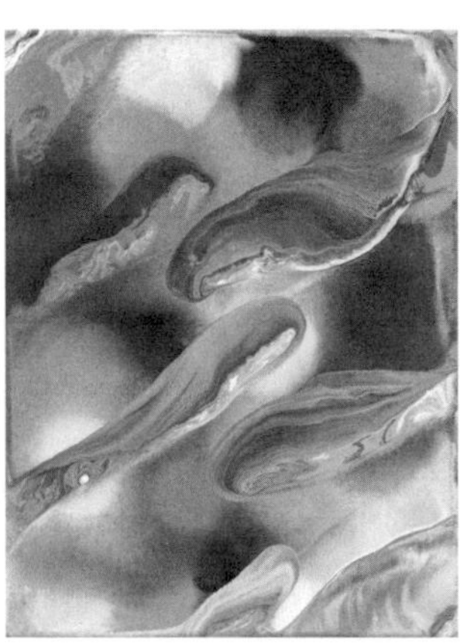

p. 81
We should take a deep breath, 2020
oil on raw linen
40 × 30 cm

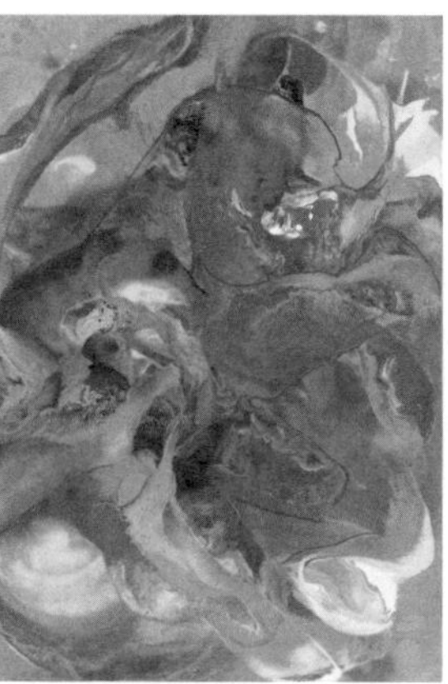

p. 82
I missed my reds (I didn't miss my reds), 2020
oil on raw linen
90 × 60 cm

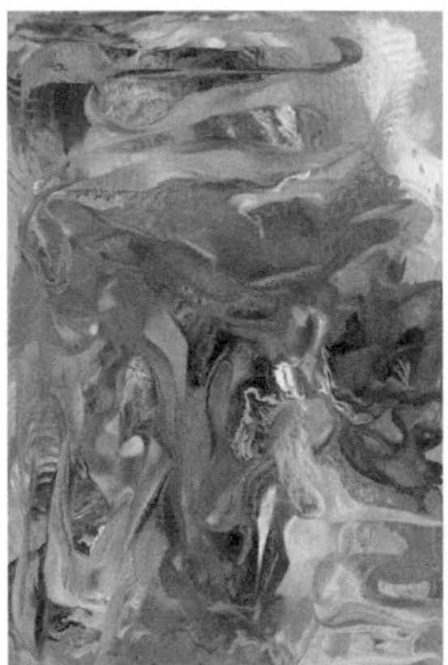

p. 83
It's a nasty piece of work, 2020
oil on raw linen
90 × 60 cm

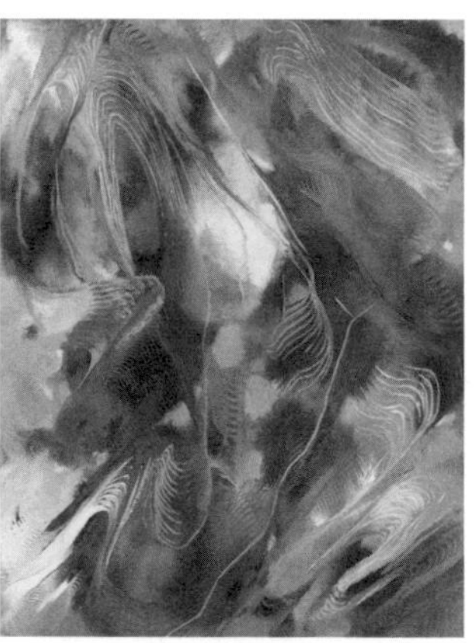

p. 84
Chemical rushes, 2020
oil on raw linen
120 × 90 cm
Private Collection, London

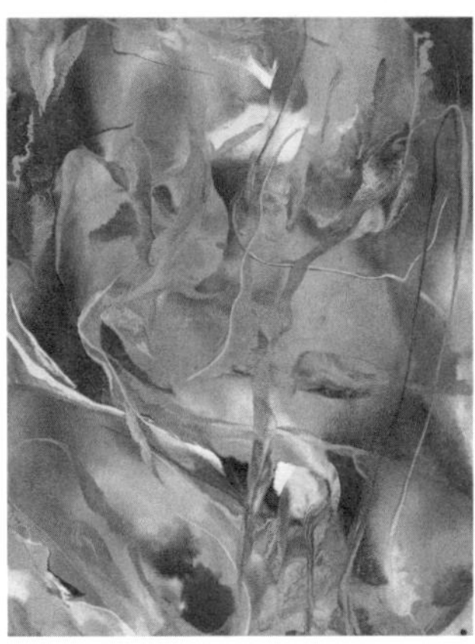

p. 85
Wake up alone!, 2020
oil on raw linen
120 × 90 cm
Collection of KORO / Public Art Norway

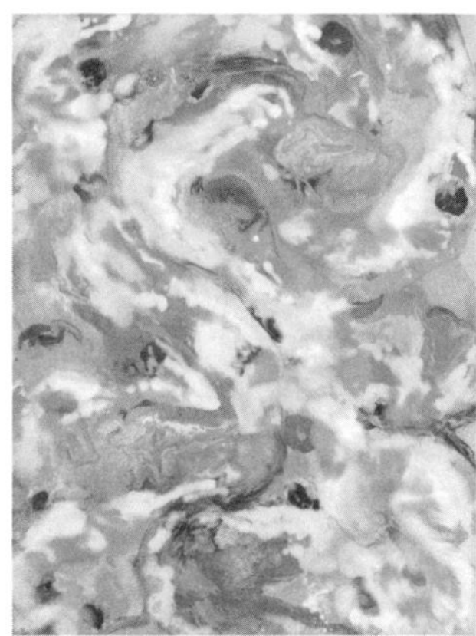

p. 87
If you want to control someone love them, 2020
oil on raw linen
140 × 105 cm
Collection of KORO / Public Art Norway

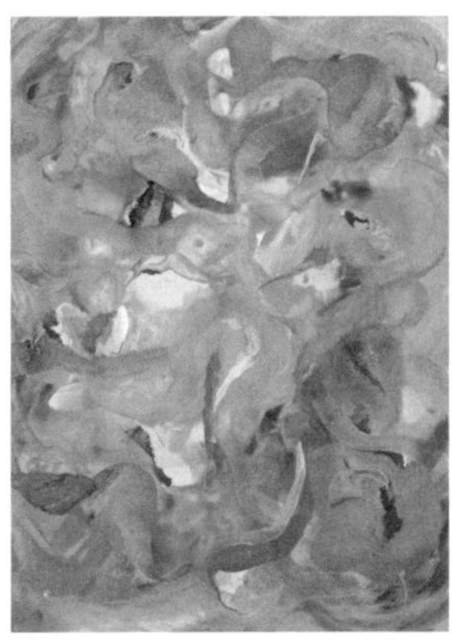

p. 88
*If you want the rainbow, you need to put up
with a little bit of rain. . .*, 2020
oil on raw linen
170 × 120 cm
Private Collection, Oslo

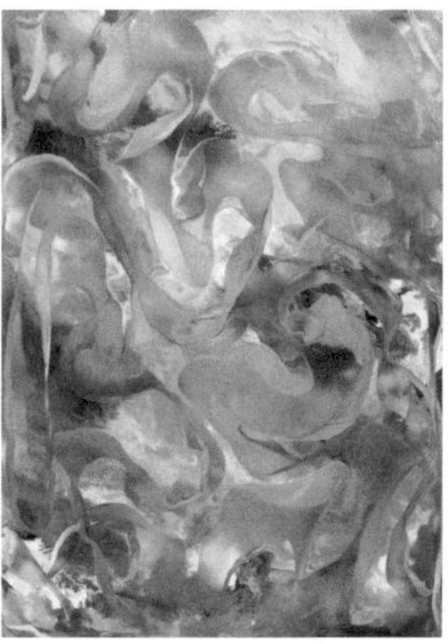

p. 89
*I want to lick you in places that leave my
tongue bacterial*, 2020
oil on raw linen
170 × 120 cm
Private Collection, Oslo

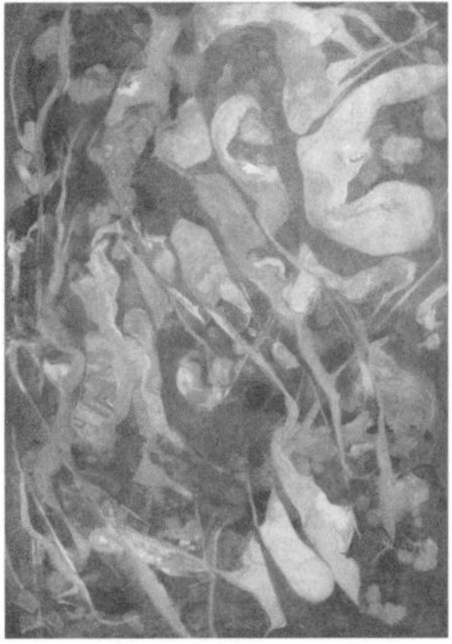

p. 91
Words I wish I had said, 2020
oil on raw linen
150 × 105 cm

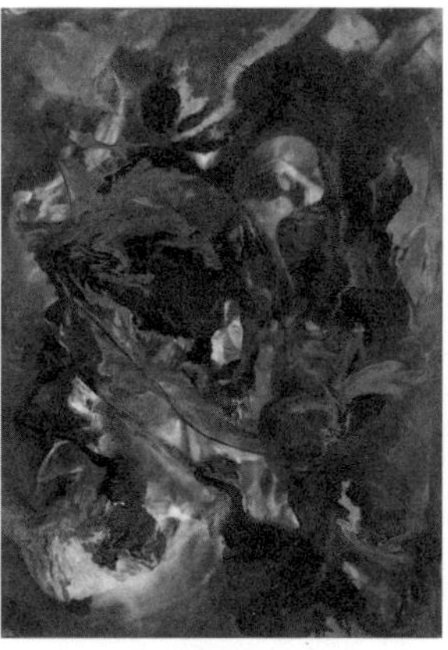

p. 92
Each burden, each great catch, 2021
oil on raw linen
170 × 120 cm

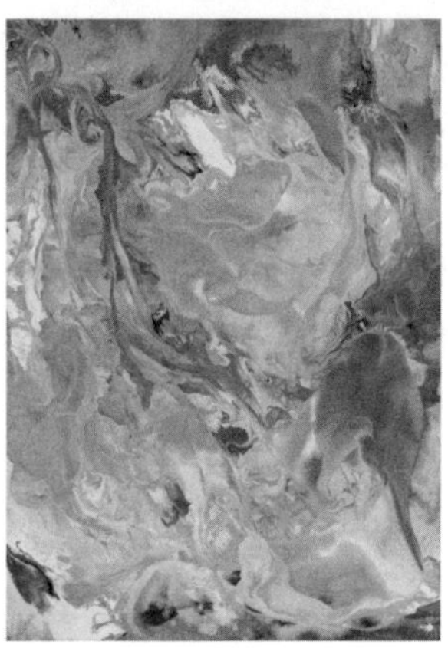

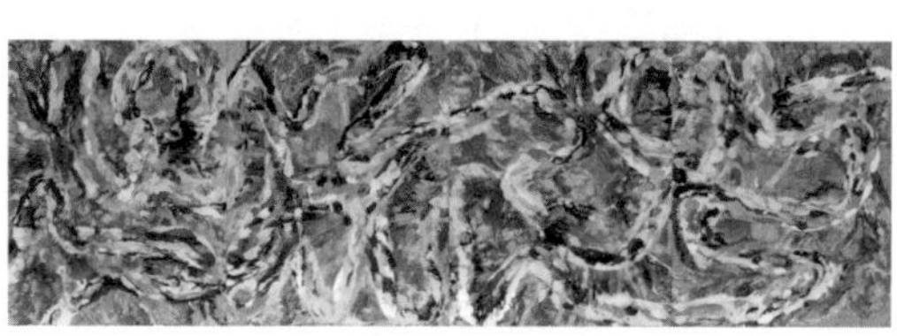

p. 93
Your loneliness is the symptom, not the sickness!, 2021
oil on raw linen
170 × 120 cm

p. 94–95
You taught me a lesson I didn't want to learn, 2020
oil on raw linen
700 × 230 cm
Public Collection, Ringerike videregående skole,
Viken fylkeskommune

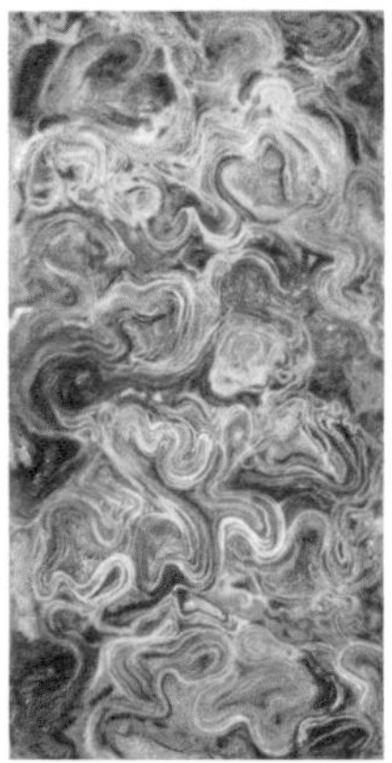

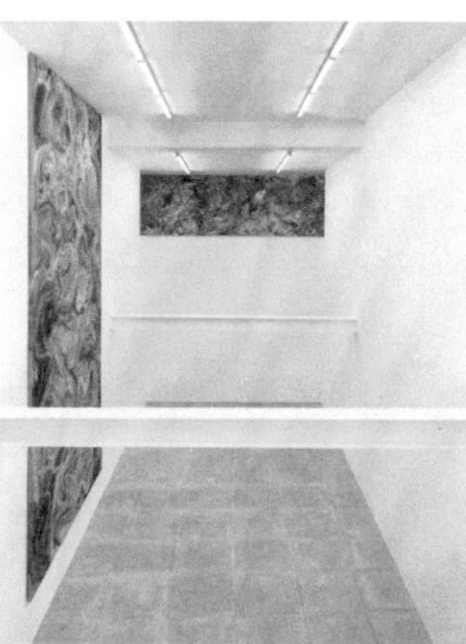

p. 97
Always the impossible as stupid as reality, 2018
oil on raw linen
500 × 250 cm
Public Collection, Vestlofoten videregående skole,
Nordlands fylkeskommune

p. 98
Will always be the opposite, 2018
installation view
The Sunday Painter

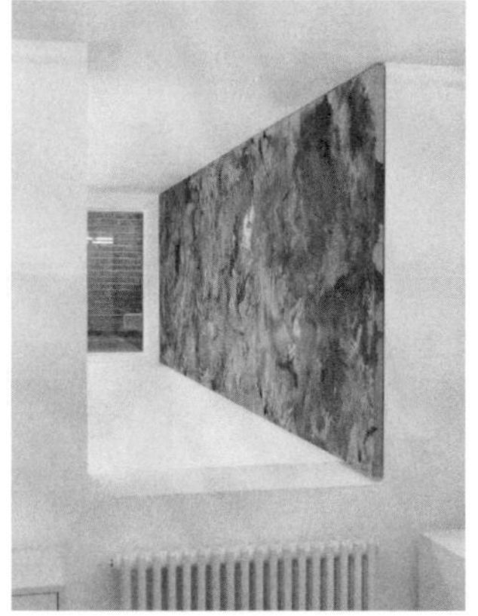

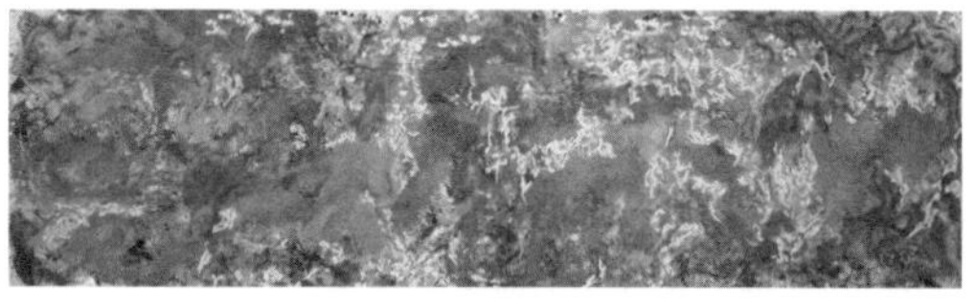

p. 99
Of course, I am not sorry, 2018
installation view
The Sunday Painter
oil on raw linen
136 × 460 cm

p. 100–101
As predictable as tides, as trainable as pets, 2018
oil on raw linen
136 × 460 cm

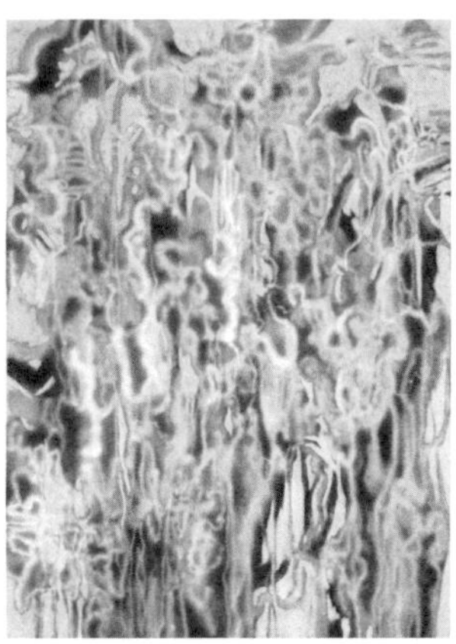

p. 102
Once bitten, twice shy, 2018
oil on raw linen
170 × 120 cm
Private Collection, London

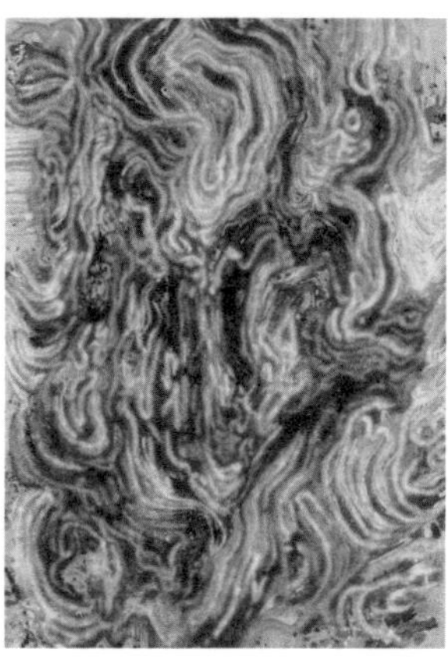

p. 103
Initially I too appear between the legs, 2019
oil on raw linen
170 × 120 cm
Private Collection, Hønefoss

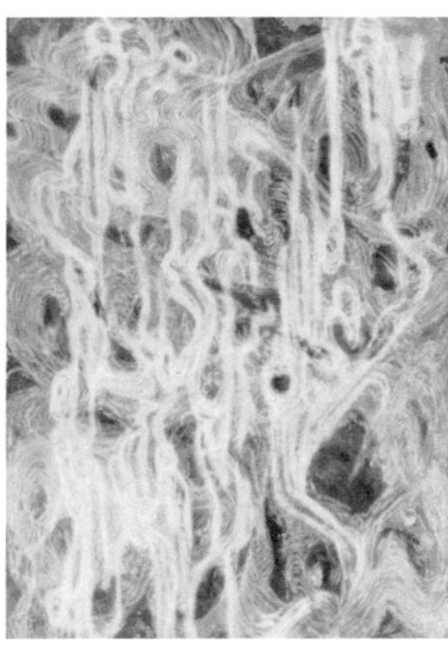

p. 104
Self-conscious sabotage, 2019
oil on raw linen
170 × 120 cm

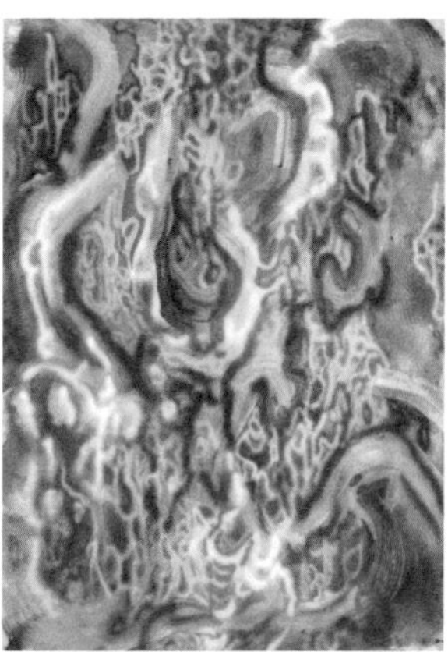

p. 105:
Raunchy humour, fairly specific sex, 2018
oil on raw linen
170 × 120 cm
The Anthony Shaw Collection l York Museums Trust,
London/York

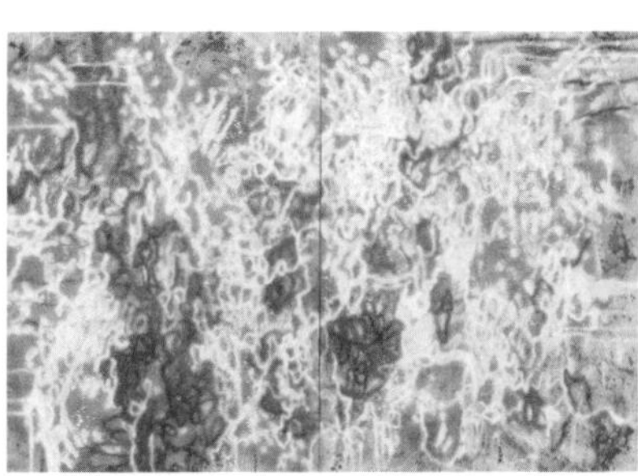

p. 106–107
Philosophy is probably homesickness, 2016
oil on raw linen
170 × 240 cm
Modern Forms Collection, London

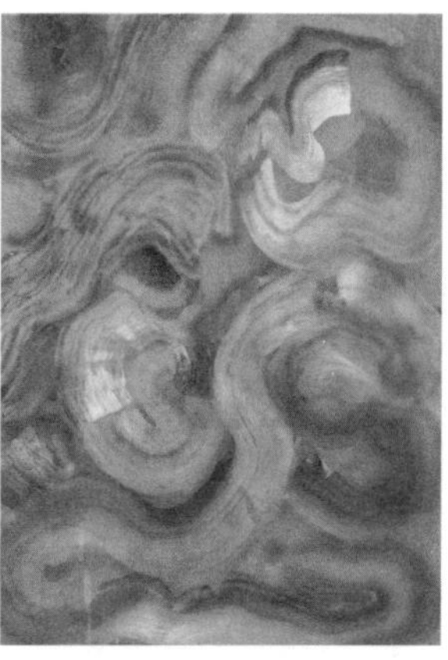

p. 109
My nipples are freer than yours, 2018
oil on raw linen
80 × 65 cm
Anna Katharina Haukeland Collection, Oslo

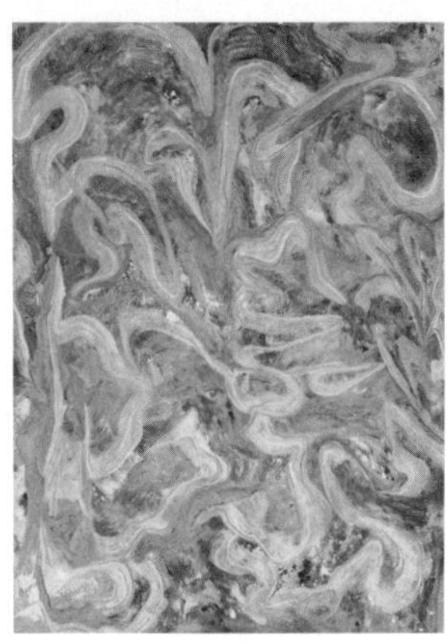

p. 110
The jokes on you I'm biding my time, 2019
oil on raw linen
170 × 120 cm

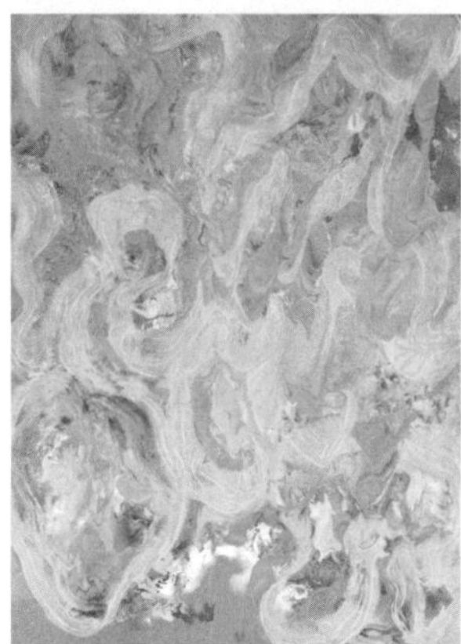

p. 111
I want it all, but slowly, 2019
oil on raw linen
170 × 120 cm
Private Collection, Berlin

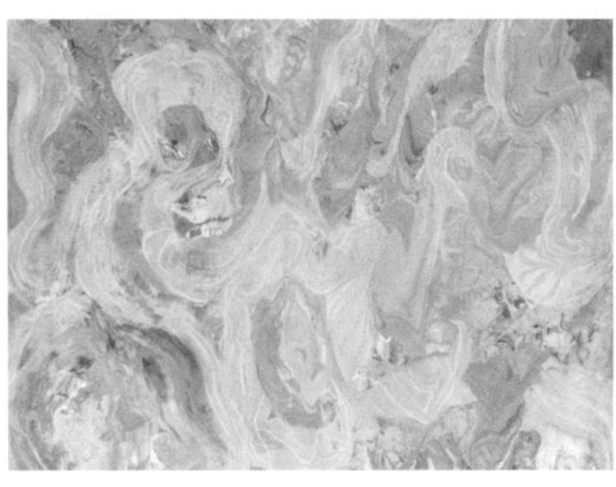

p. 112–113
I want it all, but slowly (detail), 2019

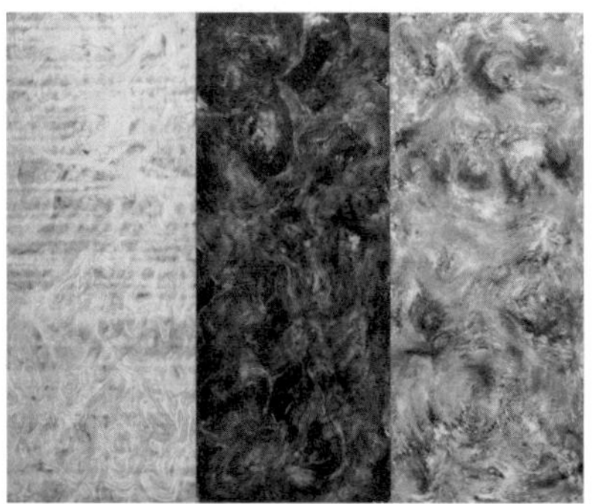

p. 114–115
installation view
Frieze New York with The Sunday Painter

Victorian promenade of self-sabotage, 2018
oil on raw linen
320 × 120 cm

You were once blue, 2018
oil on raw linen
320 × 120 cm

Glamour requires this space, 2018
oil on raw linen
320 × 120 cm
Private Collection, New York

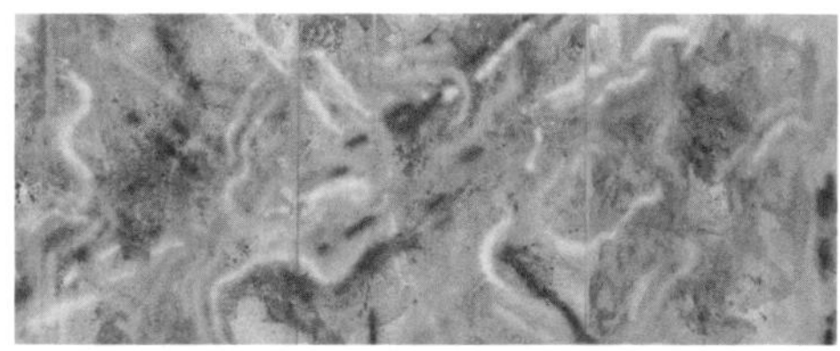

p. 116–117
When I wear a swimsuit I just don't swim, 2016
oil on raw linen
200 × 490 cm
Pangea Property Partners Art Collection, Oslo

p. 118
More than ever and once again, 2016
oil on raw linen
170 × 120 cm
Private Collection, London

p. 119
Closer scrub, 2015
oil on raw linen
170 × 120 cm
Private Collection, Oslo

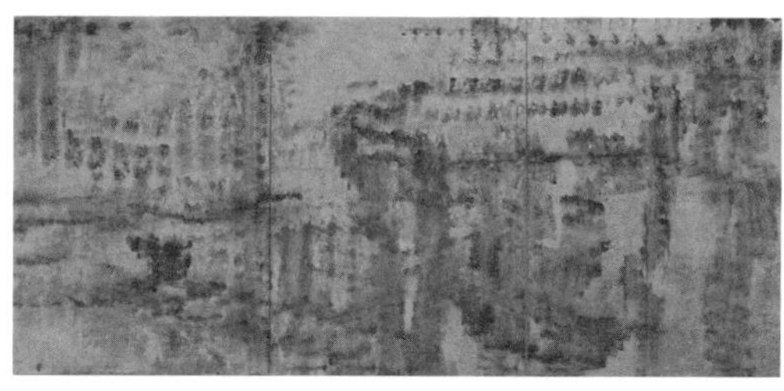

p. 120–121
Beloved are they who sit down, 2016
oil on raw linen
170 × 360 cm
Halilaj/Urbano Collection, Berlin

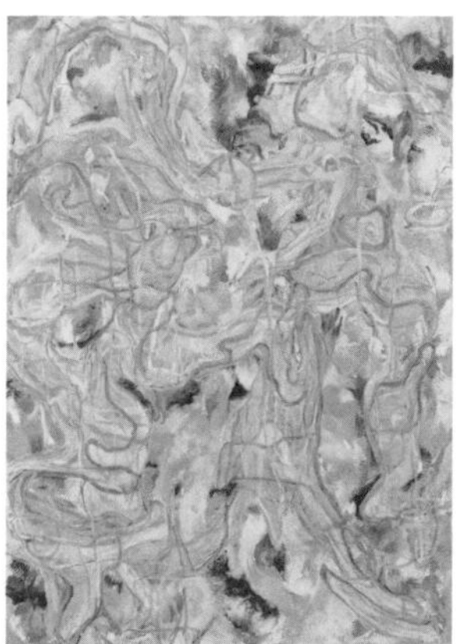

p. 123
So many unsaid things on the tip of my tongue, 2019
oil on raw linen
200 × 140 cm
Private Collection, Bergen

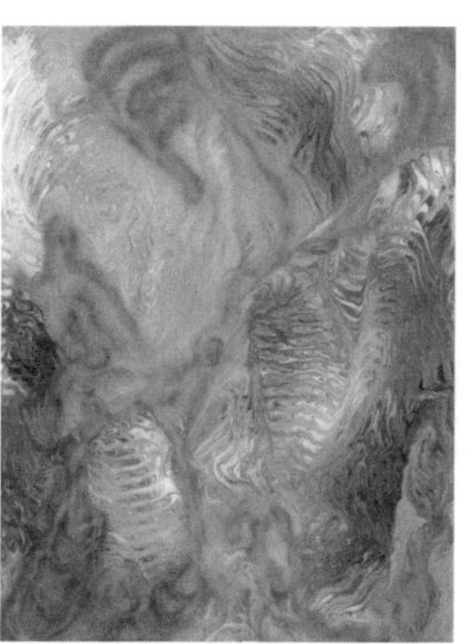

p. 124
The best is yet to come, 2019
oil on raw linen
40 × 30 cm
Private Collection, Mexico City

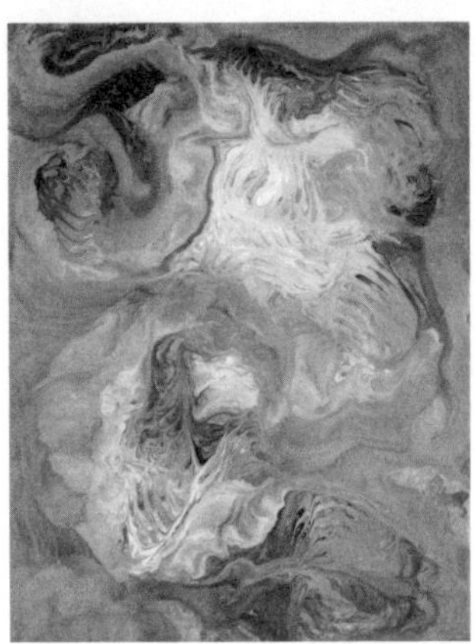

p. 125
They come, they go. . ., 2019
oil on raw linen
40 × 30 cm
Herresthal Collection, Oslo

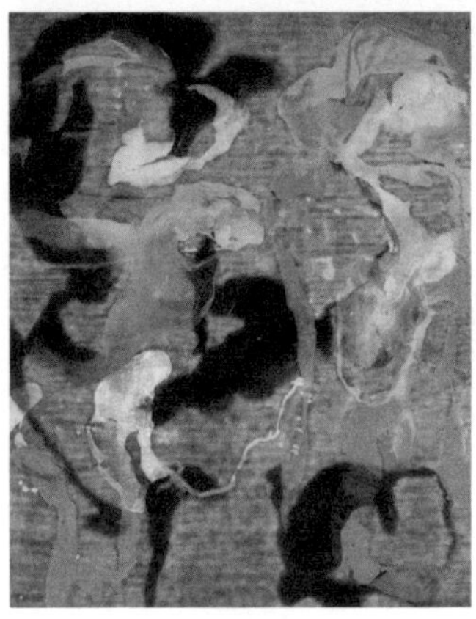

p. 127
Everything arrived as sealed, 2015
oil on raw linen
190 × 145 cm
Private Collection, Oslo

Supported by

Supported by Arts Council Norway
The Cultural Fund

SpareBankstiftelsen
RINGERIKE

Chert
Lüdde

THE
SUNDAY PAINTER

Tyra Tingleff
Of Course I'm Not Sorry

Publishing Editor
Vittoria Mieli (Mousse)

Texts
Amy Sherlock, Amy Zion,
Cooking Sections, Petter Snare

Copy Editing and Proofreading
Lindsey Westbrook, Joan Lee

Graphic Design
Massimiliano Pace (Mousse)

Published by
Mousse Publishing
Contrappunto s.r.l.
via Pier Candido Decembrio, 28
20137, Milan–Italy

Available through
Mousse Publishing, Milan
moussemagazine.it
DAP | Distributed Art Publishers,
New York
artbook.com
Vice Versa Distribution, Berlin
viceversaartbooks.com
Les presses du réel, Dijon
lespressesdureel.com
Antenne Books, London
antennebooks.com

© 2021 Tyra Tingleff,
ChertLüdde, The Sunday Painter,
and Mousse Publishing

All works by Tyra Tingleff
© Tyra Tingleff

Acknowledgments
The artist would like to thank:
Harry Beer, Jennifer Chert,
Clarissa Tempestini, Daniel
Fernández Pascual, Alon Schwabe,
Alvaro Urbano, Petrit Halilaj,
Florian Lüdde, Tom Cole, Will
Jarvis, Amy Sherlock, Amy Zion,
Petter Snare, Tim Zercie, Albin
Looström, Martin Schuessler,
Massimiliano Pace, Vittoria Mieli,
Islamiya Evans, Marit Tingleff,
Per Inge Bjørlo, Ask Bjørlo, Birk
Bjørlo, Lea Gulditte Hestelund,
Ville Bjørlo, Anna Katharina
Haukeland, Jorunn Hancke Øgstad,
Tuva Trondsdatter Trønsdal,
Gard Eiklid, Katinka Traaseth,
Morten Skrøder Lund, Absalon
Kirkeby, Louise Rosendal,
Beatriz Aragon. And for everyone
else that I should have mentioned
and forgot, I love you, but:
Of Course I'm Not Sorry.

All the photos in the book by
Renato Ghiazza, Jon Gorospe,
Ollie Hammick, Trevor Lloyd,
Victor Staaf, Christian Tunge.

First edition
2021

Printed by
ARGRAF

ISBN 978-88-6749-490-3

EUR 27 / USD 30